THE
LOST ALBUM
OF THE
BEATLES

T0019637

THE
LOST ALBUM
OF THE

WHAT IF THE BEATLES HADN'T SPLIT UP?

DANIEL RACHEL

C CASSELL

First published in Great Britain in 2021 by
Cassell, an imprint of
Octopus Publishing Group Ltd
Carmelite House
50 Victoria Embankment
London EC4Y 0DZ
www.octopusbooks.co.uk

First published in paperback in 2023
This material was previously published
as *Like Some Forgotten Dream*

An Hachette UK Company
www.hachette.co.uk

Text copyright © Daniel Rachel 2021, 2023

Distributed in the US by
Hachette Book Group
1290 Avenue of the Americas
4th and 5th Floors
New York, NY 10104

Distributed in Canada by
Canadian Manda Group
664 Annette St.
Toronto, Ontario, Canada M6S 2C8

All rights reserved. No part of this work
may be reproduced or utilized in any form
or by any means, electronic or mechanical,
including photocopying, recording or by any
information storage and retrieval system,
without the prior written permission of the
publisher.

Daniel Rachel has asserted his right under the
Copyright, Assertion in the Work Designs
and Patents Act 1988 to be identified as the
author of this work.

ISBN 978-1-78840-322-1

A CIP catalogue record for this book is
available from the British Library.

Printed and bound in the UK

10 9 8 7 6 5 4

Editorial Director: Joe Cottington
Creative Director: Jonathan Christie
Senior Editor: Alex Stetter
Senior Production Controller: Emily Noto

This FSC® label means that
materials used for the product have
been responsibly sourced.

MIX
Paper from
responsible sources
FSC® C104740
www.fsc.org

For Simon – you'll never know how much I really love you.

There was the possibility we could have carried on. We weren't sitting in the studio saying, 'Okay, this is it: last record; last track; last take.'
Ringo Starr

If people need The Beatles so much all they have to do is buy each [solo] album and put it on tape, track by track – one of me, one of Paul, one of George and one of Ringo – because otherwise, the music is just the same, only on separate albums.
John Lennon

When the spinning stops – that'll be the time to worry, not before. Until then, The Beatles are alive and well and the beat goes on.
Beatles press release, 10 April 1970

Contents

Introduction:
All My Little Plans and Schemes

It is difficult not to fall in love with The Beatles. The thrill of John asking the audience at the 1963 Royal Variety Performance, in the presence of Queen Elizabeth The Queen Mother and Princess Margaret, 'Will the people in the cheaper seats clap your hands? All the rest of you, if you'll just rattle your jewellery.' Paul's doe-eyed looks, shaking his head from side to side and screaming trademark Beatle 'oohs'. George grinning with a lopsided smile and rebuffing journalists' questions about the name of his haircut: 'Arthur,' he cuttingly replies. Or Ringo's forlorn come-and-mother-me pose, dancing bent-double, arms flailing, in *A Hard Day's Night*.

It was the way that John, Paul, George and Ringo – the four-name roll call effortlessly sliding off the tongue – stood side by side contorting their arms to spell *Help!* in flag semaphore on the album cover. The way they donned tinted shades and sat looking irrepressibly cool for the back-sleeve shoot of *Revolver*. It was Paul's joyous '1-2-3-4' introduction to 'I Saw Her Standing There', kick-starting Beatlemania, and John wisecracking to the assembled motley guests on the roof of the Apple building at the finale of *Let It Be* six years later, 'I'd like to say thank you on behalf of the group and ourselves, and I hope we've passed the audition.' It was the flirtatious presenter Cathy McGowan being reduced to a giggling pile as George charmed her on the set of *Ready Steady Go!*, revealing that they, The Beatles, sometimes watched 'private ("not dirty") films'. It was Ringo, sitting beside the actress Jessie Robins ('Auntie Jessie') on the *Magical Mystery Tour* bus, improvising and squabbling over who bought the away-day tickets.

With scene after scene of quips and japes, The Beatles played out a fantasy drama for the benefit of the cameras, and for us, the fans, to repeatedly imitate while secretly wishing for acceptance into their impenetrable gang. And then there was the music! A bounty of singles, EPs and LPs to devour and cherish – from radio-friendly chart-toppers like 'She Loves You' and 'I Want to Hold Your Hand' to the anthemic 'All You Need Is Love' and 'Hey Jude'; from the romantic 'This Boy' and 'Something' to the cool 'Rain' and the esoteric 'You Know My Name (Look Up the Number)'. One day, you might swear blind that *Sgt. Pepper's Lonely Hearts Club Band* was the greatest record ever made and the next be utterly convinced it was *Abbey Road*. And then there were those endless Beatle-themed debates: whether 'Please Please Me' was officially the group's first number one record (*New Musical Express* and *Melody Maker*: yes; *Record Retailer*: no) or if 'Yesterday' – performed by Paul accompanied only by a string quartet – was legitimately a Beatles record at all; whether George introduced Indian music to Western pop (as if the very notion could be doubted), or if John was right when he supposedly joked that Ringo 'wasn't even the best drummer in The Beatles'. [1]

---

1 This misattributed quote originates from an episode of the BBC Radio 4 comedy show *Radio Active* entitled 'Record Producer', which was written by Geoffrey Perkins and first broadcast on 5 September 1981: 'Alright,

These conversations, the arguments, the records...we had them all and wanted them to last forever. They did, and they will. But like great sex we craved more: to experience greater thrills, and to discover unknown pleasures. In this unrequited affair we made ever-increasing demands, and when The Beatles split we felt cheated. Like scorned lovers we hoped that the breakup was only temporary, an understandable trial separation, and with it came a longing for reconciliation and reunion. This erroneous fiction ended abruptly on 8 December 1980, when John Lennon was murdered in cold blood on the steps of his New York home. Taken away from us, from Yoko and from his two sons, Sean and Julian, by a single bullet. Suddenly, the possible was impossible. There could never be four Beatles again. The dream was over.

Perhaps you were an original fan from Liverpool and saw The Beatles in their earliest incarnation or witnessed the mayhem they caused in Hamburg rocking in their leather jackets. You could have bought their first single 'Love Me Do' in October 1962 or latched on to the mania 16 months later when The Beatles made their debut appearance on *The Ed Sullivan Show* on 9 February 1964. Maybe it took the Fab Four shaking off their mop-top image and embracing psychedelia or welcoming the mystical ways of Eastern spirituality. Or possibly, like me, you were born a beat too late to say 'I was there' but nevertheless were enveloped by the irresistible pull of their charm and magnetism. In time, the who, the where and the when have been

---

maybe Ringo Starr wasn't the best drummer in the world. Alright, maybe he wasn't the best drummer in the Beatles.'

surpassed by the all-encompassing joy of being consumed by Beatle fandom. A combination of books, films, art and, of course, music.

Loving The Beatles is not like being a fan of any other band. It is more like being part of a family, something akin to a cultural blood group. From the moment I consciously first heard their music as an eight-year-old, I have been infatuated by all things Beatles. By coincidence, my best friend shared this same passion, and throughout

John, Paul, Ringo and George outside their manager Brian Epstein's house in west London, 19 May 1967.

our teens and twenties we delved into one another's record collections, sharing our joint thirst for anything FAB! Our favourite game was imagining one more Beatles album. The *One after Let It Be*. Over the years, we have spent hours debating a would-be running order: accepting and rejecting tracks; replacing one song with another; discovering a new solo song by Ringo; or embracing a previously undiscovered demo recording by George. We have shouted, screamed and shared the idea with other Beatle-heads in pubs and at gigs or just with random strangers and, in doing so, discovered that imagining the unimaginable is as irresistible for others as it was for us.

We were young then, and maturity has, in time, led us away from our obsessional behaviour. Yet, now, decades later, I find the idea of a 'what if...?' Beatles album as compelling as I ever did. Of course, in those years, a whole new intensity of Beatle wisdom has spread across the globe, coupled with ingenious ways in which to keep the story alive. The internet is littered with sites and blogs preserving and reliving the Beatles years: the idea of one more record frequently explored on social media platforms across the world with imagined albums ranging from the populist to the absurd, but always presented with the loving care of a devotee. It seems that if fans can't have The Beatles in the real world, they will reinvent them in an alternative reality.

Such is the thirst for new Beatles that, in 1995, Paul, George and Ringo shocked the world and reunited to record two previously unreleased John Lennon songs, 'Free as a Bird' and 'Real Love', with fresh backing tracks, newly written middle eights, and a chorus of vocals to support John's crude original demos. Then, in 2003, *Let It Be...Naked* was released, a dressed-down version of The Beatles' last official album, without posthumous overdubs and effects. In 2018, the 'White Album' master tapes were dusted down and remixed for the modern age by the son of George Martin, Giles, and in 2019, *Abbey Road* was given a similar treatment to celebrate its fiftieth anniversary. During the writing of this book, the filmmaker Peter Jackson created a new edit of the 1969 film *Let It Be* from 60 hours of unreleased film footage and more than 150 hours of audio recordings. Then, in 2019 came perhaps one of the most bizarre reimaginings of Beatles history, *Yesterday*, a film written by Richard Curtis and directed by Danny Boyle, in which a struggling musician wakes up after a gigantic electrical storm to discover that nobody apart from him has ever heard of the songs of Lennon and McCartney, or indeed Harrison and Starr.

The Lost Album of The Beatles is dedicated to this worldwide fixation of reinvention. It is an attempt to offer a literary voice to a debate that has raged in Beatleland, and beyond, since the group originally split more than half a century ago. It asks you to imagine the following scenario: that The Beatles did not split up in April 1970; that, after releasing *Abbey Road* a year earlier, John, Paul, George and Ringo recorded a fourteenth, farewell album; and that such classic songs as 'Jealous Guy', 'Maybe I'm Amazed', 'My Sweet Lord' and 'I'm the Greatest' appeared on a single disc, under the name of The Beatles.

The seductive idea requires a great leap of faith of the reader and a willingness to reverse the clock of history. It necessitates unpicking the real-time chronology of events that led to the breakup of the group. To accept that there was a yearning, from all four Beatles, to keep the group together. In fact, despite the *Daily Mirror* headline on

10 April 1970 declaring 'Paul Quits The Beatles', and notwithstanding John's private declaration of 'a divorce' six months earlier, it is evident that there was lot more posturing and game playing than meaningful intent to end the union. Indeed, in the months following the group's dissolution, each Beatle independently expressed a belief that it was *not* over. *The Lost Album of The Beatles* asks the reader to accept that conciliatory opportunities were not missed; that differences of opinion were resolved; and that day-to-day difficulties were surmounted. In short, the book proposes a resolution to the discord in the Beatles camp and witnesses John, Paul, George and Ringo offering what the world craved: The Beatles recording together, one more time.

The pretence involves retracing the last years of the group's working relationship, from the personal and the political to the artistic and the financial. The tragic death of manager Brian Epstein, the fragmented recording of the 'White Album' and, in 1969, the problematic *Get Back / Let It Be* sessions that spawned a year of internal rancour and bitterness. By re-evaluating these areas, we catch a glimpse of an endgame where the unravelling of The Beatles was avoidable, where compromise could have trumped confrontation, where negotiation pacified provocation. An understanding of these squandered openings underpins the whole concept of the 'what if...?' fiction and makes the prospect of one more album tantalizing in its allure.

The second half of the book presents a case for the songs on a would-be final album, and, in doing so, offers a radical rewriting of pop music history. In this re-envisioned world, John, Paul, George and

Ringo agree to record a double vinyl album, *Four Sides of The Beatles*, with a side dedicated exclusively to the songs of each respective Beatle – Side One: Lennon; Side Two: McCartney; Side Three: Harrison; and Side Four: Starr – and, in the process, symbolically prepare fans for the inevitable split and solo careers that will follow.

The proposed record provides a daring solution to the pervasive inter-band complaints: that John had lost his commercial touch; that Paul's songs dominated; that George was undervalued and that Ringo was a sideman. Consequently, each Beatle is given carte blanche to fill one side of a record however they see fit: their song selections, their arrangements, their choice of producer. Moreover, the record is a reflection of the growing maturity within the group, from the mop-top days when the band led the British Invasion of the US in 1964 to the young men seeking individual identities at the dawning of a new decade: as musicians, as maturing adults, and as four young men facing the sobering reality of life in their thirties.

In choosing tracks for *Four Sides of The Beatles*, I have constructed strict criteria, which, in the main, attempt to adhere to historical feasibility. This timeframe is set from September 1969, when John proposed 'Cold Turkey' as the next Beatles single, to 31 December 1970, when Paul served a lawsuit to the High Court to sue his former bandmates and Apple Inc. Obviously, determining an exact template is contentious the paradox being that, if the group resolved their differences in September 1969, historical events that occurred thereafter are redundant. Furthermore, it is reasonable to assume that, had The Beatles agreed to make a new record, new songs would have been written for its recording.

Accepting these anomalies, *Four Sides of The Beatles* is limited to songs that are known to have existed already – be it from prior recordings, rehearsals or private demo tapes – or within the given dates. In fact, many songs selected for the proposed album were written before The Beatles officially broke up. For example, 'The Back Seat of My Car' – the closing track on Paul's second solo album, *RAM*, released in May 1971 – was introduced to The Beatles in January 1969 during the *Get Back* sessions, as was George's 'All Things Must Pass', although it was not released until December 1970. Similarly, 'Jealous Guy' was written in 1968 (then titled 'Child of Nature'), rehearsed by The Beatles in January 1969, and finally released as a John Lennon solo recording in 1971. Conversely, the rigid qualifying standard excludes many popular songs, such as 'Imagine' (written by John in 1971), 'Live and Let Die' and 'Give Me Love (Give Me Peace on Earth)' (written by Paul and George, respectively, in 1973) and 'Back Off Boogaloo' (written by Ringo in 1972).

Time and place indelibly print sounds in our memories. And to imagine songs like 'Jealous Guy', 'Another Day', 'My Sweet Lord' or 'It Don't Come Easy' stripped of our knowing their arrangements, their imagery, requires a great leap of imagination. Wouldn't 'Maybe I'm Amazed', as performed by The Beatles, be transformed if John had added harmonies and Ringo played drums on the track? Or if Paul had played bass on 'Gimme Some Truth' or George lead guitar on 'Another Day'? The proposition asks of the listener to dispense with their preconceptions of the familiar and engage with the essence of a song in its purest form: words and melody.

From a literary point of view, I have liberally selected statements made by John, Paul, George and Ringo in interviews that play to the central theme of the book. Often, this necessitated taking words out of context to serve the argument, but it is important to stress that no words have been invented. *The Lost Album of The Beatles* is illusory, and although Part 2 is a distorted application of post-Beatles history, the information used – dates, facts, interviews – is all genuine. In a similar vein, it is important to remember that opinions as to the credibility of an interview should be made in relation to the time it was recorded. For example, John's interview with Jann Wenner for *Rolling Stone* magazine in December 1970 was given within months of The Beatles' breakup and naturally is emotionally raw; added to which, the difference in the written word from the tone of his voice on the audio recording is seismic. As discussed within the book, John's state of mind was prone to change day by day, and his interview with Wenner is laced with contradictions. Tellingly, when the conversation was later published in book form, as *Lennon Remembers*, John contested it, believing that many of his attitudes had changed in the intervening years.

Inevitably, *The Lost Album of The Beatles* will engender discussion, debate and disagreement. In many ways, this is central to the book's premise. But, to reiterate, the concept of a great lost album is a fantasy and as such there can be no definitive right or wrong. The proposal is rife with incongruities and, like a Hollywood film, requires of the audience a suspension of disbelief. I therefore ask the reader to engage with the book in the spirit in which it is written: a playful game presented, I hope, with intelligence and wit. It is a love letter to the greatest band in the history of popular music. A group that continues to bring joy to the world, and, incredibly, still garners record sales in the millions. In fact, despite John Lennon singing 'the dream is over...', it is timely to remember he also sang 'it's only just begun...'

Part 1

Don't Upset the Apple Cart

1. Transition

End of Touring

I think the troubles really began when we weren't aiming anymore for the same thing, which began, I think, when we stopped touring in 1966.
Paul McCartney – *Life*, April 1971

Candlestick Park, San Francisco, 29 August 1966. The Beatles are dressed in matching stage outfits: black trousers and double-breasted coats with green velvet lapels, split buttoned cuffs, and a single-vented back. Paul screams out, 'Have some fun tonight', and with a final yelp brings the last night of The Beatles' 19-date North American tour to an end.

The band have been on stage for barely 30 minutes, ripping through 11 songs captured on cassette tape by the band's press officer, Tony Barrow, at Paul's request. Opening with a cover of Chuck Berry's 'Rock and Roll Music', followed by 'She's a Woman', 'If I Needed Someone', 'Day Tripper', 'Baby's in Black', 'I Feel Fine', 'Yesterday', 'I Wanna Be Your Man' (sung by Ringo), 'Nowhere Man' and 'Paperback Writer', and finishing with Little Richard's 'Long Tall Sally', the set is predominantly upbeat, spanning the first four years of The Beatles' recording career. The sound is amplified by the screams of 25,000 rabid fans, charged by the atmosphere and flushed at their proximity to the Fab Four.

But for those paying attention to the detail of the spectacle, The Beatles had changed. The band was no longer simply a 'rocking live act' out on the road to promote their latest record: the song arrangements had become progressively more sophisticated, reflecting a developing studio prowess, and this, coupled with the gladiatorial atmosphere of the live shows, meant that, for the group, touring was becoming increasingly tiresome. The technical innovation of the heavy bass part on 'Paperback Writer' or the chiming interplay of Rickenbacker guitars and vocal harmonies on 'Nowhere Man' was lost live, the sub-adequate PA equipment and audience screams drowning out The Beatles' ability to hear themselves think, let alone play.

John, George and Paul at Candlestick Park, San Francisco, moments before their final concert date, 29 August 1966.

There was no official announcement, no statement that The Beatles would stop touring after Candlestick Park, but, for astute audience members, the on-stage between-song banter suggested a decision had been reached. 'We'd like to carry on, now,' John said, before playing The Beatles' 1965 Christmas number one single 'Day Tripper', 'carry on together, at will – one together and all for one...' Then, as the set neared its close, Paul quipped, 'We'd like to carry on, I think, we're not really sure yet. I'd like to carry on, certainly.' 'Definitely,' replied John, 'I'd like to carry on...definitely.' Moments later, in front of a camera positioned on top of John's guitar amplifier, all four Beatles stood with their backs to the audience to pose for a photograph. It was the last time they would appear together before a paying audience. 'That's it,' George cried, later that evening on board a chartered flight from San Francisco to Los Angeles, 'I'm not a Beatle any longer.'

The world used The Beatles as 'an excuse to go mad', George reflected 30 years later for *Anthology*, 'and then blamed it on us'. In the early years of touring, the adulation had been thrilling, but as venues became bigger the music took second place to the event. The Beatles had effectively become a sideshow to the enormity of the occasion: a live touring spectacle. 'It was great at first,' George told The Beatles biographer Hunter Davies, 'but it got played out. We got in a rut. It was a different audience each day but we were doing the same things. There was no satisfaction in it. Nobody could hear. It was just a bloody big row. We got worse as musicians, playing the same old junk every day. There was no satisfaction at all.' 'It was wrecking our playing,' Ringo confirmed. 'In the end no one enjoyed touring. Once you've got to manufacture it, it doesn't work. You've got to give to receive...we didn't give anything.' John compared the process to being in the army: 'One big sameness which you have to go through,' he told Davies. 'I was thinking, "Well, this is the end, really. There's no more touring. That means there's going to be a blank space in the future." That's when I started considering life without The Beatles – what would it be?'

Adding to The Beatles' frustration on the road was the increasing banality of press conferences. Rarely asked questions of any serious depth and after years of 'playing the game', they began to crack. In the week preceding Candlestick Park, one journalist asked the group, 'One of your countrymen was here yesterday, he said he thought that American women were out of style for not wearing mini-skirts and because they didn't, their legs were ugly. I'd like to ask what you think of American women's legs.' Bemused, Ringo drily retorted, 'Well, if they don't wear mini-skirts, how do they know their legs are ugly?' John was then asked about a remark he had made six months earlier comparing the relative popularity of The Beatles with Jesus Christ. 'I've clarified it about eight hundred times,' John responded, clearly exasperated by the continued adverse publicity Maureen Cleave's interview in the *Evening Standard* in March 1966 had generated. Changing the subject, a journalist quoted a recent article from *Time* magazine claiming 'Day Tripper' was 'about a prostitute' and 'Norwegian Wood' 'about a lesbian'. 'What was your intent behind it?' he asked. 'We're just trying to write songs about prostitutes and lesbians,' Paul responded to a round of laughter. Then, when asked about the inspiration behind 'Eleanor Rigby', John, clearly bored, jibed, 'Two queers.'

When The Beatles returned home to England on 30 August 1966, everything changed. The pattern of recording and touring, established in October 1962 with the release of 'Love Me Do', was over. In four short years, The Beatles had given nearly 800 performances – plus another 1,250 if you take into account their different group set-ups, either separately or together, before signing to Parlophone. The Beatles had conquered the world and been celebrated as leaders of a cultural revolution. On Thursday, 24 November 1966 – three months after Candlestick Park – John, Paul, George and Ringo reconvened at EMI Studios to begin work on a new song, 'Strawberry Fields Forever'. And with it the axis of influence in popular music turned once again. On 1 June 1967, the ground-breaking *Sgt. Pepper's Lonely Hearts Club Band* was released, swiftly followed a month later by first 'All You Need Is Love' – introduced via a live broadcast to a worldwide audience of 400 million people – and then, in December, a new song, written by Paul, 'Hello Goodbye'. The year ended with a one-hour film made for television and an accompanying six-track double EP, *Magical Mystery Tour*. The Beatles' creative output in 1967 was staggering. But one event above all would irrecoverably change the destiny of The Beatles – the death of Brian Epstein.

Death of Brian Epstein

On 27 August 1967, Brian Epstein was declared dead from an accidental overdose of drugs. He was 32 years old. Brian had managed The Beatles since 1961, after watching them perform at the Cavern Club in Liverpool. Restyling them in suits, he secured The Beatles a recording contract with Parlophone Records and organized their live engagements. After the Beatles' final concert at Candlestick Park in 1966, Brian continued with his managerial duties, approving plans to establish Apple – a commercial venture to facilitate records, films, electronics and manufacturing (and, from a business perspective, to offset tax) – and facilitating what would become The Beatles' third film, *Magical Mystery Tour.*

George and Paul on their way to Brian Epstein's memorial service with Pattie Boyd, Mal Evans and Neil Aspinall, 17 October 1967.

In reality, Brian's active role in the day-to-day affairs of The Beatles in this 12-month period was marginalized, and his untimely passing has come to represent the moment the fate of the band was sealed. 'After we stopped touring he had nothing to do, really,' John said. Both Paul and George agreed. 'Even before we got into our own company,' Paul told *Anthology*, 'we were virtually manging ourselves. So Brian had become a bit redundant.' 'There was a huge void,' George added. 'We didn't know anything about our personal business and finances. Brian had taken care of everything. It was chaos after that.' 'We collapsed,' John told *Rolling Stone* in 1970. 'I knew that we were in trouble then. I didn't really have any misconceptions about our ability to do anything other than play music. And I was scared. I thought, "We've fuckin' had it."'

With Brian gone, it soon become apparent that The Beatles' contractual legacy was bound up in paperwork owned by the Epstein estate and filtered down through a sea of accountants and solicitors. Over the next two years, The Beatles became mired in a business imbroglio which slowly ate at the soul of their creative existence. In 1985, Hunter Davies wrote in the postscript to his authorized biography of the band, 'I had never imagined that the end of The Beatles, whenever it happened, would simply come in a welter of legal tangles, financial quibbling, trivial personality clashes, slanging matches, ridiculous recriminations, juvenile insults and silly squabbles.'

Reflecting on the establishment of Apple as an attempt to break from capitalist convention and offer sanctuary to artists of all backgrounds from big business, John told the *New Musical Express* on 13 December 1969, 'I know now that the original concept of helping everybody doesn't work in its purest form. All you get are the bums and freeloaders everybody else turns down.'

Under different circumstances, Brian would have managed Apple and kept The Beatles at arm's length from its demands. As it was, Apple, in effect, gave The Beatles control of their future and exacted responsibility for their individual actions. Where they had once lived in a cossetted world, protected by Brian to concentrate on songwriting, recording and touring, outside demands now penetrated their daily lives, disrupting their carefree lifestyle. Symbolically, 'Brian's boys' had become men of 'Swinging London'. In the second half of the 1960s, as popular culture embraced psychedelia, so The Beatles' outlook obscured and with it hitherto unwelcome guests were invited into their fold. As Neil Aspinall observed in *Anthology*, 'Suddenly, the lunatics had got hold of the asylum.'[1]

Yoko Ono

Yoko Ono's arrival in John Lennon's life in 1966 is a polemical moment in The Beatles' story, the resulting shockwaves irrevocably transforming the group's previously impenetrable four-way dynamic. Almost immediately, John underwent a dramatic metamorphosis that affected both his personal and professional behaviour. For those looking for an easy target, Yoko's entry into The Beatles' inner circle provided the perfect scapegoat for the group's protracted

---

1   In March 1961, Aspinall was taken on as the Beatles' van driver and roadie. He later rose to the position of personal assistant and, by 1976, was managing director of Apple Corps.

disintegration. Dismissing the chaos around Apple, Hunter Davies argued that the ongoing legal rows were a 'result', not a 'cause', of the split. 'If there was one simple reason why The Beatles split up when they did,' Hunter boldly asserted, 'it was not the argument over who should run their affairs, but the arrival into John's life of Yoko Ono.'

On 19 May 1968, Yoko visited John at his marital home in Weybridge, Surrey. Taking advantage of Cynthia Lennon's absence, the couple spent the night creating electronic noises and tape loops – later released as *Unfinished Music No. 1: Two Virgins*.[2] In the morning, John and Yoko consummated their union, as John proudly revealed to the *Rolling Stone* journalist Jann Wenner in 1970: 'It was midnight when we started…and then we made love at dawn. It was very beautiful.'

Three days later, on 22 May 1968, the couple, making their first public appearance, attended the launch party of Apple Tailoring at the Club Dell'Aretusa on Chelsea's King's Road, where, notably, George Harrison was also in attendance.[3] Although she was now introduced as John's partner, it was by no means Yoko's first foray into The Beatles' orbit. Having sought out Paul in 1965 while in search of original handwritten manuscripts as a birthday present for the composer John Cage, two years later Yoko attended a Beatles recording session for 'The Fool on the Hill'.[4] A black-and-white photograph, snapped on

---

2 A former student at the Liverpool College of Art, Cynthia Powell married John Lennon on 23 August 1962.

3 On 7 December, 1967, The Beatles opened a clothes boutique at 94 Baker Street. A second shop, Apple Tailoring (Civil and Theatrical), opened on 23 May 1968 on the King's Road.

4 Paul recounted the story to Howard Stern on SIRIUS XM Radio on 18 October 2001: 'We were in London [in late 1965] and Yoko came around

the day – 25 September 1967 – shows John holding an acoustic guitar dressed in a matching white polo neck and trousers sitting opposite Yoko who is dressed in black.[5] On 30 May 1968, Yoko once again was present at a Beatles recording session, on this occasion invited by John to spend an afternoon in Studio Two at EMI's Abbey Road as work began on 'Revolution'. The Beatles cut a fiery ten-minute version of the song complete with sound effects and on-mic moans courtesy of Yoko and the repeated line 'you become naked' – later immortalized on the finished 'White Album' recording.

During this period, John and Yoko stayed at Paul's house on Cavendish Avenue in St John's Wood. In her memoir *Body Count*, published in 1972, Paul's then girlfriend, Francie Schwartz, gave a less than flattering account of the host's behaviour. '[Paul] sent them a hate letter once, unsigned, typed,' Schwartz wrote:

> I brought it in with the morning mail. Paul put most of his fan mail in a big basket and let it sit for weeks, but John and Yoko opened every piece. When they got to the anonymous note, they

to my house, knocking on the door. "There's this Japanese lady outside," I said, "Okay, let her in." She came in and she said, "It's John Cage's birthday and us artists want to collect a bunch of manuscripts to give him." I thought, "I don't want to do this." But I said, "My friend John might." I said, "He lives here," and she went to see him.' As a result of the meeting, John donated the original handwritten lyrics of 'The Word' from *Rubber Soul*.

5 On the same afternoon, two Japanese journalists, Rumiko Hoshika and Koh Hasebe, interviewed and photographed the Beatles for *Music Life*. The picture was later used for the Japanese picture sleeve issue of 'Hello Goodbye'. Despite their shared nationality, it is believed Yoko did not speak to either Hasebe or Hoshika; the latter assumed Yoko to be Chinese.

Yoko Ono and John during the recording session for 'The Fool on the Hill' at EMI Studios, 25 September 1967.

looked puzzled, looking at each other with genuine pain in their eyes. 'You and your Jap tart think you're hot shit,' it said. John put it on the mantle, and in the afternoon, Paul hopped in, prancing much the same self-conscious way he did when we met. 'Oh I just did that for a lark...' he said in his most sugar-coated accent. It was embarrassing. The three of us swivelled around, staring at him. You could see the pain in John.

Historically, strangers had not readily been welcomed into The Beatles' inner circle. But, in the glow of love, John wantonly ignored any perceived group protocol, despite the growing unease of Paul,

George and Ringo. Yoko's arrival further signified the end of John's marriage to Cynthia. The couple divorced on 8 November 1968, and thereafter Yoko was a permanent presence, not only in John's day-to-day life, but in all Beatle activities. Wherever John was, Yoko sat beside him. No explanation was offered beyond John's stated desire that they wanted to spend every minute with one another. Not surprisingly, a simmering resentment spread among the three other Beatles. 'There was a definite vibe,' George recalled, for *Anthology*, 'a wedge that was trying to drive itself deeper and deeper between him and us.' With the close possessive bond The Beatles had with one another being challenged, confrontation was nevertheless avoided, leading to what Ringo referred to as 'talking in corners'. 'We didn't get it,' Paul simply said in the 1997 biography by Barry Miles, *Many Years from Now*, 'and it put a strain on it.' With nobody prepared to tackle the issue openly, an air of resentment festered even as Yoko was begrudgingly tolerated.

In January 1969, a mere two months after the release of the 'White Album', The Beatles commenced work on a new project at Twickenham Studios. Despite an atmosphere of apparent appeasement, and with John seemingly placated and engaged, Yoko's all-pervasive presence was slowly stretching people's patience. Disclosing his thoughts to the film director Michael Lindsay-Hogg, Paul ventured, 'There's only two answers. One is to fight it and fight her and the other thing is just to realise John's not going to split with her just for our sakes.' Reasoning that an obstacle is only such if you recognize it as one, Paul deduced that, if forced to make a choice, John would pick Yoko over The Beatles. Advocating tolerance,

Paul said. 'Let the young lovers stay together. It's silly neither of us compromising.' George was not convinced. 'There were negative vibes at that time,' he said in *Anthology*. 'John and Yoko were out on a limb. I don't think he wanted much to be hanging out with us, and I think Yoko was pushing him out of the band, inasmuch as she didn't want him hanging out with us.'

Before meeting John, Yoko had belonged to Fluxus, a loose, international collective of experimental artists, poets and musicians. Based in downtown New York, Yoko staged a series of conceptual performance pieces including *Painting to Be Stepped On* (1960), *Cut Piece* (1964) – in which members of the audience were invited to cut off small pieces of her clothing as she sat alone on a stage dressed in a black suit – and *Sky Piece to Jesus Christ* (1965) as well as making the risqué *Film No. 4*, also known as *Bottoms* (1966–7). Yoko was an established artist and perhaps in some respects considered herself an equal to The Beatles. Unlike many visitors to the group's inner sanctum, Yoko did not cower or show undue humility. Her arrival, along with her privileged upbringing – she was born into a wealthy, elite family and had attended Tokyo's private Gakushuin University, renowned for educating the children of Japan's Imperial aristocracy – understandably rankled with Paul, George and Ringo. For John, it was a liberation. 'Yoko freed me completely to realize that I was me and it's alright,' he told Jann Wenner in 1970. 'And that was it. I started fighting again, being a loudmouth again, and saying, "Well, I can do this, fuck you," and "this is what I want," and "Don't put me down."'

As rehearsals in the cavernous film studio progressed, the mood darkened. Over lunch on 10 January, after an alleged argument with

John, George walked out. John went on the attack. 'Yoko only wants to be accepted,' he said, 'she wants to be one of us. It's hateful that someone can be treated with so much hostility just because they love someone.' 'Well, she's not a Beatle, John,' Ringo retorted, 'and she never will be.' The next morning, Paul asserted a need for diplomacy, acknowledging John's tendency to go overboard with things new. To question John's decision-making carried a risk of him saying, 'Well, screw you,' and quitting, Paul said. It was a scenario he was determined to avoid.

Through all the years of fan mania, The Beatles had endured an acutely pressurized existence and, like any longstanding relationship, they had become attuned to each other's minutest foibles and sensitivities. Anticipating how history might interpret their decline, Paul joked, 'It's going to be such an incredible, comical thing in fifty years' time: they broke up because Yoko sat on an amp...you see, John kept on bringing this girl along...' In December 1980, John reflected upon the situation in an interview with Andy Peebles for BBC Radio 1. 'I understand it all now, but Yoko just wanted to join in everything. Suddenly we were together all the time; in a corner mumbling and giggling. And there were Paul, George and Ringo saying, "What the hell are they doing? What's happened to him?" My attention completely went off them. But I understood how they felt.'

With The Beatles now approaching their thirties, predictably, relationships outside of music began to impact on their day-to-day lives. Nonetheless, girlfriends had always been an integral part of their lives. In August 1962, John married Cynthia Powell – three months before the release of 'Love Me Do'. In February 1965, having met her at the Cavern Club, Ringo married Maureen Cox. A year later, George married Pattie Boyd after meeting her when she was in character as a schoolgirl on the film set of *A Hard Day's Night*. On 12 March 1969, Paul married Linda Eastman at Marylebone Register Office, and eight days later, John and Yoko married 'in Gibraltar near Spain', as described in The Beatles' single 'The Ballad of John and Yoko'.

But, unlike Pattie, a blonde English model, or Maureen, with her unassuming girl-next-door looks, neither Linda nor Yoko fitted neatly into a glossy Beatle narrative. Linda was American, a photographer who eschewed the fickle world of entertainment, and who, in 1967, photographed The Beatles during promotion for their new album, *Sgt. Pepper's Lonely Hearts Club Band*. At the time, Paul was engaged to the actress Jane Asher. On 20 July 1968, Asher made an unexpected announcement on *Dee Time*, a BBC television show. 'I haven't broken it off,' she told presenter Simon Dee, 'but it is broken off, finished. I know it sounds corny, but we still see each other and love each other, but it hasn't worked out. Perhaps we'll be childhood sweethearts and meet again and get married when we're about seventy.' Unlike Asher, who was popular among Beatle fans, Paul's new girlfriend, Linda, was confronted with frequent mouthfuls of jealousy-fuelled abuse outside Paul's north London home whenever she visited.

Being Japanese and a conceptual artist, Yoko was similarly cast by fans as a misfit, unsuited to the perceived role Beatle girlfriends were expected to fulfil. On 17 July 1971, television presenter Michael Parkinson asked Yoko, and John, about The Beatles' split: 'Another reason for people taking a dislike of you is because you've become known, again through the newspapers in this country, as the woman who broke up The Beatles. But that's not true?' 'That's not true,' John replied. 'Listen, I'll tell you. People on the street and the kids do not dislike us. It's the media.' Beneath the surface lay an uneasy xenophobia. Accused of single-handedly causing the breakup of The Beatles, John was incensed. 'Yoko didn't split The Beatles,' he told Jann Wenner. 'But she's a woman and she's Japanese, there's racial prejudice against her and there's female prejudice against her. It's as simple as that.'

In The Beatles' story, the judgement of women, and particularly Yoko, has historically carried a measure of misogyny and prejudice. This is hardly surprising considering that the majority of books about The Beatles have been written by white male writers, myself included. The fact was that Yoko awoke in John a vitality that had long been supressed. Ever since The Beatles stopped touring, John had struggled to motivate himself. As he told *Newsweek* in September 1980, he surrounded himself with 'sycophant slaves who were only interested in keeping the situation as it was'. Comparing his post-touring years to those of Elvis Presley, John said, 'I was too frightened to step out of the palace. The king is always killed by his courtiers. He is overfed, overindulged, overdrunk to keep him tied to his throne. Yoko showed me what it was to be Elvis Beatle.'

Speaking on *The Last Resort with Jonathan Ross* in October 1987, George said, 'At the time we split up, there was too many other people trying to get in the group. We could have had two groups, The Beatles and The Beatles' wives.' Yoko may have been a catalyst in the breakup process, but each of The Beatles asserted a growing need for independence from the group, be it through forming new relationships, making solo records or venturing into film projects. By late 1968, The Beatles as a collective concern was in need of a radical shake-up. If they were to survive the upheavals of the year ahead, a fresh approach and a new way of presenting themselves were urgently needed.

The 'White Album'

The year 1968 was a zenith in the songwriting career of The Beatles. The total number of songs written and recorded by the group combined with those given to other artists was greater than in any other year of their existence. But the year also marked a world stage of angry voices. In the UK, on 20 April the Conservative MP Enoch

Paul at the Apple office on Wigmore Street, with press officer Derek Taylor and Ronald Kass, head of Apple Records, 13 June 1968.

Powell made the iniquitous 'Rivers of Blood' speech calling for the voluntary repatriation of non-white UK residents, forecasting that 'in fifteen or twenty years' time the black man will have the whip hand over the white man'. A week later, the Abortion Act came into effect, legalizing termination under certain conditions, and in May, the Kray Twins were arrested. In the US, Martin Luther King Jr. was assassinated, and two months later, on 5 June, Robert Kennedy was shot dead at the Ambassador Hotel in Los Angeles. In Czechoslovakia, the Prague Spring entered its fifth month of resistance, and at the Mexico Olympics Tommie Smith and John Carlos bowed their heads and raised their fists to salute the Black Power movement. 'The tensions arising in the world around us had their effect on our music,' Paul McCartney wrote for *We, The Beatles* in July 2018, 'but the moment we sat down to play, all that vanished and the magic circle within a square that was The Beatles was created.'

In February 1968, perhaps as a reaction to a counterculture radically embracing psychedelic drugs and a contradictory angrier new world order, The Beatles accepted an invitation from the spiritual guru Maharishi Mahesh Yogi to visit India and study Transcendental Meditation. Set in the foothills of the Himalayas, the ashram at Rishikesh was a welcome sanctuary of solace and retreat from the demands of Western culture. Rising with the sun, The Beatles attended morning lectures with the Maharishi to learn about the ancient mysteries of higher consciousness. In the afternoons, they relaxed and meditated. 'We wrote about thirty new songs between us,' John remarked after his return from India. 'Paul must have done about a dozen. George says he's got six, and I wrote fifteen. And look what meditation did for Ringo – after all this time he wrote his first song.'[6]

Returning to London in late spring, The Beatles began work on their ninth studio album. Recorded over a five-month period – between 30 May and 17 October – *The Beatles*, which because of its unadorned plain sleeve became widely known as the 'White Album', was the first Beatles record where the distinct identities of the individual songwriters noticeably came to the fore. 'Paul was always upset about the *White Album*,' John told authors Peter McCabe and Robert Schonfeld in September 1971. 'He never liked it because, on that one, I did my music, Paul did his and George did his. At first, he didn't like George having so many tracks, and second, he wanted it to be more of a group thing, which really meant more Paul.' During the sessions, The Beatles would usually arrive at EMI at two o'clock in the afternoon and work through in to the early hours. In the studio, a set of green and red fluorescent lamps were displayed to liven up the sterile environment, together with the smell of burning Aparajita incense – made from a blend of Ayurvedic herbs – adding a distinctive aroma to the sessions.[7] Typically, backing tracks were recorded by all four members of the band, but as the recording of the album stretched out over the summer, overdubs were often added by individuals as

---

6   A reference to 'Don't Pass Me By', which, as we will discover in a later chapter, was actually written by Ringo six years earlier.

7   Introduced by Ravi Shankar to George Harrison while on a trip to India in 1966, a joss stick was subsequently lit at all Beatle sessions from *Sgt. Pepper* onwards. Having accepted George as a student of the sitar, Shankar later signed to Apple Records and, despite never recording with The Beatles, released the soundtrack album *Raga* in December 1971.

THE LOST ALBUM OF THE BEATLES

outside engagements began to fracture the working group unity.

On 7 June, George and Ringo flew to California to make a guest appearance in a scene in Ravi Shankar's film *Raga*, leaving Paul to work on 'Blackbird', written as a tribute to the Civil Rights movement. Shortly after, Paul absented himself for five days, to attend a Capitol Records conference in Los Angeles to launch Apple and in doing so missed the ongoing recording and mixing of John's experimental sound collage 'Revolution 9'. Having returned to London, George also missed the final day of mixing, opting instead to produce 'Sour Milk Sea' for Jackie Lomax.[8] On 17 July, all four Beatles took a day off to attend the premiere of *Yellow Submarine* at the London Pavilion cinema in Piccadilly Circus. In early August, sessions transferred to Trident Studios in Soho to make use of an eight-track machine deemed suitable for the mixing of 'Hey Jude'. A week later, The Beatles returned to Abbey Road to record 'Not Guilty', after which its composer, George, took a four-day break in Greece.

As the ad-hoc work practice continued through a dull and wet summer, and with the album deadline looming, The Beatles began to work independently, pragmatically making use of Abbey Road's three separate studios: on 10 October, while strings were being recorded for both George's song 'Piggies' and John's 'Glass Onion' in Studio Two, Paul was in Studio Three adding finishing touches to 'Why Don't We Do It in the Road?' The resourceful methodology reflected the growing maturity of The Beatles. While enabling an abundance of material to

---

8   Employed by Apple as an in-house songwriter, Lomax was set up with a two-track Revox recorder on the top floor of the Apple Boutique at 94 Baker Street. After hearing a set of demos, George offered to produce Lomax's first record.

be recorded and subsequently paving the way for a double-disc release, the practice of working individually also had the advantage of deftly avoiding growing rancour.

The 'White Album' sessions are often regarded – by the band, EMI staff and music historians – as a difficult period for The Beatles when the growing strains of interpersonal relationships were tested and stretched to breaking point. On 22 August, Ringo quit the band feeling disillusioned and undervalued.[9] 'I left because I felt two things,' Ringo reflected in *Anthology*. 'I felt I wasn't playing great, and I also felt that the other three were really happy and I was an outsider, but then I realised that we were *all* feeling like outsiders, and it just needed me to go around knocking to bring it to a head.'

In fact, Ringo was not the first to walk out on a Beatles recording session. On 21 June 1966, Paul upped sticks during a nine-hour session for the as yet untitled track for the *Revolver* album 'She Said She Said'.[10] 'I think it was one of the only Beatle records I never played on,' Paul told Barry Miles in *Many Years from Now*. 'I think we'd had a barney or something and I said, "Oh, fuck you!" and they said, "Well, we'll do it." I think George played bass.' Why Paul quit the session has never been satisfactorily explained, but a brief exchange caught on tape between John and Paul during a lunchtime break on 13 January 1969,

---

9   In Ringo's absence, the remaining three Beatles – with Paul playing drums – recorded 'Back in the USSR', 'Dear Prudence' and 'While My Guitar Gently Weeps'. When Ringo agreed to return a fortnight later to film the 'Hey Jude' and 'Revolution' promotional videos, George decorated the studio in flowers.

10 The song took its title from an acid experience in Los Angeles when John overheard the actor Peter Fonda recounting a story about being shot as a ten-year-old, claiming, 'I know what it's like to be dead.'

during the *Get Back* sessions, verifies the spat from three years earlier. 'The only regret I have about past numbers is because I've allowed you to take it somewhere I didn't want it to go,' John said. 'Then my only chance was to let George take over because I knew he'd take it as is.' 'Like on "She Said She Said",' Paul replied.[11]

What is interesting about 'She Said She Said' is how the sound of the group could be manufactured without the involvement of all four Beatles. Indeed, there are many examples of tracks recorded by fewer than all four members of the group participating, and yet the finished song clearly belongs to The Beatles: in 1965, 'Yesterday' featured only Paul, accompanied by a string quartet; in 1968, John and Ringo didn't play on 'Martha My Dear' nor did John on 'While My Guitar Gently Weeps' or 'Long, Long, Long'; in 1969, 'The Ballad of John and Yoko' was recorded entirely by John and Paul; and during the recording of *Abbey Road*, Paul, George and Ringo cut four tracks – 'Golden Slumbers', 'Here Comes the Sun', 'Oh! Darling' and 'Maxwell's Silver Hammer' – while John was recuperating from a car crash in Scotland. The question is: what constituted a Beatles recording? Was it who contributed to the track or was it simply just the stamp on the record label?

When the 'White Album' was released on 22 November 1968, it came in a plain white sleeve, designed by the British artist Richard Hamilton. White was the colour of hope, symbolizing a fresh start. For all the supposed difficulties reported during its making,

11 Paul's grievances in June 1966 were quickly resolved when a united Beatles set out on a short tour of West Germany, Japan and the Philippines immediately after the final mix of *Revolver* was completed.

the finished album revealed a band at the height of its creativity. Simultaneously topping the charts in the US and the UK, the music within contained an abundance of joyfulness and harmonious interplay: John's quirky ad-libs on 'Ob-La-Di, Ob-La-Da', Ringo screaming 'I've got blisters on my fingers' at the end of a charged 'Helter Skelter', George's sublime 'Long, Long, Long', or the note-perfect vocal pastiche of the Beach Boys during the middle passage of Paul's 'Back in the USSR'. When the album's outtakes were issued – over three CDs in 2018 – the studio banter was thick with humour and warmth. And in the five decades since its release, the 'White Album' has repeatedly been cited by artists and musicians as one of the most influential albums in rock and pop history.

The events of 1968 had been prodigious, with The Beatles' output being publicly characterized as a seamless outpouring of innovation and unrivalled creativity. Despite not having played live for over two years and with a music scene in radical transformation, progressing from psychedelia and rock to the birth of a British blues explosion, the commercial success and the affection held for the band was never greater. By the year's end, 'Hey Jude' became the sixth Beatles single to surpass one million sales.[12] Yet, all was about to change. The year 1969 would prove to be the year that broke The Beatles.

---

12 The six Beatles records with UK sales above one million are: 'She Loves You' (1.92 million), 'I Want to Hold Your Hand' (1.78 million), 'Can't Buy Me Love' (1.54 million), 'I Feel Fine' (1.42 million), 'Day Tripper'/'We Can Work It Out' (1.41 million) and 'Hey Jude' (1.11 million).

2. *Get Back* Sessions

Twickenham Studios

Astonishingly, whenever The Beatles started work on a new album the band's previous record would be at the top spot in the UK national chart. And so it was in January 1969, with the 'White Album' enjoying an eight-week tenure at number one, Paul challenged The Beatles to begin a new venture: to write, rehearse and record an entirely new set of songs for a television special. Under the scrutiny of film lenses and rolling audio tape, January 1969 was the most documented month in the history of The Beatles. A film of the period, *Let It Be*, theatrically released in cinemas in May 1970, depicted a downbeat Beatles scratching their way forward amid minor squabbles and a lot of facial hair. It was a sombre presentation. Yet, in the intervening years, more than a hundred hours of sound and assorted visuals, latterly dubbed the *Get Back* sessions, have flooded the online market. Mostly released unofficially, they reveal a pronounced disparity between the officially presented version of events and an apparent powerful period of intense creativity. Moreover, Peter Jackson's 2021 three-part documentary *Get Back* clearly shows The Beatles as a working, cooperative unit.

The *Get Back* sessions spanned 22 working days and witnessed The Beatles writing, rehearsing and recording a plethora of thrilling music. They played songs from their earliest days – 'I Fancy Me

Chances with You', 'Too Bad about Sorrows', 'Because I Know You Love Me So' – alongside previous hits – 'Love Me Do', 'Michelle', 'Help!' – mixed in with traditional songs and favourite cover versions from 'Frère Jacques' and 'The House of the Rising Sun' to Buddy Holly and Chuck Berry standards. On top of this, more than a dozen new songs were written for a proposed live television performance, and many more that would later appear on *Abbey Road*. Although there are no overt fully blown arguments or fundamental disagreements during the sessions, two key events have come to historically define the period: George Harrison walking out on 10 January and an impromptu gig on the roof of the Apple building on 30 January. It is these two incidents that hold the greatest bearing on the final year of The Beatles.

Rehearsals began on Thursday, 2 January 1969 at Twickenham Studios, where The Beatles had filmed the motion pictures *A Hard Day's Night* and *Help!* The sound stage was more than double the size of The Beatles' familiar recording surroundings at Studio Two, Abbey Road. Surrounded by cameras, lights and intermittent draughts, The Beatles set up facing one another in an ad-hoc circle with Ringo's drum kit elevated on top of a two-foot riser. To accommodate the film crew, director Michael Lindsay-Hogg imposed a rigid schedule.[1] The Beatles were expected to arrive at ten o'clock in the morning, work through

1   Lindsay-Hogg had worked with The Beatles on *Ready Steady Go!* and the promotional films of 'Paperback Writer', 'Rain', 'Hey Jude' and 'Revolution'. In December 1968, he directed *The Rolling Stones Rock and Roll Circus* featuring John Lennon performing 'Yer Blues' with an all-star band, including Keith Richards on bass, Mitch Mitchell on drums and Eric Clapton on lead guitar.

until one, and then, after an hour's lunch break, until five or six o'clock in the evening. The strict timetable was reminiscent of the group's earliest days at EMI Studios as fresh-faced youths, when George Martin upheld a disciplined work ethic. The controlled recording environment had remained largely unchallenged throughout their recording career until the death of Brian Epstein in 1967 after which an emboldened Beatles asserted their independence. 'George Martin no longer had an equal in The Beatles camp,' Giles Martin wrote in the introduction to *The Beatles White Album Anniversary Edition* in 2018. 'In 1968 he lost the classroom.'

The Twickenham experience began positively with the introduction of many new songs. On day one, John arrived with 'Dig a Pony' and 'Don't Let Me Down', Paul with 'I've Got a Feeling' (with a section written by John), 'Two of Us' and 'Oh! Darling', and George with 'Let It Down' and 'All Things Must Pass'. Over the next two days, John introduced 'Gimme Some Truth', Paul 'Teddy Boy', 'Maxwell's Silver Hammer' and '(She Came in through the) Bathroom Window', George 'Hear Me Lord' and Ringo fragments of two new ideas, 'Picasso' and 'Taking a Trip to California'. By this point, the majority of the material introduced was either mid-paced or slow, prompting John to call out 'Has anyone got a fast one?' The following day, perhaps in a conscious reaction to John's request, Paul initiated a one-chord stomp. Seated opposite George and Ringo, Paul tentatively strums a rhythm on the bass while searching for words and a melody. Incredibly, the basis of a new song emerges. It is immediately seized upon by Ringo who provides a rolling backbeat as Paul picks out the line 'Get back', much to the delight of the gathered entourage who begin to sing along to the infectious chorus.

Up-tempo and simple, 'Get Back' was the first song to firmly take hold at Twickenham and inject a sense of purpose into the rehearsals. Reacting to the positive atmosphere, Paul seized the moment to pass comment. 'There's some really great songs,' he said to John, 'I just hope we don't blow any of them.' Although speaking with a lightness of touch, Paul is clearly anxious. Seemingly admonishing himself for his own shortcomings, he makes reference to a past incident in an attempt to avoid its repetition. 'You know how often on albums we sometimes blow one of your songs because we come in in the wrong mood, and you say, "This is how it goes *I'll be back*," and we go, "Urghhhh".'[2]

Perhaps intuitive to a brooding malaise, on the third day at Twickenham Paul and George unexpectedly stopped communicating. Initially buoyant about The Beatles' new project, George's sanguinity soon soured, and he retrospectively described the experience as 'coming back to the winter of discontent'. Despite it being the New Year and with a fresh unorthodox approach to recording, little had changed since the group had last been in the studio together. 'It was going to be painful again,' George told *Anthology* in 1995. 'There was a lot of trivia and games being played.'

On Monday, 6 January, George arrived early and in good spirits. 'I wrote a gospel song over the weekend!' he exclaims. After playing 'Hear Me Lord', which George will later record in 1970, for his first solo album, *All Things Must Pass*, attention turns to John's new song, 'Don't

---

2 Possibly a reference to 'I'll Be Back', recorded for *A Hard Day's Night* in 1964.

Let Me Down'. Presented with a simple structure, Paul instinctively begins to add texture and nuances to its melody, which John subtly adopts over repeated run-throughs. As the song begins to sharpen with tighter-fitting words and more ambitious musical passages, Paul hits upon an idea to overlap the end of each verse with a counter melody, doubled by George, 'love for the first time in my life'.

Across the next hour, as The Beatles wrestle over the song's arrangement, Paul's dogged determination and astute musical sense begin to rub against his perceived dictatorial behaviour. 'Start off with a corny one,' Paul proposes. 'I think the words should be corny,' John responds, 'because there's no clever words in it.' 'The corny bits,' George adds, 'I thought, were the notes, how we were doing it, not the words.' Attempting to move forward, Paul suggests playing the passage again, to see 'if it's all right'. John and Paul repeat the line, but George is not convinced. 'That bit is even cornier,' he says. 'The harmony – it's too pretty.' Undeterred, Paul continues, 'We can make it better as we go along. Do it once more. *1-2-3-4...*' Unimpressed by what he hears, George complains, 'It sounds like the same old shit.' 'I like the same old shit,' John retorts, deadpan. Ignoring a gnawing edge of cynicism, Paul struggles to articulate what he is hearing in his head and, perhaps feeling an inward frustration, becomes increasingly authoritarian in his manner. 'I give up,' he eventually submits.

The testy exchange is typical of a band in rehearsal: new ideas being tried and rejected to a backdrop of barbed comments from musicians overfamiliar with one another. Paul is at the centre of the process, energized and driven, attempting to stretch the possibility of the song and broaden its boundaries. As his ideas are played and tested, the rhythm track begins to fall into place. It is riveting listening. But what an audio tape or film archive cannot capture is the atmosphere and the body language in the room. It leaves unanswered questions: is this how The Beatles always behaved and spoke to one another? Or is there a new dynamic at play? Commenting on his relationship with Paul, George told the *New Musical Express* in March 1971:

> That period was the low of all time. We were all getting a bit fed up with our surroundings. To get a peaceful life, I always had to let Paul have his own way – even when it meant songs of mine weren't being recorded. At the same time, I was helping to record Paul's own songs, and into the bargain I was having to put up with him telling me how to play my own instrument. Matters came to a head when Paul started getting at me about the way I was playing.

In the afternoon – 6 January – The Beatles rehearse 'Two of Us' but, as with the morning session, Paul becomes frustrated by the direction the song is taking and complains that the harmonies are not together. George suggests that they keep playing it until 'we can find the bit'. 'Or we can stop and say it's not together,' Paul says. The niggling jabber continues until Paul reluctantly admits 'it's complicated…if we can get it simpler,' he says, 'and then complicate it where it needs complications…' 'It's not complicated,' George rebuffs. 'I know,' Paul says, 'but I mean, you know…' 'I mean,' George continues, determinedly talking over Paul, 'I'll play just the chords, if you'd like, and…' 'No, come on, George,' Paul interrupts, attuned to

George's propensity for self-pity, 'you always get like that.' Downcast, George finishes his sentence, '...that's all I'm trying to do.'

In a strained atmosphere, Paul attempts to ease George's discomfort. 'You always get annoyed when I say that. I'm trying to help you, but I always hear myself annoying you, and I'm trying to...' 'No,' George interjects, 'you're not annoying me.' Hesitantly, Paul continues, 'I get so I can't say...' 'You don't annoy me, Paul,' George interrupts again. 'But you know what I mean,' Paul says. 'Well,' George adds stubbornly.

As with many fallings-out, the subject of an argument is rarely the source of its animosity but rather disguises festering resentments unspoken but imbued between the lines. Above all, George sought recognition – not necessarily as a Beatle but as a musician. Indeed, each of the frontline Beatles – John, Paul and George – were flirting with how best to advance their transitioning futures while reconciling, albeit subconsciously, the prospect of taking control of their artistry as solo musicians against the benefits of working collaboratively within the group.

Having suggested playing a different song, Paul acquiesces to George's wish and they soldier on with 'Two of Us'. But once again discontent rears up. 'I've learnt that bit,' George grumbles, 'and I'm trying to take those chords along with it.' 'I only want to ask you,' Paul retorts, attempting to pacify the situation. Having abstained from the squabble, John finally intervenes. 'It's your song,' he says. 'You don't have to do it exactly how [George] wants to do it. You say, "Don't play that...play that." It's up to you. You just sort of take it. It's your scene.' Thankful for John's matter-of-fact intervention, Paul discloses, 'But now I'm scared of that; to be the boss. And I have been for a couple of years. We all have. There's no pretending about that.'

Knocked by John's observations and George's complaints, Paul returns to the matter later in the day: 'I just can't think of any solution out of here. The trouble is...we should all arrange our own tunes.' 'That's the best way,' George snaps. 'This is not just to do with playing music,' Paul says, unnerved. 'It's far further reaching.' With suppressed irritation, George crackles, 'It's always the further reaching end of it.' Dismayed, Paul protests. 'I daren't put my foot anywhere.' The tone of the exchange remains calm, conversational even, and yet, the undercurrent tension is overt until George eventually bites, 'I don't mind. I'll play what you want me to play or I won't play at all if you don't want me to play. Whatever it is that'll please you, I'll do it.'

In the ensuing five decades, the incident has prompted a vast wealth of analysis and examination. And yet, strangely, the legendary disagreement, which is persistently cited as the reason for *Let It Be* being an unmitigated disaster, occurred four days before George walked out on the band. Indeed, the following afternoon – 7 January – when George expressed a grievance that his songs were being overlooked, Paul's response was conciliatory. 'It doesn't matter what's gone wrong,' he said, 'as long as the four of us notice it. And instead of just noticing it, determine to put it right. That's what I'm into.'

Singled out, from hours of recorded dialogue, these moments bear greater weight than they perhaps deserve, but clearly there is a creative power struggle at play. Yet, over the next few days, there is scant evidence of antagonism between Paul and George. Indeed, The Beatles continued to work productively, introducing and rehearsing a clutch of new songs, including 'Get Back', 'I've Got a Feeling', 'Maxwell's Silver Hammer', 'One after 909', 'I Me Mine', 'The Long and Winding Road', 'Let It Be', 'For You Blue', 'Across the Universe' and 'Teddy Boy'.

Friday, 10 January – the day George walked out and four days after the spat with Paul – started in good humour. Sitting around drinking tea, Paul, Ringo, engineer/producer Glyn Johns and Michael Lindsay-Hogg gossip about Peter Cook being rude to Zsa Zsa Gabor on *The Eamonn Andrews Show* the previous evening. When George and John arrive, work begins on 'Get Back' but an uneasy debate ensues over a seventh chord George plays on the guitar. 'It's passé,' Paul complains. 'It's just a chord,' George responds. Soon after, despite the seeming innocuousness of this exchange, George, perhaps feelings undervalued, says out of the blue, 'You need Eric Clapton.' 'You need George Harrison...' John flashes back. 'George Harrison just doing simple things,' Paul adds. The flashpoint passes, and the rehearsal continues in a positive mood. An hour's break is taken for lunch but when they return to the studio, George makes a shocking declaration. 'I'm leaving the band.' 'When?' John asks. 'Now. You can replace me. Put an ad in the *New Musical Express*.'

That night, George wrote in his dairy: 'Got up went to Twickenham, rehearsed until lunch time – left The Beatles – went home – had chips later at Klaus.'[3] What prompted George's decision to leave has over the years been the subject of much speculation. 'I decided I'd had enough and I told the others I was leaving the

---

3 A reference to Klaus Voormann, a friend of The Beatles. In 1966, Voormann designed the album sleeve for *Revolver*.

group,' George told the *New Musical Express* in March 1971. Then, referencing film footage of his departure, he added. 'The next scene, I'm not there, and Yoko's just screaming, doing her screeching number. Well, there's where I had left.' Writing in his memoir *Luck and Circumstance*, Michael Lindsay-Hogg described the events preceding George's announcement, implying the exchange with John happened over, rather than after, lunch:

At the morning rehearsal, I could tell by his [George's] silence and withdrawal that something was simmering inside him and so, in my role as documentarian, I'd asked our soundman to bug the flower pot on the lunch table. We'd finished the first course when George arrived to stand at the end of the table. We looked at him as he stood silent for a moment. 'See you 'round the clubs,' he said. That was his good-bye. He left. John, a person who reacted aggressively to provocation, immediately said, 'Let's get in Eric. He's just as good and not such a headache.'

With George gone, the band returned to the live room where John launched into a rendition of The Who's mini-opera 'A Quick One (While He's Away)', repeating the phrase 'soon be home' with knowing scorn. 'Okay, George,' he says sarcastically in the guitarist's absence, 'Take it!' An ensuing monotone jam soon descends into a cacophony of noise: Paul generating howls of feedback from his bass cabinet; Ringo thrashing at the drums; and Yoko, sitting in George's seat, screaming 'John, John' among a barrage of indecipherable vocal gyrations. Over 20 minutes, the three Beatles exorcise their pent-up frustration until John eventually calls out, 'Okay, "I've Got a Feeling".' Starting up the song's riff, John sings in a range of lampooning styles. He then stumbles through takes of 'Don't Let Me Down', Eddie Cochran's 'C'mon Everybody' and an exaggerated comical rendition of Paul's 'Maxwell's Silver Hammer'. Further half-hearted attempts at 'Don't Be Cruel', 'On a Sunny Island' and 'It's Only Make Believe' all follow as John and Paul clown about, amusing themselves by putting on silly voices. When Paul improvises Samuel Barber's Adagio for Strings at the piano in a moment of relative calm, John parodies an America preacher, 'Every day I think what fun we had when we was The Beatles playing and rocking around the world.'

While Paul bangs out 'Martha My Dear', John joins a discussion concerning forthcoming plans. 'If George doesn't come back by Monday or Tuesday we ask Eric Clapton to play,' John says. 'The point is if George leaves do we want to carry on The Beatles? I do.' Attempting to make good of a rapidly disintegrating situation, Michael Lindsay-Hogg makes a suggestion. 'Maybe for the show you can say George was sick.' 'No,' John cuts back. 'If he leaves, he leaves.' 'What is the consensus?' Lindsay-Hogg asks presumptuously. 'Do you want to go on with the show and the work?' 'Yes,' John snaps. 'If he doesn't come back by Tuesday we get Clapton.' Breaking the conversation, Yoko suddenly starts relentlessly screaming 'JOHN... JOHN...JOHN!' over and over. 'WHAT? WHAT!' John shouts back. 'Anything you want...anything you say, dear.' 'JOHN... JOHN...JOHN,' Yoko persists. 'Yoko...Yoko,' John replies in a high-pitched voice. Then trying a new tactic, he shouts to Yoko, '...YES!'

and finally, 'Stop that!' Ignoring the incessant wailing, Lindsay-Hogg asks the others how they feel about carrying on. Answering on behalf of the group, John says, 'We should just go on as if nothing's happened.'

Significantly, any meaningful discussion addressing George's departure or obvious unhappiness is avoided. Of course, the English are renowned for their reserved nature and guarded emotional articulateness. Added to which, it must be remembered that these are young men, still only in their twenties, learning the art of compromise and struggling to expose their inner feelings in positive expression. In the desperate void, The Beatles stumbled towards an inevitable demise, desperately in need of an experienced guiding hand.

The day ends with Paul sitting at the drum kit, John playing guitar and Yoko bawling over a formless improvisation. Leaning into the microphone, Ringo provides a running commentary. 'Yeah, rock it to me, baby! That's what I like! You may think this is a full orchestra but if you look closely you can see there's only two people playing and one person singing. I know it sounds like Benny Goodman but don't worry it's the big sound of 1969. You bet your life! Oh, sock it to me, sock it to me!'

Following a weekend break – and with George still absent – the Monday morning session begins with a discussion about a band get-together held at Ringo's Tudor mansion in Elstead, Surrey, the previous afternoon. 'The meeting was fine,' Ringo relays to Lindsay-Hogg, 'but then it all sort of fell apart in the end.' Briefly changing the subject, Paul makes a suggestion that the day's rehearsal should be spent writing words for incomplete songs. 'For what?' Ringo asks glumly. 'It doesn't matter,' Paul says ambiguously. 'If we do an extra week and then we decide to chuck it in...then if we really split, see you in a year's time.'

Pondering over Sunday's meeting, Neil Aspinall attempts to make sense of a particular critical exchange: 'John said to George, "I don't understand you" and George said, "I don't believe you."' 'That was a key moment,' Paul says wryly. Continuing, Aspinall offers an explanation, 'I think John knew what he was talking about. 'Sure he did,' Paul says. Aspinall persists, 'That's why George said it twice. It's like the bullshitting thing.' 'The thing is,' Paul says, 'John does bullshit. I bullshit. But they mean it, him and Yoko.' Adopting a candid tone, Paul explains how John and Yoko's relationship is affecting his songwriting. 'I start writing songs about white walls because I think John and Yoko would like that!' Admitting it was a mistake to take Linda and Heather to Ringo's house at the weekend, Paul adds, 'We were seeing it as a family outing. It should have just been the four of us.' Defending Paul's judgement, Linda says, 'Yoko was doing all the talking. She was talking for John.' 'In the middle of all that,' Paul says, picking up the story, 'George went. And said, "I'll see you."' 'He was waiting for it to stop,' Linda adds. 'You need to have a meeting without Yoko.' 'That's a big crunch,' Paul replies.

After two hours of conversation – with it becoming evident that George's grievances are directed pointedly at John, and by default Yoko – the accused pair arrive at the studio. Captured on tape by a discreetly placed microphone, the discussion continues over lunch. 'I don't think The Beatles revolves around four people,' John says, amid the noise of clattering cups and plates. 'The only answer is to do it on your own but that's too hard.' Sympathizing with John, Linda says, 'It's really hard working in a relationship.' 'I know,' John agrees. 'It's like all of us are dissatisfied with The Beatles' LPs. I think, individually, there's far more inside us.'

Hearing John out, Paul then addresses his own behaviour in rehearsals, acknowledging a desire to perfect arrangements, until John cuts in to say, 'The point that we both know is how George plays won't be like how you want him to play.' Further acknowledging Paul's annoyance at him (John) for being arrogant during the making of the 'White Album', John explains how it was better to just let George play whatever he liked. 'Within ourselves,' Paul surmises, with humility, 'we reach something that's nearly perfect.'

Buoyed by John's pep talk reminder that The Beatles work best when they each contribute freely to a song, Paul returns to the rehearsal room, with an idea. 'Let's go now, shall we,' he says. 'Let's go and see George.' 'We should phone and see if he's there,' Ringo suggests. 'He's gone to Liverpool,' Mal Evans interjects.[4] Undeterred, John and Paul spend the remainder of the afternoon writing words for 'Get Back'. The following day – Tuesday, 14 January – Paul and Ringo arrive early and hit upon an idea to write and film a play in a day. Enamoured of the idea, John and Yoko happily play along. Little music is played beyond short renditions of 'Mean Mr. Mustard' and 'Get Back', and when the cameras are switched off two days later, the ten days The Beatles have spent at Twickenham Studios come to an unceremonious end.

---

4 Evans became The Beatles road manager after Brian Epstein offered him the job in 1963. After The Beatles stopped touring, Evans became a personal assistant and, by 1968, an executive at Apple.

The two-week rehearsal period at Twickenham had been defined by George's disillusionment and growing inner frustration with John's kowtowing to Yoko and Paul's officious manner. Perhaps, as much due to the tight bond of friendship and respect that united The Beatles, the outlet for their disquiet was as subtle as it was spiky. Certainly, the intensity of working in an unnatural creative environment magnified a developing weariness, but simultaneously it highlighted the strength of the group to filter petty grievances into making dynamic music – rich in body and deep with emotion.

Apple: The Rooftop Performance

On 20 January 1969, The Beatles reunited at Apple, a newly built studio in the Georgian townhouse basement of 3 Savile Row, Mayfair, where they would spend the next 11 consecutive days completing the *Get Back* project. The grievances that had marred George's experience at Twickenham had seemingly been resolved. Indeed, five days earlier – on Wednesday 15 January – John, Paul and Ringo had met at George's house. But beyond reaching a decision to abandon the planned TV special, little has surfaced of the day's conversation. 'The others asked me to return,' George would offer as a brief explanation to the High Court in February 1971, 'and – since Paul agreed he wouldn't try to interfere or teach me how to play – I went back. Since the row, Paul has treated me more as a musical equal. I think this whole episode shows how a disagreement could be worked out so that we all benefited.' 'There's that famous old saying,' Ringo told *Scene and Heard*, '"You always hurt the one you love" and we all love each other and we all know that. We still sort of hurt each other occasionally...and it builds up into something bigger than it was.'

The Beatles' worldwide success and its accompanying round-the-clock demands had rendered playing music just for sheer fun near impossible. At Twickenham, and then Apple, setting up in a studio, face to face, and playing from morning till night afforded The Beatles the opportunity to rediscover their roots. For the first time in many years, The Beatles were a group again: hanging out, writing, rehearsing, playing songs together. Rejecting production ingenuities, which so many of their earlier recordings had been celebrated for, The Beatles embraced a return to recording live. 'The idea of us just doing it and there's no overdubs or you can't get out of it,' George enthused to his bandmates, 'is much better really. Because you know that all the time recording, you're thinking, "Ah, it's all right, we can do that later," so you never get even the most out of that moment, really.'

Nevertheless, an end result was both expected and desired by The Beatles. But it did not prevent the group from enjoying themselves. On a daily basis, they would happily switch from rehearsing their own songs to playing rock 'n' roll standards and random oddities from their formative years. The importance of this process cannot be underestimated. Jamming is the equivalent of schoolboys playfighting or actors improvising – a form of non-verbal communication to break down barriers and a bonding exercise to unite people through a shared common language. By repeatedly playing covers and revisiting their earliest attempts at songwriting, The Beatles cultivated their growth. It was a musical form of reconnection and, albeit subconsciously, a way to strengthen the band's inner core. 'We stopped touring and we'd only get together for recordings,' John said in 1970:

> So therefore the recording session was the thing we almost rehearsed in as well – it's like an athlete: you really have to keep playing all the time to keep your hand in. We'd be off for months and we'd suddenly come into the studio and be expected to be spot on again. It would take us a few days getting loosened up and playing together. That's what we all missed.

In some respects, in January 1969, The Beatles reverted to being like an amateur band – rehearsing for an upcoming show and, for the most part, without the distraction of recording equipment. For the first time in many years, The Beatles developed ideas playing live and in the moment.

On the third day at Apple – 22 January – a surprise guest, Billy Preston, dropped by. He was a friend from their Hamburg days, where on one occasion George had invited him to join them on stage; Preston had politely declined, fearful of word getting back to his employer, Little Richard. Nevertheless, a strong friendship developed, and when George saw Preston on stage at the Royal Festival Hall, playing keyboards in Ray Charles's band, he 'put the word out' for him to visit Apple. Preston's timely arrival was captured on film, and John is seen sharing a joke with Preston, who is beaming with delight. After playing through 'Dig a Pony', Preston is invited to play along on 'Don't Let Me Down', which he does, effortlessly complementing the sound. In a blink of an eye, The Beatles had become a five-piece.[5]

Having spent much of the morning reciting Martin Luther King Jr.'s celebrated 'March on Washington' speech, John wantonly attempted to incorporate the historic soundbite 'I have a dream'[6] into 'I've Got a Feeling'. Enthralled by Preston's sudden appearance, John exultantly shouts out King's call for racial integration, liberally peppering songs throughout the day with King's slogan. It has been suggested by some Beatle historians that, by bringing Preston into the fold, George was subtly redefining the creative parameters of the *Get Back* project and, by default, diluting Paul's perceived 'overbearing' control. It is a notion that has no supporting evidence. The arrival of Preston is also often cited as the tonic that lifted the mood in a decaying atmosphere. Again, it is an argument without substantiation. Before Preston's arrival, there was a wholesome spirit among The Beatles, with them regularly adopting silly voices, sharing jokes or playing their songs at a comedy double

---

5   Preston's involvement was the first time The Beatles had operated as a five- piece since July 1961, when Paul switched from playing piano to bass to accommodate Stuart Sutcliffe joining the band. In the intervening years, and since reverting to a four-piece, guest appearances on Beatle tracks extended to less than a handful of familiar names – Brian Jones on 'You Know My Name (Look Up the Number)', Nicky Hopkins on 'Revolution', Ronnie Scott on 'Lady Madonna' and Eric Clapton on 'While My Guitar Gently Weeps' – all of them uncredited. Yet, in an unprecedented show of gratitude, when 'Get Back' was released as a single in April 1969, the sleeve credit proclaimed 'The Beatles with Billy Preston'.

6   King's birthday, 15 January, had been a week earlier, and on 21 January, ITV replayed Michael Grigsby's documentary *Deep South* showing the 1963 'March on Washington' speech. Ray Charles had recorded a song called 'I Had a Dream' in 1958, not to be confused with the song 'I Had a Dream' written by David Porter and Isaac Hayes and recorded by Johnnie Walker in 1966.

speed. More often than not, John was at the centre. '"I Dig a Pygmy" by Charles Hawtrey and the deaf-aids,' he randomly shouts out before a rehearsal of 'Dig a Pony'. 'Phase one, in which Doris gets her oats!' Nevertheless, Preston's arrival is keenly felt, and the joy The Beatles take from his keyboard virtuosity is tangible. Over the following week, Preston's input expands the dynamic of the music and provides the missing link The Beatles had been searching for.

Jean-Luc Godard was keen to collaborate with The Beatles. In late 1968, the acclaimed French director attended a meeting at Savile Row to explore the possibility of making a film with the band. Godard had recently made the pseudo-documentary *1 + 1* showing The Rolling Stones recording 'Sympathy for the Devil' at Olympic Studios, intercut with didactic scenes featuring the American revolutionary organization the Black Panthers. After its release, Godard travelled to New York where, on 19 November, he filmed a performance by the rock group Jefferson Airplane on the roof of the Hotel Schuyler on 57 West 45th Street. The impromptu appearance attracted a crowd on the street below, luring residents to lean out of apartment windows to catch a glimpse of the spectacle. Jefferson Airplane's five-minute performance was met with polite applause, prompting singer Grace Slick to skip on the roof of the hotel with joy. As members of the band leaned over the railings to view the scene below, Godard's camera team capture actor Rip Torn being arrested by the New York Police Department for alleged harassment. Amid shouts and jeers, a lone voice calls out, 'If they continue the music, lock 'em up!'

Godard's proposal to The Beatles to create a similar happening in London was rebuffed but perhaps not altogether forgotten. On

21 January, having batted around ideas for several days, The Beatles discussed the possibility of an unspecified spontaneous performance. 'What's your practical answer to the problem now, regarding tomorrow?' John asked. 'I think we'd be daft to not do it, try and do something. Even if it's a grand dress rehearsal and see how it went.' Reflecting on being filmed for the past three weeks, Paul asks rhetorically, 'Is it a documentary of us doing another album, which it is...it isn't a TV show anymore...it's an album, that's what I've got to get in my head.' 'All that footage and film,' George concludes, 'could make about half a dozen films.'

How the film should end had been the subject of continuous debate since the start of the project. Suggestions ranged from Yoko's idea to play to an empty auditorium in a London theatre to John's notion of sailing towards the horizon on a ship, 'timing it,' he said, 'as the sun came up on the middle eight'. Protesting that 'we'd be stuck with a bloody big boat of people,' George declared the idea 'insane!'. When the idea of a rooftop performance was floated, Paul expressed concern that it would be an anticlimactic ending to the preceding month. 'It's too far,' he says the day before the proposed show. 'It puts us in the open air on a little roof with wind, and rain if it rains because we haven't got the end. I've got a feeling that we're just going to go off like we did at the end of the last album, and think, "Not another fucking album".'

Attempting to explain Paul's reservations, John compares the ownership of the *Get Back* venture to writing a song. 'Say it's *his* number, this whole show, but it's a compromise so it's actually turned into *our* number more than *his* number, that's all...' 'And that's all right,' Paul says. '...It's all right,' John continues. 'That's what's bugging you, really, because it's a different number. It's turned into a rock number as opposed to a quiet number or something like that...I would dig to play on stage. If everything was all right and there was no messing and we're just going to play on stage. That's why I said yes to the TV show, I didn't want the hell of doing it...I like playing that's why I went on the Stones show...but I don't want to go on the road again.'[7] 'I just feel as though we are on the road again,' Paul says, 'but we're in the studio.' Interjecting, George says – in stark contradiction to his comment a fortnight earlier, 'I don't want to do any of my songs on the show. They'll just turn out shitty.' – 'This is the nicest place I've been for a long time. I can just feel my fingers getting lose again...really, I just wanna play.' Enthused, John adds, 'It's such a high when you get home.' 'Yeah, it's great isn't it?' George grins.

And so, before lunchtime on 30 January 1969, The Beatles stepped out on to the reinforced wooden planked roof of 3 Savile Row with a casual insouciance. Among a jumble of cables and amplifiers, John stood centre stage looking over the London skyline wearing a brown fur coat and black trousers. Paul, to his right, in a black suit and open-necked white shirt. Stage left, George sporting green trousers and a black fur coat. Behind the drum kit, Ringo wearing a red plastic mac, purloined from his wife, Maureen, and, nestled behind Paul, Billy Preston sitting at an electric keyboard robed in a knee-length black leather trench coat.

It is almost two and a half years since The Beatles gave their last public performance at Candlestick Park, in August 1966. More in

---

7   The 'Stones show' was *The Rolling Stones Rock and Roll Circus*, held on
    11 December 1968.

the spirit of a rehearsal than a commercial concert, the 42-minute performance is relaxed and informal; there are three attempts at 'Get Back', two versions of both 'I've Got a Feeling' and the aptly named 'Don't Let Me Down', and one rendition of 'Dig a Pony' and 'One after 909'. A modest audience witnesses the event. People clamber up onto adjacent buildings – including four young men stood in a line dressed in matching black suits (a mirror image of John, Paul, George and Ringo five years earlier at the height of Beatlemania) – while on the street, five storeys below, a mixture of fans and disgruntled citizens objecting to the disturbance gather. The Beatles are relaxed and treat the impromptu happening without fuss or fanfare. There are false starts, in-between song banter, snatches of additional songs – 'I Want You', 'Danny Boy', 'God Save the Queen' and Irving Berlin's 'A Pretty Girl Is Like a Melody' – and, finally, a murmur of mild amusement when the police appear from the stairwell behind Billy Preston's keyboard to bring proceedings to an end. The scene is neatly rounded off by John's much lauded ad-lib, 'I'd like to say thank you on behalf of the group and ourselves and I hope we've passed the audition.'

After the performance, The Beatles reconvened in the basement studio of Apple to listen back to the live recording. There was a general sense of satisfaction and talk of 'taking over London' and 'pretending the police' had forced the show to end. It was agreed to record the songs not performed on the roof and the following day – Friday, 31 January – The Beatles spent a final session at Apple doing precisely that. The day commenced with a ten-minute improvised medley of country songs, led by John, including Lonnie Donegan's 'Take This

Hammer' and 'Lost John' and a brief version of John's 'Run for Your Life' from *Rubber Soul*. Attention then turned to recording 'Two of Us' in between which Paul sings 'Step inside Love' – written for Cilla Black in 1967 – and John improvises ad-hoc renditions of Johnny Cash and Elvis Presley songs. An hour was spent recording 19 takes of 'The Long and Winding Road' interrupted by a flash play-through of 'Lady Madonna' and a brooding five-minute acid-rock version of 'I Want You'. John and Paul harmonize through three versions of 'Oh! Darling', and plans to record 'Teddy Boy', 'For You Blue' and 'All Things Must Pass' are discussed. Paul leads The Beatles through 26 takes of 'Let It Be' – still without the song's third verse – before writing the missing lyrics at the end of the day. 'Ohhhh, yes!' Paul joyfully chirps, as the final C major chord of 'Let It Be' rings out. It was the last sound after a month of recording and one of the most dramatic four weeks in the life of The Beatles' recording career. As machines are turned off and the film lights shut down, Michael Lindsay-Hogg is heard poignantly asking, 'How was that?'

To answer Lindsay-Hogg's question, The Beatles had, within the space of a calendar month, written a new album – *Let It Be* – and much of the material for what would become *Abbey Road*. They had overcome George walking out on rehearsals and rounded off the episode by playing a stunning live set of original songs for the first time since 1966. While dramatically bringing an enclave of central London to a standstill, The Beatles had shown that, in the face of adversity, collective endeavour was the answer to their future creative prosperity.

3. The End Game

Arrival of Allen Klein

We're always waiting for the big man with a cigar.
John Lennon – press conference, 1965

On 7 January 1969, during a break in rehearsals at the *Get Back* sessions at Twickenham Studios, George shares a nagging concern. 'Ever since Mr. Epstein passed away, it hasn't been the same.' Agreeing, Paul says, 'We've been very negative since Mr. Epstein passed away. That's why all of us, in turn, have been sick of the group. There's nothing positive in it. It is a bit of a drag. But the only way for it to not be really a drag, is for the four of us to say, "Should we make it positive or should we fuck it?"'

There was nothing unusual about The Beatles broaching contentious issues. Problems were often casually aired and then passed off with casual detachment. It gave difficult matters space to dwell in preparation for later discussion. Astutely recognizing that, where leadership is lacking, disorder prevails, Paul raised the issue of management with Michael Lindsay-Hogg. 'Your daddy goes away at a certain point of your life and you stand on your own feet,' Paul said:

> That's all we've been faced with: Daddy's gone away now, and
> we're on our own at the holiday camp. And I think we'd rather

go home. Or we do it. It's discipline we like. For everything you do, if you want to do it well, you got to have discipline, we all think that. But for this, we've never had discipline. Mr. Epstein said, 'Get suits on,' and we did…and so we were sort of always fighting that discipline. But now it's silly to fight the discipline because it's our own self-imposed, these days. So we put in as little as possible. But I think we need a bit more if we are going to get on with it.

'After Brian died,' John was later to comment in *Rolling Stone*, 'we collapsed. Paul took over and supposedly led us. But what is leading us, when we went round in circles?' In 1964, Allen Klein had approached Brian Epstein to co-manage The Beatles. His offer was politely refused. A year later, Klein renegotiated The Rolling Stones' record contract with Decca, boasting, 'I can find you money you never even knew you had.' Having established an influence in the music industry working for The Animals and Herman's Hermits, Klein subsequently negotiated advantageous deals for The Kinks and The Small Faces. Then, in August 1967, at the moment the death of Brian Epstein was broadcast on American radio, and while driving across the George Washington Bridge, Klein allegedly shouted, 'I've got them!'

Gaining access to The Beatles inner circle was difficult. When John gave an interview to *Disc & Music Echo* in January 1969, he told Ray Coleman, 'We've haven't got half the money people think we have. It's been pie in the sky from the start. Apple's losing money every week because it needs close running by a big businessman. If it carries on like this, all of us will be broke in six months.' Seizing the initiative, Klein engineered a meeting with John and Yoko. Held at the Harlequin Suite of the Dorchester Hotel on 27 January 1969, the conversation stretched into the early hours. John and Yoko were impressed by Klein's intricate knowledge of The Beatles' music and his 'street' manner, lapping up stories of Klein producing films in Hollywood and working with The Rolling Stones. They heard how his mother had died when he was a child – like John's and Paul's – and how he had spent his boyhood in a Jewish orphanage. 'One of the things that impressed me about Allen, and obviously it was a kind of flattery as well, was that he really knew which stuff I'd written,' John told Peter McCabe and Robert Schonfeld in September 1971. 'Not many people knew which was my song and which was Paul's, but he'd say, "Well, McCartney didn't write that line, did he?" I thought, anybody who knows me this well, just by listening to records, is pretty perceptive. I'm not the easiest guy to read, although I'm fairly naive and open in some ways, and I can be conned easily. But in other ways I'm quite complicated, and it's not easy to get through all the defences and see what I'm like.'

The following day, The Beatles spent the morning rehearsing 'I've Got a Feeling' until Paul had to leave for a lunchtime meeting and suggested that John should take over lead vocals. Accepting Paul's proposal, John's approach was fascinating, lending Paul's melody a more overt blues bent. After a couple of perfunctory attempts, his thoughts turned to his encounter with Klein. 'I wanted to tell you all at once,' John raved to George and Ringo. 'I just think he's fantastic. I'd just like you to see him and talk...a lot of interesting news that we don't know half about.' 'About us?' George asks. 'Yeah!' John enthuses:

> He'll tell you all that. He knows everything about everything, on everyone. He's that big. I was there till two in the morning. I was thinking, 'Fuckin' hell, I've got to see him.' I put him off last time. He knows things that you can't believe…he even knows what we're like. The way he described each of us…he knows me as much as you do. We were both stunned.

With glowing admiration, John describes how Klein had negotiated The Rolling Stones a better royalty than The Beatles and planned to donate the money from *The Rolling Stones Rock and Roll Circus* to children in need in Biafra.[1] After lunch, Paul returns and The Beatles spend a productive afternoon rehearsing half a dozen songs. Clearly invigorated, John plays a heavy blues riff and Billy Preston sings 'I want you, I want you so bad' over the top, locked into John's cascading guitar notes. The idea develops and 'I Want You' – later to be recorded for *Abbey Road* – appears, as if from nowhere. Thrilled, The Beatles jam around the intoxicating riff into the evening until John shouts out, 'Allen Klein's here – look out!'

Enthralled by the prospect of a manager lifting the burden of Apple from The Beatles' shoulders, John sent a handwritten note to

---

1   The Republic of Biafra in eastern Nigeria was declared independent on 30 May 1967. On 7 January 1969, at Twickenham Studios, Paul suggested, 'We should send planes to Biafra and rescue all the people. Play at the airport as they come in. Do a show for them.'

the chairman of EMI Records, Sir Joseph Lockwood. 'Dear Sir Joe,' it read, 'from now on Allen Klein handles all my stuff.' With immediate effect, Klein was charged with auditing The Beatles' accounts and effectively granted control of the group's management. Nevertheless, John's unilateral declaration broke an unwritten agreement between the four Beatles and, in doing, constituted a decisive moment in the band's relationship, effectively driving a wedge between himself and Paul. 'In the very early days of The Beatles,' Paul told *Rolling Stone* in April 1970, 'we sort of thought of ourselves as a democracy. But nothing ever came to a vote – the chemistry of the four of us made the decisions naturally. John dominated the group in making the decisions and John and I dominated the group musically. What's happened now is that each of us has become very strong individuals in our own right.'

In a written affidavit, submitted to the High Court in December 1970 after the breakup of The Beatles, John argued that grounds for consensus was no longer practical. 'Of necessity, we developed a pattern for sorting out our differences, by doing what any three of us decided. It sometimes took a long time and sometimes there was deadlock and nothing was done, but generally that was the rule we followed and, until recent events, it worked quite well.' Further drawing attention to the death of Brian Epstein, John pointed out that, resultantly, 'Apple was full of "hustlers" and "spongers"'. Within weeks of Klein's appointment, John wrote, 'He dismissed incompetent or unnecessary staff; the "hustling" and lavish hospitality ended; and discipline and order appeared in the Apple offices.' Explaining further the personal differences between

The Beatles, despite walkouts and arguments, John said that they remained 'close as we had ever been'. 'After Mr. Epstein's death,' he wrote, 'Mr. McCartney and me, in particular, tried to be business-like over Apple's affairs, but we were handicapped by our ignorance of accounting, business practice and our preoccupation with our musical activities...We needed a business man. No Beatle can spend his days here checking the accountants,' John concluded. 'That was just the irreconcilable difference between us,' Paul told *Life* in 1971, conscious of his own misgivings and John's infatuation with Klein. 'Klein is incredible. He's New York. He'll say "Waddaya want? I'll buy it for you."'

On 4 February 1969 – the day after John, George, Ringo and a reluctant Paul instructed Allen Klein to conduct an audit of their financial affairs – Lee Eastman and his son John, respectively the father and brother of Linda Eastman, were officially offered the position as The Beatles' lawyers. Paul's wish to employ his prospective in-laws was met with resistance from the three other Beatles, not least because of the Eastmans' middle-class roots. 'We were all from Liverpool,' George said in *Anthology*. 'We favoured people who were street people. Lee Eastman was more of a class-conscious type of person. As John was going with Klein, it was much easier if we went with him too.' Exploring the issue in a radio interview with Howard Smith in 1970, George added, 'You imagine that situation if you were married and you wanted your in-laws to handle certain things. It's a difficult one to overcome because...well, you can think of the subtleties. When I go home at night I'm not living there with Allen

Klein, whereas in a way, Paul's living with the Eastmans.'[2]

Categorically opposed to the Eastmans' involvement, John expressed his view in unpleasant and scandalous terms to *Rolling Stone* magazine in December 1970. But such was the severity of his damnation that the passage was cut from the published interview.[3] 'Eastman's a WASP Jew, man!' he ranted, 'and that's the worst kind of Jew on earth, that's the worst kind of WASP too – he's a WASP Jew, can you imagine it!'

In Paul's mind, John's desire to favour Klein had been whetted by a coy seduction of Yoko. 'Allen had a very good way of persuading people,' Paul explained in *Anthology*. 'In Yoko's case, she wanted an art exhibition and she was having some difficulty maybe getting it on. I think Allen Klein said, "Okay, you got it. Exhibition? No problem!" So we all ended up paying for her Syracuse exhibition – a quarter each – and she wasn't even in the group.'

---

2   The issue of partisan involvement dated back to 1962, when George's mother suggested that his brother Peter should replace Neil Aspinall as their manager. 'She didn't understand there was no fucking way Peter could have done my job,' Aspinall explained in Mark Lewisohn's *All These Years*. 'What would have happened if he was driving the van and one of them said, "Aw fuck off, Pete?" What was George gonna do? Say, "Hey, that's my bother you're talking to?" It becomes a family thing, when really everything had to be equal or it couldn't have worked.' Clearly attuned to the pitfalls of artist agreements, when Brian Epstein took over management of the group in 1962, he reneged on signing a management contract. In his memoir, *A Cellarful of Noise*, Epstein noted, 'I wanted to free The Beatles of their obligations if I felt they would be better off."

3   John's anti-Semitic comment was reinstated when the transcript of the interview was issued its entirety in November 1971, as *Lennon Remembers*. Ironically, Allen Klein was also Jewish.

Convinced of Klein's nefarious ways, Paul revealed a startling source of disquiet in his affidavit to the High Court in February 1971. 'Mr. Lennon had challenged my statement that Mr. Klein had sowed discord within the group,' Paul wrote, 'but I recall a telephone conversation in which Mr. Klein had told me, "You know why John is angry with you? It is because you came off better than he did on *Let It Be*."' Mr. Klein also said to me, "The real trouble is Yoko. She is the one with ambition." I often wonder what John would have said if he heard the remark.'

On Friday, 9 May 1969, The Beatles were booked for a recording session at Olympic Studios, in Barnes, south-west London. Arriving with a three-year management contract in hand, Allen Klein insisted that all four Beatles sign it. John, George and Ringo signed. But Paul refused, incensed at Klein's demand for a 20 per cent royalty fee. Notwithstanding the fact that Lee and John Eastman and Allen Klein were Jewish and willing to work on a Sabbath, Paul fairly judged that a legal contract was unlikely to be acted upon over a weekend. When Paul proposed a reduction to 15 per cent 'they all accused me of stalling,' Paul told *Club Sandwich*'s Mark Lewisohn in 1992. 'In my mind I was actually trying to save our future, and I was vindicated later, but at the time I was definitely "the dark horse, the problem".'

Deaf to Paul's protestations – denying Klein an official position within The Beatles' management – John, George and Ringo were incensed. 'That was actually the night we broke The Beatles,' Paul explained to Lewisohn. 'That was the big crack in the liberty bell, it

Paul and Linda McCartney arrive at the High Court, London to dissolve The Beatles' partnership, 19 February 1971.

never came back together after that one.'[4] Shortly after, Paul composed the wistful 'You Never Give Me Your Money' lambasting Allen Klein. 'I was having dreams that Klein was a dentist,' Paul said in *Many Years from Now*:

> I remember telling everyone and they all laughed, but I said, 'No, this was a fucking scary dream!' I said, 'I can't be with the guy any longer. He's in my dreams now, and he's a baddie.' He was giving me injections in my dreams to put me out and I was thinking, fucking hell! I've just become powerless. There's nothing I can do to stop this rot. So I decided to just get out, but they wouldn't let me out, they held me to that contract.

At this critical juncture, could The Beatles have rejected both Allen Klein and the Eastmans' involvement and found a mutually acceptable candidate to manage the group? It seems attempts were made to do exactly that with a view to remedying John's and Paul's opposing preferences. In 1962, Dr Richard Beeching published a report entitled 'The Reshaping of British Railways' recommending the closure of unprofitable routes to increase revenue, resulting in the closure of one-third of Britain's railway lines. Decorated by the Queen, the newly titled Lord Beeching was approached by John – at Paul's request – to manage The Beatles affairs, but, understandably, the

---

4   The Liberty Bell was a historical reference to the first public reading of the American Declaration of Independence on 8 July 1776. The bell was cast by Lester and Pack in Whitechapel, London, but had to be recast on two separate occasions, owing to the discovery of a crack in the bell after a test strike.

conversation never seriously progressed; an ageing peer was always an unlikely candidate to manage a freewheeling pop group. Nonetheless, the conciliatory attempt illustrates a willingness to explore alternatives, and demonstrates how a successful outcome would have changed the course of Beatle history.

Contrarily, if the ongoing business wrangling suggested ill-feeling among The Beatles with the potential to grind activity to a halt, the reality was surprisingly sanguine. 'The outcome of this whole financial business doesn't matter.' John told the *New Musical Express* on 3 May 1969. 'We'll still be making records, and somebody will be copping some money, and we'll be copping some money, and that'll be that.' 'I don't like doing the business bit that much but you can't avoid it,' Paul told journalist David Wigg. 'We were once just a band but because we were successful money came in – you can't help that. When money comes in, income tax has to be paid so you can't really help just turning into a business man. It's just force of circumstance.' Three days after the Klein showdown at Olympic Studios and being told to 'fuck off' by his fellow bandmates, Paul was asked by Roy Corlett on BBC Radio Merseyside if there was a 'great bond of friendship'. 'Yes, sure there is,' Paul replied, 'They're my three best friends. They're good lads, I tell you.'

The Beatles' readiness to bounce back from business acrimony spoke highly of their tight attachment to one another. In a further show of solidarity, the group gathered on 13 May in a stairwell at EMI's offices on Manchester Square for a photo shoot to re-create the pose on the cover of *Please Please Me*. As they had done six years earlier – in March 1963 – and with a knowing degree of irony, The

Beatles leaned over an upper-level balcony into the lens of Angus McBean's camera below. Gone were the freshly shaved smiling faces, the matching suits and the neatly knotted ties – Ringo's smartly combed quiff replaced by shaggy shoulder-length hair; Paul's cheery smile darkened by a hint of a grimace; George's affectionate grin weighted by a knowing stare; and John's glistening mop grown out, substituted with heavy facial hair and a tailored white suit. It was the second time The Beatles had attempted to 'get back' having re-created their Pierre Cardin collarless shirt 'fab' pose for the 'Hello Goodbye' promotional video – directed by Paul – in November 1967. Eighteen months later, the sense of happy reminiscence was substituted by an image of forbearance.[5]

As recording sessions continued so the business standoff limped on. 'Klein is certainly forceful to an extreme,' John said, 'but he does get results. So far as I know, he has not taken any commission to which he was not entitled.' Freshly charged and keen to validate John's flattering endorsement, Klein asserted his business acumen by successfully renegotiating a contract with EMI/Capital and increasing The Beatles' royalty rate from 17.5 per cent to an unprecedented 25 per cent. Significantly, the agreement assented, whether individually or collectively, that The Beatles would deliver the minimum of two albums a year until 1976. And although all four Beatles had been contracted collectively and financially for ten years – since July 1967 – with songwriting exempted from the deal, it meant all royalties from future solo releases would be shared four

---

5   The resulting photographs were used for the covers of the 1976 compilation albums *The Beatles 1962–1966* and *The Beatles 1967–1970*, respectively.

ways within the defined contractual period.

The deal was due to be signed on 20 September 1969 at Savile Row. In the week leading up to the document agreement, all four Beatles came together to discuss voting rights and share options. And, as will later be discussed, the occasion also marked a decisive turning point in The Beatles' history. 'I wasn't gonna tell you till after we'd signed the contract,' John announced, repeating a precedent set by Ringo and then George. 'But I'm leaving the group.'

John in negotiation for control of shares in The Beatles' publishing company, with Allen Klein and Yoko Ono, 29 April 1969.

Abbey Road

In February 1969, three weeks after performing on the Apple roof, and despite George temporarily walking out during the *Get Back* sessions, the festering disagreements over the arrival of Allen Klein and the management affairs of the Apple business empire, The Beatles began work on what would become their thirteenth studio album, *Abbey Road*. Sessions began at Trident Studios on Saturday, 22 February and continued sporadically throughout the spring before an intense period of recording during the summer to complete the record.

A sequence of photographs, taken by Ethan Russell, shows The Beatles at Trident at the outset of the project.[6] John is wearing a brown woollen polo neck, Paul, clean-shaven, is dressed in a light-blue denim shirt, George in dark-blue jeans and a white sweater holding a newly acquired red Gibson Les Paul, and Ringo sat behind his kit with a tea towel over the snare drum and to his left, handwritten lyrics on a metal-framed music stand. Before him, Yoko is sitting beside Paul's stepdaughter, six-year-old Heather, who is playfully engrossed with a white painted cone.

The Beatles spent the February weekend, working into the early hours, on 'I Want You (She's So Heavy)' while fielding a complaint from a local neighbour who claimed that the music was disturbing the peace. 'It's his own fault,' Paul responds, unsympathetically, 'for getting a house in such a lousy district.' 'Well, we'll try it once more,'

---

6 *Let It Be* was released on 8 May 1970 as a boxed set including a lavish book with colour photographs of The Beatles at Twickenham, Apple and Trident.

John suggests, 'very loud, and then if we don't get it we'll try it quiet, like it might do it the other way. Okay, last chance to be loud.' Crashing into a final take, 'I Want You' was loud and heavy, emotively building over seven minutes around George's dexterous guitar riff, John's hard blues vocal delivery, Paul's atmospheric bass runs; a menacing white noise; and a mesmeric Billy Preston organ solo – overdubbed on 20 April at Abbey Road.

Two days later, *Oliver!* won the Best Motion Picture Musical Award, and Barbra Streisand Best Actress for her role as Fanny Brice in *Funny Girl* at the 26th Golden Globe Awards. It seemed as if the distance between The Beatles and mainstream taste could not have been greater. But, on 11 April, a new Beatles single was released which duly entered the charts at number one on both sides of the Atlantic.

'Get Back' and 'Don't Let Me Down' had both been recorded in January during the *Get Back* sessions, and the single was the first opportunity for the public to hear The Beatles' new direction. 'Why did we spring "Get Back" on the public so suddenly?' John rhetorically asked in an *NME* interview. 'Well, we'd been talking about it since we recorded it, and we kept saying "That's a single." Eventually we got so fed up talking about it we suddenly said, "Okay, that's it. Get it out tomorrow."'

Three days later – on 14 April – John and Paul recorded 'The Ballad of John and Yoko'. 'John and Yoko came round to see me, and John said, "I've got this song about me and Yoko and I'm hot to record it, I'd like to ring up the studio, get some time and we could do it right now. You could play bass and you could play drums."' Impulsively the pair nipped round to Abbey Road and recorded the song, described by John as 'like an old-time ballad…it's the story of us going along getting married, going to Paris, going to Amsterdam, all that,' John explained to the *NME*'s Alan Smith. 'It's "Johnny B. Paperback Writer",' he added, playfully merging a Beatles song with Chuck Berry's 'Johnny B. Goode'. In the studio, John quipped to Paul, 'Go a bit faster, Ringo.' 'Okay, George!' Paul replied.

By 11 o'clock, and after 11 takes, the track was finished and mixed to stereo.[7] 'The story came out that only Paul and I were on the record,' John explained to the *NME*, 'but I wouldn't have bothered publicizing that. It doesn't mean anything. It just so happened that there were only two of us there – George was abroad and Ringo was on the film [*The Magic Christian* with Peter Sellers] and he couldn't come that night.' 'I didn't mind not being on the record,' George nonchalantly informed *Anthology*, immune to any implied rift within the band. 'If it had been "The Ballad of John, George and Yoko" then I would have been on it.' Over the following weeks, The Beatles recorded 'Old Brown Shoe', 'Something', 'Oh! Darling', 'Octopus's Garden' and 'You Never Give Me Your Money' before taking an early-summer break. Returning to Abbey Road on 1 July, The Beatles embarked on an intensive eight-week period of recording.

If the *Get Back* sessions were to be remembered for inter-band politics, walkouts and petty squabbles, the following two months witnessed the pinnacle of The Beatles' collaborative endeavour: lyrically, musically and technically. In keeping with their recent

---

7   The first Beatles single to be offered in such a format.

Ringo with American actress Raquel Welch during the filming of *The Magic Christian*, February 1969.

history, the new record – *Abbey Road* – would be a reaction to their last – *Let It Be*. In 1966, *Revolver* had built on the sophistication of *Rubber Soul*. In 1968, the 'White Album' had offered a liberated release from the production trickery of the preceding *Sgt. Pepper*. And in the summer of 1969, *Abbey Road* was a reaction to the amorphous *Get Back* sessions.

During the first three weeks of July 1969, neither John nor Yoko attended the recording sessions at Abbey Road after being involved in a motoring accident while on holiday in Scotland. When John was discharged from Golspie's Lawson Memorial Hospital – after six days and seventeen facial stitches – he arranged for a double bed, ordered from Harrods, to be delivered to the EMI Studios for Yoko to convalesce; having not only sustained facial cuts and a back injury, she would also suffer a second miscarriage.

Briefly popping into the studio on 9 July, while Paul, George and Ringo were recording 'Maxwell's Silver Hammer', John fully returned to the fold on Monday, 21 July, by which time, nine of the seventeen songs for *Abbey Road* had been recorded.[8] If there was any lingering concern over Paul and George's working relationship in the wake of their squabble at Twickenham Studios, it was quashed in this intensely creative period.

In possession of a new mixing console and, for the first time, an

---

8   Their combined contribution included recording the backing for 'Golden Slumbers' (George playing bass), 'Carry That Weight' (Paul playing rhythm guitar), 'Maxwell's Silver Hammer', 'Oh! Darling', 'Here Comes the Sun', 'Something', and a peppering of many songs with harmonies including the nautical vocal effects on 'Octopus's Garden'.

eight-track tape machine, The Beatles experimented, introducing a range of effects and production techniques not previously heard on their recordings, from the futuristic sound of the Moog synthesizer and the piercing shrill of white noise to daring edit cuts and an epic concluding mini-operatic song cycle. A marathon two-day session on Friday, 1 August and Monday, 4 August was spent working on a new song written by John. It exemplified The Beatles' indefatigable thirst for innovation. 'Because' was a tour de force of complex vocal harmonies recorded as a three-piece ensemble and tracked twice over by John, Paul and George to create the swell of a human chord. The dedication and endurance of the three vocalists were testament to their commitment to The Beatles, and, moreover, illustrated the healing power of music to transcend simmering resentments. 'Suddenly, when we were working on something good,' Ringo reflected in *Anthology*, 'the bullshit went out the window and we got down to what we were doing really well.'

Curiously, during the recording of 'Because' – and, indeed, again later in the month when John, Paul and George recorded duelling guitar solos for the side-two medley of *Abbey Road* – Yoko was not present in the studio. It was as if The Beatles, when left to their own devices, free of distraction, retreated to an instinctive base camaraderie, allowing the bond between them to ignite their creative powers.

Apart from 'Octopus's Garden' – written by Ringo – and 'Something' and 'Here Comes the Sun' – both written by George – the songs on *Abbey Road* were all original compositions by either John or Paul. And although all but five tracks on the finished record had been introduced during the *Get Back* sessions, the apparent cohesive sound of the finished piece, coupled with the enthusiasm with which it was recorded, disguised the manipulative agendas of the chief songwriters.[9] In hindsight, it seems apparent that John, Paul and George were manoeuvring to showcase their individual contributions and, in doing so, laying the foundations for what a next Beatles presentation could be.

'By the time we made *Abbey Road*,' Paul told *Life* magazine in April 1971, 'John and I were openly critical of each other's music and I felt John wasn't much interested in performing anything he hadn't written himself.' 'We made the album from a large number of songs,' John told Barry Miles in September 1969:

> You see, each of us has got, maybe, ten songs to contribute to an album, but we won't get them all on, so when it's your turn on record, as it were, you've got to pick the one you want on the most. I like singles myself. I think Paul has conceptions of albums, or attempts it, like he conceived the medley thing. I'm not interested in conceptions of albums. All I'm interested in is the sound. I like it to be whatever happens. I'm not interested in making the album into a show. For me, I'd just put fourteen rock songs on.

---

9   It cannot be overstated that during the making of *Abbey Road* an incredible wealth of songs, recorded earlier in the year during the *Get Back* sessions – including 'Two of Us', 'Dig a Pony', 'I Me Mine', 'Let It Be', 'I've Got a Feeling', 'One after 909', 'For You Blue' and 'The Long and Winding Road' – remained unreleased.

In 2019, Apple released an anniversary edition of *Abbey Road* containing two discs of outtakes. The collection of alternate versions and studio banter suggests that the recording of *Abbey Road* was conducted in an atmosphere of harmony and unity. Still, antagonism was easily roused. On one occasion, 17-year-old Gill Pritchard, one of the latterly named Apple Scruffs, witnessed Paul clearly distressed 'racing out of the studio in tears'.[10] 'The next day he didn't turn up at all,' Pritchard told *Mojo* magazine in 1996. Paul's unusual and unaccounted-for behaviour was corroborated by fellow Scruff, Wendy Sutcliffe, who after seeing John storm out of the studio followed him as he marched towards Paul's house. 'John was really angry,' she says. 'When he got there he banged on the door calling for Paul to open up.' Undeterred by Paul's silence, John climbed over the gate and hammered on the front door. According to Sutcliffe, a screaming match soon ensued, with John shouting that both George and Ringo 'had come in from the country' and Paul hadn't had the grace 'to let anyone know he couldn't make the session'.

John's irregular behaviour was mirrored two years later, when, in March 1971, following the High Court decision to dissolve The Beatles' partnership and, as a result, serving notice on Allen Klein's position as manager of The Beatles, John allegedly drove round to Paul's house and threw a brick at his front window. If the story is true, it would have required John to throw a brick quite some distance over the high perimeter garden wall to the front of Paul's house – perhaps

---

10 A small group of fans who dedicated themselves to long hours of pilgrimage outside Beatles studios. In 1970, George immortalized the coterie when he wrote 'Apple Scruffs' for his solo album *All Things Must Pass*.

as much as 75 metres (just over 246 feet) – and with enough force on impact to smash a pane of glass.

Further suggestions of fracas in the studio during the recording of *Abbey Road* are described by engineer Geoff Emerick in his controversial account of The Beatles' recording practices, *Here There and Everywhere*. 'If George Martin hadn't been there, the four Beatles probably would have gone at it hammer and tongs,' Emerick wrote. Nevertheless, he was in no doubt that the group would carry on:

> It never occurred to me that we were working on the last Beatles album. No one had said anything to that effect, and frankly, the idea seemed inconceivable to me. Of course I realised that they were growing apart and arguing a lot, but they were also still making great music together...and they were clearly still a going commercial success...My sense was that they would take some time off and sort their differences out and that in another six months we'd be back doing another album.

Elsewhere, Emerick writes of witnessing 'the nastiness that plagued the "White Album" sessions' and 'the horror show that was *Let It Be*'. Yet, his account of The Beatles' mood has been verified by very few first-hand witnesses. Rather, like many a long-lasting relationship, The Beatles were capable of airing grievances, facing up to them, and moving on. If the 'White Album' had been beset by unpleasantness, The Beatles happily reconvened within months to work on *Get Back*. Likewise, for all the grumblings and reports that the sessions at Twickenham Studios had been treacherous, The Beatles almost immediately set to work on recording new tracks for what would become *Abbey Road*. Discussing the record with *Anthology* in 2000, George said, 'I didn't know at the time that it was the last Beatle record that we would make. I remember liking the record and enjoying it, but I don't recall thinking that was it because there was so much going on all the time.'

Abbey Road was released on 26 September 1969 and in its first year sold more than five million copies – two million more than *Sgt. Pepper's Lonely Hearts Club Band* had sold. The Beatles were producing some of the best music of their career: writing together, collaborating and setting new standards for the long-playing record. 'Show me any other group packing so much originality of composition and honest pop music on to one album. Show me!' fizzed the *New Musical Express*.

Get Back. Phil Spector. *Let It Be*

In the summer of 1969, with The Beatles working on *Abbey Road*, the uncertainty surrounding the Twickenham Studios/Apple recordings demanded resolution. Over 150 hours of audio had been recorded in January 1969, leaving the daunting task of assembling the music into a digestible presentation. On 10 March, John and Paul called Glyn Johns to Abbey Road to share a proposition. 'Remember that idea you had about putting together an album,' they said pointing to a pile of boxes. 'There are the tapes, go and do it.' 'We just said, "Do it",' John told Jann Wenner in 1970. 'None of us could be bothered going in and nobody called anybody about it. It was twenty-nine hours of tape, it was like a movie. I mean just so much tape. Ten, twenty takes of everything. Nobody could face looking at it.'

Glyn Johns had built an impressive reputation working as an engineer with artists such as The Pretty Things, the Small Faces and The Rolling Stones before graduating to the role of producer. Then, despite having little personal knowledge of their career to that point, Johns was invited by Paul to work with The Beatles at Twickenham Studios as an engineer in preparation for a live television special.[11] That changed when the proposed live performance was shelved and The Beatles moved to Apple Studios and began to record their newly written material.

Ingratiating himself with The Beatles, Johns enjoyed what he would describe as 'a positive atmosphere' in the studio. Each morning, Johns played back mixes of the previous day's recordings to The Beatles, often sequencing tracks intercut with banter from the studio floor. Acetate discs were cut for home listening, which slowly evolved into the concept of a record presenting The Beatles unfettered: no overdubs; no studio trickery. 'The idea,' Johns told Richard Buskin in 1988, 'was to present the opposite of what the public expected.'

Relishing the chance to compile a record, Johns studiously listened through the hours of recorded audio. A pilot album was completed on 28 May 1969 at Abbey Road – overseen by George

---

11 As a record producer was not needed for live television, it is often assumed that George Martin was not involved with *Get Back*. In fact, Martin attended at least 14 of the 22 sessions across January 1969.

Harrison – and subsequently mixed at Olympic Studios, overseen by George Martin. A test disc of the proposed *Get Back* album was then given to each of The Beatles with the following running order: A-side – 'One after 909', 'Medley: I'm Ready (aka Rocker) / Save the Last Dance for Me'[12] / 'Don't Let Me Down', 'Dig a Pony', 'I've Got a Feeling' and 'Get Back'; B-side – 'For You Blue', 'Teddy Boy', 'Two of Us', 'Maggie Mae', 'Dig It', 'Let It Be', 'The Long and Winding Road' and 'Get Back (Reprise)'.

'It's a strange album. There's bits of us mumbling and chatting and singing old rockers and all sorts of messing about,' John explained to Howard Smith on WABC radio in New York in 1969. 'It'll be a single LP – and we also made a sort of documentary of us making the album: all the traumas and the paranoia, all the different things that happen to you when you try and make a record.' 'He'd done a very straightforward mix, very plain,' Paul told Mike Read in October 1987. 'But I loved it because it was just The Beatles. It was us and it had a lot of character.' 'It's very rough in a way,' George informed BBC Radio 1 listeners in March 1970:

It's nice because you can see our warts. You can hear us talking, you can hear us playing out of tune, and you can hear us coughing and all those things. It's the complete opposite to this sort of clinical approach that we've normally had, you know,

---

12 'Rocker' was ostensibly Fats Domino's 1959 song 'I'm Ready', and alongside 'Save the Last Dance for Me' – first recorded by The Drifters in 1960 – would have been the first cover versions to appear on a Beatles record since 'Act Naturally' and 'Dizzy Miss Lizzy' featured on the 1965 album *Help!*

studio recording, the balance, everything is just right, the silence in between each track. This is really not like that.

Get Back with 'Let It Be' and 11 other songs was pressed and manufactured, only for technicalities to scupper its intended release date, later blamed on difficulties in the production of an accompanying lavish book. Two months later, under the heading 'August LP surprises', Mal Evans wrote a track-by-track analysis of the album for *Beatles Book Monthly* No. 72, concluding, '*Get Back* is The Beatles with their socks off, human Beatles kicking out their jams, getting rid of their inhibitions, facing their problems and working them out with their music.' As further release dates came and went, an acetate of the album reached two North American FM radio stations, prompting a flurry of bootleg copies to flood the black market. Speculation as to the source of the leak pointed to John Lennon, who in September 1969 visited Canada to perform at the Toronto Rock and Roll Revival festival (an event of much significance, as we will see).

In the meantime, on 20 July, all four Beatles watched the first cut of the *Let It Be* film, including a scene of John, Paul and Ringo jamming with Yoko after George's sudden walkout. Although it was later cut from the film, over time George seemingly conflated this sequence, which came after his spat with John, and his argument with Paul four days earlier. 'It was a very, very difficult, stressful time, and being filmed having a row as well was terrible,' George recounted in *Anthology* in 1995. 'I got up and I thought, "I'm not doing this anymore. I'm out of here." So I got my guitar and went home.' Informed by a distorted recall of events, George consequently vetoed the commercial release of *Let It Be*, which at the time of writing has been kept from both the VHS and DVD/Blu-Ray market.

As with George, Paul also came to believe that the *Get Back* sessions were a period of time dogged with arguments and group despondency. And whereas Paul complained that the film was biased towards John and Yoko, John argued that the film was cut to serve Paul. 'He had this idea that we would rehearse and then make the album,' John told *Rolling Stone* in 1970:

> And, of course, we're lazy fuckers and we've been playing for twenty years, for fuck's sake, we're grown men, we're not going to

George at Apple, January 1969.

sit around rehearsing. I'm not, anyway. And we couldn't get into it. We put down a few tracks and nobody was into it at all. It was a dreadful, dreadful feeling in Twickenham Studios, and being filmed all the time. I just wanted them to go away, and we'd be there, eight in the morning. You couldn't make music at eight in the morning or ten or whatever it was.

Reviewing the film rushes, Michael Lindsay-Hogg was taken by footage of John and Yoko waltzing in time to the Spanish-infused rhythm of a new song, 'I Me Mine'. George introduced the song, written in the first week of January 1969, as 'a heavy waltz'. Consisting of a single verse and a guitar flourish, played in a flamenco style, the song lasted little more than a minute and a half. 'It's very quick,' George conceded. 'We'll use it for a commercial,' John replied. Finishing the song with an emphatic 'I – Me – Mine', George remained silent. 'We're a rock and roll band, you know…I'll get on the barrel organ,' John teased, then adding in a conciliatory tone, 'Okay George, have you any idea what we'll play?'

Handled by Paul and Ringo, 'I Me Mine' gradually blossoms from an acoustic base into a dynamic rock song. When, at the end of the second verse, George strikes a sustained A minor chord, Ringo fills the space with a three-quarter rhythm played at double time on the ride cymbal. Paul and George latch on to the idea and within minutes a newly written bridge evolves over a 12-bar chord structure providing a dynamic juxtaposition to the somnolent verses. 'Sounds like it'll be a good rock bit,' Paul enthuses, 'because it gets out of the idea of the waltz.'

Despite a tangible level of excitement, 'I Me Mine' was then left untouched for the duration of the *Get Back* sessions. Then, a year later, Lindsay-Hogg requested a version of 'I Me Mine' be recorded for the *Let It Be* film soundtrack. '[It's] a very strange song,' George told Radio 1 listeners on 30 March 1970. 'It took five minutes just from an idea I had. I went into the studio and sang it to Ringo, and they happened to film it. And that film sequence was quite nice, so they wanted to keep that sequence in the film, so we had to go in the studio and re-record it.'

Booked for Saturday, 3 January 1970, Paul, George and Ringo laid down 16 basic takes. [13] Before take 15, George read out a satirical press statement to the handful of people in the studio to mark John's absence and, perhaps, to comment on the growing rumour that he (John) had, in fact, by then quit the group. 'You all will have read that Dave Dee is no longer with us,' George announced. 'But Micky and Tich and I would just like to carry on the good work that's always gone down in number two.' [14] Significantly, the following day – Sunday,

---

13 John missed the session because he was on holiday in Denmark. In light of his barbed comment at Twickenham a year earlier – 'a collection of freaks can dance along with George's waltz...there's no place in the group's playlist for a Spanish waltz' – it is debatable whether this was due to design or unfortunate timing.

14 George's namecheck was a reference to the million-selling British band Dave Dee, Dozy, Beaky, Mick & Tich. In fact, the lead singer, Dave Dee, had a fascinating connection to a piece of pop history. Formerly a police cadet known as David Harman, he attended the road accident in Chippenham on 17 April 1960 that killed the rock 'n' roll star Eddie Cochran and injured Gene Vincent. In a strange turn of events, Cochran's Gretsch guitar was impounded after the fatality and subsequently purloined by Harman. Having taught himself to play the instrument, he returned it to the Cochran family.

4 January – was dedicated to finalizing mixes of 'Let It Be' and would be the last Beatles session at Abbey Road for 25 years.

On 6 January 1970, Glyn Johns compiled a new 44-minute master tape of *Get Back* as a soundtrack to the anticipated film release. The revised running order omitted Paul's 'Teddy Boy' to accommodate the inclusion of 'I Me Mine' and John's 'Across the Universe', both featured in the *Let It Be* film. Elsewhere 'Dig It' was edited down from its original five minutes to barely one.[15] 'We got an acetate each and we'd call each other and say, "What do you think?"' John ventured before dismissing the record and its producer:

> We were going to let it out with a really shitty condition,
> disgusted. I didn't care. I thought it was good to go out to
> show people what had happened to us. Like this is where we're
> at now, we can't get it together and don't play together anymore.
> Leave us alone! Glyn Johns did a terrible job on it, 'cause he's
> got no idea.

By this point, The Beatles' investment in *Let It Be* was at best ambivalent, if not dangerously close to surrendering antipathy. Yet, if concern was exacerbated by John's prolonged absenteeism, a postcard addressed to Paul, Linda, Mary and Heather arrived at

---

15 The modified listing was as follows: A-side – 'One after 909', 'Medley: I'm Ready (aka Rocker) / Save the Last Dance for Me' / 'Don't Let Me Down', 'Dig a Pony', 'I've Got a Feeling', 'Get Back' and 'Let It Be'; B-side – 'For You Blue', 'Two of Us', 'Maggie Mae', 'Dig It', 'The Long and Winding Road', 'I Me Mine', 'Across the Universe' and 'Get Back (Reprise)'.

7 Cavendish Avenue, postmarked 15 January 1969. It simply read: 'We love you and will see you soon. Hi! It's snowing now in Denmark.' Decorated with hearts drawn in orange pen, coloured in with blue, and signed by John, Yoko and Kyoko (Yoko's daughter from a previous marriage), the warm message was perhaps enough for Paul to believe that his relationship with John was still intact. Meanwhile, behind the scenes, John was plotting the future *Let It Be*.

Back in November 1969, Allen Klein had organized a second screening of *Let It Be* for The Beatles and their wives. Later, over dinner, Klein informed Paul, George and Ringo that Phil Spector had visited him in New York and had expressed a wish to work with The Beatles. The idea was met with a general nod of approval. 'When Spector came around,' John told *Rolling Stone* magazine, 'it was like, "Well, alright, if you want to work with us go and do your audition, man." In a blatant rejection of Glyn Johns's prior work, and without the knowledge of the other Beatles, John entrusted the master tapes of *Get Back* to Spector. 'He worked like a pig on it,' John said. 'He'd always wanted to work with The Beatles and he was given the shittiest load of badly recorded shit ever. And he made something out of it. It wasn't fantastic, but I heard it, I didn't puke. I was so relieved after six months of this black cloud hanging over me that this was going to go out. I thought it would be good to let the shitty version out because it would break The Beatles, it would break the myth.'

Commencing work on 23 March 1970, Spector extended the recording of 'I Me Mine' by 51 seconds – doubling the first section of the song – added strings and choral voices, and finished off by making stereo mixes of 'I've Got a Feeling', 'Dig a Pony', 'One after 909' and 'Across the Universe'.[16] With the record complete, Spector sent a letter to all four Beatles to gain their approval. 'If there is anything you'd like done to the album let me know and I'll be glad to help,' he wrote. 'Naturally little things are easy to change, big things might be a problem. If you wish, please call me about anything regarding the album tonight.'

In response to Spector's efforts, George told BBC Radio 1 listeners:

> There's really good songs on it – 'Let It Be', 'Don't Let Me Down', 'The Long and Winding Road' and a great song of John's, 'Dig a Pony'. People may think we're not trying because it's really like a demo record. But, on the other hand, it's worth so much more than those other records because you can actually get to know us a bit more. It's a bit more human than the average studio recording.

In a separate interview, Paul was not so pleased. 'You can't blame Spector. He was hired in and he thought we all agreed and knew what was happening. But in actual fact I wasn't too happy about the whole thing.' Talking to *Melody Maker* on 7 August 1971, Ringo broke ranks and informed readers, 'We all said yes. Even at the beginning Paul said yes. I spoke to him on the phone, and said, "Did you like it?" and he said, "Yeah, it's okay," he didn't put it down.'

---

16 Unbeknown to both parties, Paul was in Studio Three, Abbey Road, at the same time that Spector was overseeing copy masters of his solo record *McCartney*.

With *Let It Be* completed, Allen Klein insisted that the film be released in advance of the album, much to the chagrin of Paul. 'I don't like *Get Back* being held back so long,' he told *Rolling Stone* on 30 April 1970. 'This is one of the reasons I don't want Klein. It is silly to blame him but the holding of the *Get Back* album now is humorous. The LP is looking to be a joke, for it is a bit of a cliffhanger. I would like to have seen it out three months ago and now I don't even remember making it.' A month earlier, George told afternoon listeners on the BBC Radio 1 programme 'The Beatles Today': 'It's been held up because we're trying to put the film out in about forty different cities throughout the world all at once, rather than put on a premiere in New York and then let the critics say, "Oh well, we think it's this and we think it's that."'

Let It Be was released on 8 May 1970. 'This is a new phase BEATLES album...' read the description on the back of the album. 'Essential to the content of the film, LET IT BE was that they performed live for many of the tracks; in comes the warmth and the freshness of a live performance; as reproduced for disc by Phil Spector.' 'There was a bit of hype on the back of the sleeve for the first time ever on a Beatles album,' Paul told *Melody Maker*.[17] 'It said it was a "new-phase Beatles album" and there was nothing further

---

17 Contesting his claims, on 24 November 1971 John wrote an open letter to Paul – published in *Melody Maker* on 4 December 1971 – stating, 'One other little lie in your "It's only Paulie" MM bit: *Let It Be* was not the "first bit of hype" on a Beatle album. Remember Tony Barrow? And his wonderful writing on *Please Please Me* etc. etc. the early Beatle Xmas records! Also, we were intending to parody Barrow originally, so it was hype...anyway, enough of this petty bourgeois fun.'

from the truth. That was the last Beatles album and everybody knew it...[Allen] Klein had it re-produced because he said it didn't sound commercial enough.'

'A betrayal,' George Martin declared, in a rare pique of anger during an *Arena* documentary in 2016. Incensed at his omission from the production credit, Martin recommended to EMI that an alternative album by-line should have read, 'Produced by George Martin. Over-produced by Phil Spector.' 'If anybody listens to the bootleg version, which was pre-Spector and listens to the version Spector did,' John countered, 'they would shut up. Spector did a terrific job.' The music press did not agree. Writing in the *New Musical Express*, Alan Smith argued, 'If the new Beatles' soundtrack album *Let It Be* is to be their last then it will stand as a cheapskate epitaph, a cardboard tombstone, a sad and tatty end to a musical fusion which wiped clean and drew again the face of pop music.'

On 20 May 1970, a morning screening of *Let It Be* was viewed by press and close friends. Then, in the evening, invited guests, including Mary Hopkin, Lulu, Spike Milligan, film director Richard Lester and members of Fleetwood Mac and The Rolling Stones, attended a star-studded premiere of the 'Bioscopic Experience' at the London Pavilion, Piccadilly Circus. 'It was set up by Paul, for Paul,' John fumed in *Rolling Stone*. 'That's one of the main reasons The Beatles ended. I can't speak for George, but I pretty damn well know – we got fed up with being sidemen for Paul. After Brian died, that's what happened to us. And on top of that, the people that cut it, cut it as "Paul is God" and we're just lying around there. I felt sick.'

Accepting that 'there are scenes in it like the rooftop concert that were good', George's assessment of the film was nonetheless damning. 'Most of it makes me so aggravated. It was a particularly bad experience that we were having at that time and it's bad enough having it, let alone having it filmed and recorded so you've got to watch it for the rest of your life. I don't like it.' In a conciliatory tone, Paul told *Rolling Stone*, 'The *Get Back* film is a good film, and it is a real film. The troubles are in it as well as the happy moments.' The film industry agreed and awarded *Let It Be* a Grammy for 'Best Original Score Written for a Motion Picture'. [18]

But by then The Beatles, as a working band, no longer existed.

---

18 The award was accepted by Paul and Linda on 16 March 1971. Handed four
    Grammys – one for each Beatle – Paul simply said, 'Thank you. Goodnight'.
    'Let It Be' was also nominated as best song and album of the year, losing out in
    both categories to Simon & Garfunkel's 'Bridge over Troubled Water'.

4. **The Love We Make**

Divorce

By the time we got to Let It Be *we couldn't play the game anymore. We could see through each other, suddenly we didn't believe. It'd come to a point where it was no longer creating magic.*
John Lennon

Why did The Beatles break up? Let us surmise. The end of touring in August 1966 disconnected The Beatles creatively from their audience. A year later, the death of Brian Epstein left the group not only without a manager but vulnerable to the predacious instincts of Allen Klein and furthermore coincided with the sale of Northern Songs, the publishing company controlling the songs of Lennon and McCartney.[1] In 1968, the arrival of Yoko Ono diverted John Lennon's energy from the group. This, coupled with artistic differences, drove John, Paul and George to covet individual control of their songs. Moreover, The Beatles were maturing, forming new relationships and increasingly pursuing activities outside of the band. Then on Friday, 10 April 1970, a front-page headline changed everything.

'PAUL QUITS THE BEATLES', declared the *Daily Mirror*.

---

1   It became known subsequently that Paul had bought additional shares in the company without the knowledge of the other Beatles.

The article, written by tabloid journalist Don Short[2] and published in flagrant contravention of a press embargo, which, according to The Beatles' press officer, Derek Taylor, was 'taking roughly a 9–4 gamble on getting away with it', was based on a typed questionnaire, included in promotional copies of Paul's debut solo album, *McCartney*. Asked about the future of The Beatles, Paul responded with a measured degree of ambiguity, neither denying nor confirming a breakup:

Q: Are you planning a new album or single with The Beatles?

A: No.

Q: Is this album a rest away from The Beatles or the start of a solo career?

A: Time will tell. Being a solo album means it's 'the start of a solo career...' and not being done with The Beatles means it's just a rest. So it's both.

Q: Is your break with The Beatles temporary or permanent, due to personal differences or musical ones?

A: Personal differences, business differences, musical differences, but most of all because I have a better time with my family. Temporary or permanent? I don't really know.

Q: Do you foresee a time when Lennon–McCartney becomes an active songwriting partnership again?

A: No.

---

2   On 18 October 1968, Short alerted John to a planned raid at his central London flat ahead of a visit by the drug squad.

In all, Paul answered 41 questions, divided into two sections: a status appraisal and a track-by-track breakdown of his new record. Over lunch with *Evening Standard* journalist Ray Connolly, Paul attempted to explain the meaning of the press release:

I never intended it to mean I'd quit. It was a misunderstanding. We got some people at the office to ask some questions just on paper, and they sent them over to our house and I just filled them out like an essay, like a school thing. When I saw the headlines, I thought, 'Christ, what have I done? Now we're in for it,' and my stomach started churning up. I never intended the statement to mean 'Paul McCartney quits Beatles'. I didn't leave The Beatles – The Beatles have left The Beatles, but no one wants to be the one to say the party's over.[3]

Besieged by media attention, Apple issued an immediate press release – dictated by Derek Taylor and typed by his secretary, Mavis Davies:

Spring is here and Leeds play Chelsea tomorrow and Ringo and John and George and Paul are alive and well and full of hope. The world is still spinning and so are we and so are you. When the spinning stops – that'll be the time to worry, not before. Until then, The Beatles are alive and well and the beat goes on, the beat goes on.

---

3 The questions were written by Apple employee Peter Brown, at Paul's request.

'I absolutely did believe as millions of others did, that the friendship The Beatles had for each other was a lifesaver for all of us,' Taylor clarified in *Anthology*. Nevertheless, the *Daily Mirror* exclusive had caused irrevocable damage and, despite a counter-response in *The Times* stating 'MCCARTNEY SPLIT WITH BEATLES DENIED', history has marked the moment as the official end point of The Beatles.

But while, for many, Paul's press release was a shock, in reality, it merely reflected the artistic and financial stalemate The Beatles had languished in since September 1969. 'The world reaction was like "The Beatles Have Broken Up – It's Official!",' Paul said in *Anthology*. 'We'd known it for months.' Unknown to the general public, John had quit the group six months earlier, and as he told *Rolling Stone*, 'A lot of people knew I'd left, but I was a fool not to do what Paul did, which was use it to sell a record. I wasn't angry. I was just – "shit".'

On 13 September 1969, John announced to a close circle of friends, including Eric Clapton, Klaus Voormann and journalist Ray Connolly, that he was leaving The Beatles. 'I was speechless,' recalled Connolly in a *Daily Mail* interview. 'I knew that the breakup of The Beatles would be the biggest story I would ever get in my life. John, however, had something more to say, "Don't tell anybody yet."' Connolly's conversation with John had taken place mid-flight between London and Canada as they travelled to the Rock and Roll Revival concert that John had impetuously agreed to perform at. The one-day festival organized by promoter John Brower was to be headlined by The Doors supported by an impressive cast of rock 'n' roll stars from Bo Diddley and Jerry Lee Lewis to Chuck Berry, Gene

DON'T UPSET THE APPLE CART

Vincent and Little Richard. The day before the festival, fearing empty seats in the 20,000-capacity arena, Brower phoned Apple to offer eight tickets to The Beatles and friends. By chance, John took the call and, to Brower's amazement, offered to perform at the event. 'We got this phone call on a Friday night that there was a rock 'n' roll revival

John and Yoko at Heathrow Airport on their way to Canada to promote *Live Peace in Toronto*, 16 December 1969.

show in Toronto with a 100,000 audience, or whatever it was,' John recollected. 'They were inviting us as king and queen to preside over it, not play – but I didn't hear that bit. I said, "Just give me time to get a band together," and we went the next morning.'

Billed as The Plastic Ono Band[4] and backed by Klaus Voormann, Alan White and Eric Clapton,[5] John and Yoko performed covers of 'Blue Suede Shoes', 'Money' and 'Dizzy Miss Lizzy', The Beatles album track 'Yer Blues', 'Cold Turkey', 'Give Peace a Chance', and two Yoko compositions 'Don't Worry Kyoko (Mummy's Only Looking for Her Hand in the Snow)' and 'John, John (Let's Hope for Peace)'. It had been eight months since The Beatles' rooftop performance and three years since The Beatles' last professional engagement at Candlestick Park in August 1966. 'I dug performing at Toronto,' John told Barry Miles for *OZ* magazine on 23 September 1969. 'And I didn't have that Beatles mystique to live up to, which is the drag about performing with The Beatles. You've got to *be* The Beatles. But performing is a groove.' Miles then asked John if he would do anything like that again. 'Yes, sure,' John replied. 'I'm bound to now I've had a taste of it.'

Despite the success of the event, on the return flight home, Allen

---

4 Named by John based on an idea by Yoko featuring a set of mechanized Perspex figurines. To that point the Plastic Ono Band existed only in name, not as a functioning live unit. The group was parodied by Paul in 1980 when he created the fictitious Plastic Macs for the video of his solo single 'Coming Up', combining 'Plastic Ono Band' with 'The Dirty Macs', the super-group established for *The Rolling Stones Rock and Roll Circus* performance.

5 Declining John's invitation to join the band, George said in *Anthology*, 'I didn't really want to be in an avant-garde band. I knew that was what it was going to be.'

Klein advised John to keep his decision to quit The Beatles under wraps until advantageous business arrangements had been made. John agreed. But when he attended a band meeting at Savile Row on 20 September, diplomacy failed him. With George away visiting his unwell mother in Liverpool, conversation turned to the group's future. Backed up by Ringo, Paul proposed that they should return to playing small gigs. 'We should get back to our roots,' Paul said. 'We're a damn good little band.' Sitting to his left, John was unconvinced. Becoming increasingly belligerent, he brazenly rejected Paul's suggestions, suddenly blurting out. 'I might as well tell you. I'm leaving the group.' Shocked, Paul asked, 'What do you mean?' 'I want a divorce,' John confirmed, 'like my divorce from Cynthia.'

A stunned silence filled the room. 'That just hit everyone,' Paul told *Life* magazine in 1971. 'All of us realized that this great thing that we'd been part of was no longer to be. This was the chop.' Then, John added that he was not yet ready to make a public announcement. A visibly shaken Paul stirred. 'Oh well, that means nothing's really happened if you're not going to say anything.'

Common knowledge to those close to him, John's state of mind was precarious and increasingly subject to distraction. Unquestionably, the situation was exacerbated by the omnipotent presence of Yoko and the couple's flirtation with heroin. Resultantly, John's stated desire for a 'divorce' was passed off by the other Beatles as rashness. 'If you disagreed with what John said one week,' George professed, 'just speak to him the next week instead.' 'I blab off,' John told Jann Wenner in 1971, 'some of it makes sense, some of it is bullshit, some of it's lies and some of it is God knows what I'm saying.'

In fact, John was not the only one who had suggested that The Beatles' time was up. On 3 January 1969 – The Beatles second day at Twickenham Studios – John proffered a plan: 'When we've done a month of this and we do the album…let's do an album after,' he enthusiastically suggested. 'Get to good peak playing and then we split.' Four days later, the matter arose again in a telling exchange between George and Paul. 'We should have a divorce,' George said, somewhat out of the blue. 'Well, I said that at the last meeting,' Paul responded. 'But it's getting near it.' 'Who'd have the children?' John piped up, lightening the mood. 'Dick James,'[6] Paul replied, as the band launched into 'I've Got a Feeling' with the poignant opening line 'I've got a feeling…deep inside'.

A week later, Paul shared a fantasized dramatic ending to The Beatles in a conversation with Michael Lindsay-Hogg:

> I was talking to Neil [Aspinall] last night about the idea of a TV show, which was that while we were rehearsing the show ourselves we should have alongside us, say the editor of the *Daily Mirror*, a real hard news nut, rehearsing a team of really hard, incredible news men with films, so that on the night of the show in-between all of our songs is news; the fastest, and the hottest from every corner of the earth, so, 'We've just heard there's been an earthquake in so-and so,' just like incredible news in-between each thing so it's like a red hot news programme. And at the end the final bulletin is, 'The Beatles have broken up'.

---

6   A reference to The Beatles' music publisher.

The Beatles steered on, but it begged the question: would Brian Epstein have been able to prevent the growing disenchantment? Certainly, the arguments and resentments, triggered by the Klein/Eastman debate, would have been curbed. Likewise, Brian would have provided a much-needed outlet for Paul, George and Ringo's antipathy towards Yoko, and furthermore the uncertainty surrounding the *Get Back/Let It Be* project. As it was, Brian's death precipitated a chain of events that would dramatically overshadow The Beatles' future. Firstly, the establishment of Apple created to manage The Beatles' affairs was, within two years, beyond its artistic endeavours, an unmitigated failure, catastrophically losing The Beatles millions of pounds. As a desperate rear-guard measure, Allen Klein was invited to step in and stop the rot setting in. 'If Brian was around today he would be managing us,' Ringo said in *Anthology*, 'and if we'd been with Brian we wouldn't have had to go through Allen Klein to be our own men.' It was a point of view shared by Barry Miles. 'With the introduction of Allen Klein into The Beatles equation,' he wrote in *Many Years from Now*, 'it was now inevitable that they would split up.'

'Nobody could break The Beatles up,' John contested:

We broke ourselves up. When Brian died we got a bit lost because we needed a manager, all of us are artists and we're nothing else. We can't manage ourselves or look after ourselves in that way. But it's a lot for four big heads like The Beatles to stay together for such a long time. In the early days there was the thing of 'making it big', or breaking into America and we had that goal together…but when we reached twenty-eight or twenty-nine…our personalities developed and they were a bit stifled with The Beatles.

Nevertheless, the intimacy between John, Paul, George and Ringo had been fostered over a decade and was never going to be an easy union to break. Relationships can bear many struggles, but the ties that bind people together are complex and deeply interwoven, shaped by time and cemented in unique shared experiences. 'By the time The Beatles were at their peak,' John told David Wigg in 1971, 'we were cutting each other down to size. We were limited in our capacity to write and perform by having to fit it into some kind of format.' Further believing that The Beatles were restricting his growth, John was quick to read the early warning signs. 'So, like people do when they're together,' he said, 'they start picking on each other. It was like, "It's because of you – you got the tambourine wrong – that my whole life is a misery."'

'It was like a wind down to a divorce,' Ringo remembered in *Anthology*. 'A divorce usually doesn't just happen suddenly, there are months and years of misery until you finally say, "Oh, let's end it."' In keeping with the metaphorical analogy, Paul compared the state of affairs to a Gene Vincent song that The Beatles used to cover in their early days. 'It was like an army song,' he told *Q* magazine in 1986, 'and for us The Beatles became the army. We always knew that one day "Wedding Bells" would come true.' Interestingly, six years earlier, John referenced the same song in an interview with David Sheff. 'You know the song *those wedding bells are breaking up that old gang of mine*,' John said in 1980. 'That was it. The old gang of mine was over the moment I met Yoko.'

On 26 November 1969, John's attention turned to two unreleased songs recorded in August 1968 and April 1969. According to Geoff Emerick, '[John] asked me to go into Abbey Road with him to help mix and edit two songs that had been sitting on the shelf for a long time: "You Know My Name (Look Up the Number)" and "What's The New Mary Jane".' Intent on releasing both songs as a double A-side, John persuaded Apple to announce a rush-release date for 5 December. An accompanying press release cryptically stated that the recording featured John and Yoko singing '[with instrumental support from a group] of many of the greatest show business names of today'. '"You Know My Name (Look Up the Number)" is probably my favourite Beatles track just because it's so insane,' Paul told Mark Lewisohn in 1988. 'I mean, what would you do if a guy like John Lennon turned up at the studio, and said, "I've got a new song". I [Paul] said, "What's the words?" and he replied "You know my name look up the number." I asked, "What's the rest of it?" "No, no other words, those are the words. And I want to do it like a mantra!"' Discussing the song's release in relation to The Beatles' future, John told the *New Musical Express*, 'It's my escape valve and how important that gets, as compared to The Beatles, for me, I'll have to wait and see.'

Despite Paul's enthusiasm for John's song, the record was put on hold in favour of The Beatles Fan Club annual Christmas release. Given the conversations over the past months, and in particular John's wish for 'a divorce', a new collective Beatles recording was not only unexpected but shocking. Making the record necessitated that Radio 1 disc jockey Kenny Everett edit together four individually recorded contributions:[7] John and Yoko in conversation walking in the grounds of Tittenhurst Park – their home since May 1969; Paul singing a yuletide greeting from his home in St John's Wood accompanied on acoustic guitar; George speaking directly from the offices of Apple; and Ringo plugging his new film, *The Magic Christian*, from his home in Ascot.

With all the ongoing activity, fans had every reason to believe that the New Year held great promise for The Beatles. But on 7 November 1969, two months after John's private 'divorce' proclamation, Paul seized the initiative and made a startling revelation to *Life* magazine. 'The Beatle thing is over,' he told journalist Dorothy Bacon. 'We make good music and we want to go on making good music. But the Beatle thing is over. It has been exploded, partly by what we have done, and partly by other people.'

Astonishingly, Paul's statement was ignored. It was as if the breakup of the world's most famous group had been prophesized by T S Eliot's line in 'The Hollow Men', 'The world ends not with a bang but a whimper'. In fact, it transpired that Paul's disclosure followed a phone conversation with John. 'I told him I was leaving The Beatles, too,' Paul recounted to *Life* in 1971. 'He said, "Good! That makes two of us who have accepted it mentally."'

---

7   Credited as Maurice Cole.

Indecision

A flower on its own is pretty; a flower in a garden is beautiful.
George Harrison – handwritten note

Ciphering through who said what, when and to whom may help to apportion blame for the demise of The Beatles. Yet, beyond the rancour and bitterness between the warring factions, what emerges is a story of frustration and a despairing cry for resolution. Despite the arguments and the walkouts, each Beatle in turn indicated their desire to continue. The question is: was there a decisive moment when The Beatles' difficulties could have been resolved and agreement reached enabling them to record together again?

Coming after the glut of songs written and recorded during the *Get Back* sessions, the release of two chart-topping standalone singles – 'Get Back' and 'The Ballad of John and Yoko' – and the universal praise heaped upon *Abbey Road*, John's decision to quit The Beatles could not have been more shocking. In the absence of an official statement, an uneasy quiet followed. Paul, George and Ringo each phoned one another to discuss John's passive play of attrition, while half expecting him to retract his notice. 'Everybody had tried to leave,' George reflected in *Anthology*, 'it was nothing new. Everybody was leaving for years.' In an attempt to appreciate what they had, George pinned a poetic note on the wall inside the Apple office. It simply read: 'A flower on its own is pretty; a flower in a garden is beautiful.'

And soon John's initial certainty began to fluctuate. Recollecting a business meeting between John and Paul held upstairs at the Apple offices in October 1969, Anthony Fawcett, John's personal assistant, wrote: 'After a confrontation, John burst into the room, red in the face and fuming with rage: "That's it – it's all over!"' Then two months later – on 13 December – when asked by the *New Musical Express* about forthcoming Beatles music, John painted an optimistic impression. 'It just depends how much we all want to record together,' he said. 'I go off and on it.'

Unsurprisingly, as the protracted stalemate wore on, rumours of a group division reached the media. Suggesting that the problem lay between John and Paul, George told Howard Smith of the *Village Voice*, in March 1970, 'It'll all be okay. Just give 'em time because they do really love each other. We all do.' Desperate for a scoop, a student journalist, Alanna Nash, tracked down John's surrogate guardian, Aunt Mimi, at her home in Sandbanks, Poole. 'I don't know what all this business between John and Paul is about,' she told Nash. 'I don't dare ask John. I did ring Paul about it, and he told me things would straighten up. The boys have been friends for so long. I remember them coming home from school together on their bikes, begging biscuits. I'm sure they'll get back together again. This is just a phase they're passing through.'

Talking on WABC-FM radio, George downplayed the notion of a power struggle, describing John and Paul's squabbles as childish and 'just being bitchy to each other', adding, 'we've been so close and through so much together. But the main thing is, like in anybody's life, they have slight problems. And it's just that our problems are always blown up and shown to everybody.' Perhaps in recognition of his own relationship difficulties with Paul, George remained positive.

'It's just a matter of time, just for everybody to work out their own problems and once they've done that I'm sure we'll get back 'round the cycle again.'

'When John and I used to meet during that period,' Paul told Barry Miles in 1997, 'he'd say, "Do they try and set you against me like they try and set me against you?" And I'd say, "Yes, often. People'll say, 'Oh, did you hear that Lennon threw up before he went on stage in Toronto?' They'd always tell me the juicy things, in case I wanted to go, "Did he? What a bastard! Well, serve him right, ha, ha, ha."' Ever the source of sincerity and frankness, John compared the situation to a broken marriage. 'It's like when people decide to get a divorce,' he told David Wigg:

> Quite often you decide amicably, but then when you get your lawyers and they say, 'Don't talk to the other party unless there's a lawyer present,' that's when the drift really starts happening. It's really lawyers that make divorces nasty. If there was a nice ceremony like getting married for divorce it would be much better. But it always gets nasty because you're never allowed to speak your own mind. You get frustrated and you end saying and doing things you wouldn't do under normal circumstances.

Central to rescuing the ailing relationship was the issue of songwriting. The majority of Beatle songs had been written by Lennon and McCartney, but in later years, as George began to write prolifically, so his claim for greater representation on records increased. In 1968, the 'White Album' had been an attempt to accommodate such grievances. For the first time, The Beatles issued a double album with 30 songs spread over two discs – thirteen of John's, twelve of Paul's, four of George's and one of Ringo's. But, much to John's frustration, it had resultantly and dramatically extended the recording period. Two months later, The Beatles began work at Twickenham Studios, effectively writing and recording not only *Let It Be* but the majority of songs that would appear nine months later on *Abbey Road*. 'I don't want to spend six months making an album I have two tracks on,' John complained to the *New Musical Express* in December 1969, 'and neither do Paul or George probably. That's the problem. If we can overcome that, maybe it'll sort itself out.' Rather than 'overcoming' the problem, the issue was left to fester. At a board meeting at Apple, on 9 September 1969, recorded on a Philips C-60 cassette by John, in Ringo's absence – and 17 days before the release of *Abbey Road* – the subject of songwriting ruptured in a tense exchange.[8]

'We always carved the singles up between us,' John said to Paul. 'We have the singles market. George and Ringo don't get anything. We've never offered George "B" sides; we could have given him a lot of "B" sides, but because we were two people you had the "A" side and I had the "B" side.' Imperturbable, Paul countered, 'Well the thing

---

8   This meeting is often dated 8 September. But an article in *Melody Maker* ['Ringo taken ill – 13 September 1969'] suggests otherwise: 'Ringo was due to attend a big meeting at London's Apple headquarters on Tuesday [9 September] when The Beatles were discussing their plans for the future...the meeting was still being held – but without him.'

is I think that until now, until this year our songs have been better than George's. Now, this year, his songs are at least as good as ours.' Incensed, George retaliated, 'Now that's a myth 'cause most of the songs this year I wrote last year or the year before. Maybe now I just don't care whether you are going to like them or not, I just do 'em...If I didn't get a break I wouldn't push it. I'd just forget about it. Now for the last two years, at any rate, I've pushed it a bit more.'

Sympathetic to George's position, John responded, 'I know what he's saying 'cause people have said to me you're coming through a lot stronger now than you had.' 'I don't particularly seek acclaim,' George continued. 'That's not the thing. It's just to get out whatever is there to make way for whatever else is there. You know, 'cause it's only to get 'em out, and also I might as well make a bit of money, seeing as I'm spending as much as the rest of you, and I don't earn as much as the rest of you. Most of my tunes I never had The Beatles backing me.' 'Oh, c'mon, George!' John exclaimed, losing his patience. 'We put a lot of work in your songs, even down to "Don't Bother Me", we spent a lot of time doing all that and we grooved. I can remember the riff you were playing, and in the last two years there was a period where you went Indian and we weren't needed.'[9] 'That was only one tune,' George retorted. 'On the last album [the 'White Album'] I don't think you appeared on any of my songs – I don't mind.' 'Well, you had Eric or somebody like that,' John countered.[10]

---

9 'Don't Bother Me', recorded in 1963 for *With The Beatles*, was George's first attempt at songwriting.

10 A reference to Eric Clapton's uncredited guest appearance as lead guitar player on 'While My Guitar Gently Weeps'.

Sensing the mood spiralling, Paul says, 'When we get in a studio, even on the worst day, I'm still playing bass, Ringo's still drumming, and we're still there, you know.' 'It's nothing new the way things are,' John adds dismissively. 'It's human. We've always said we've had fights. It's no news that we argue. I'm more interested in my songs. Paul's more interested in his and George is more interested in his. That's always been.'

Traditionally, the choice of songs rehearsed by The Beatles replicated an unspoken pecking order, corresponding in equal part to age and tenure within the group. First was John, who formed The Beatles and by default was leader. Second Paul. And third George, recruited by Paul, who in turn brought in Ringo as Pete Best's replacement. But increasingly, since The Beatles had stopped touring in 1966, George had stockpiled an impressive reserve of unrecorded songs. Whereas, in the past, he had been intimidated by the quality of John and Paul's collaboration, by 1969 he was challenging their assumed supremacy, albeit surreptitiously. 'What I do is bring out the numbers I think are the easiest to get across,' George told the *New Musical Express*. 'The ones I think will take the shortest time to make an impact.'

Having presented 'All Things Must Pass', 'Isn't It a Pity', 'Let It Down' and 'Hear Me Lord' in the first week of the *Get Back* sessions, with little or no enthusiasm from John or Paul in the second week at Twickenham Studios, George had more success with 'For You Blue' and 'Old Brown Shoe' – the former perhaps for its standard and easy-to-play 12-bar blues structure, and the latter for its appealingly up-tempo charm.

'Even on *Abbey Road*,' George told WABC-FM on 1 May 1970, 'we'd record about eight tracks before I got round to doing one of mine. You say, "Well, I've got a song," and then with Paul, "Well I've got a song as well and mine goes like this *diddle-diddle-diddle-duh*," and away you go.' 'The trouble is that we've got too much material,' John told *Melody Maker* in September 1969. 'Now that George is writing a lot we could put out a double album every month. After *Get Back* is released in January [1970], we'll probably go back into the studio and record another one. It's just a shame that we can't get more albums out faster.'

Between the words, the subtext of the ongoing resentments and circling debates was the radical notion of dividing the next album

Ringo takes a break from recording, April 1964.

equally between the four songwriters. 'Even before they began [*Abbey Road*],' engineer Phil McDonald recalled in *The Complete Beatles Recording Sessions*, 'I remember John saying that he wanted all of his songs on one side and all of Paul's on the other.' The idea had gained traction. During the heated board meeting at Apple in September 1969, John went on the attack. 'It seemed mad for us to put a song on an album that nobody really dug, just because it was going to be popular.' Citing 'Ob-La-Di, Ob-La-Da' and 'Maxwell's Silver Hammer', John told Paul those songs should be given to artists who would appreciate them more. 'People who like music like that,' he said, 'like Mary [Hopkin].'[11]

Musical differences had beset The Beatles since their earliest days. 'Paul preferred "pop-type" music,' John wrote in his court affidavit in 1971, 'and George and I preferred what is now called "underground".' Then, recognizing the benefit of varied influences, John clarified his stance: 'Musically speaking it contributed to our success.' Perhaps checking himself, John then made a spectacular suggestion. 'All right, let's move on,' he said at Apple on 9 September 1969. 'We'll do another album. We'll all do four songs. How's that? That's fair.'

It was an incredible volte-face. Yet, surprisingly, the response from Paul and George was muted. 'All right,' John continued, undeterred. 'How about a Christmas single? Y'know, we finish it with a Christmas

---

11 After appearing on the television programme *Opportunity Knocks*, Mary Hopkin was brought to the attention of Paul by the model Twiggy. Her debut single, 'Those Were the Days' – produced by Paul – was released in the UK on 30 August 1968 and went on to sell over five million copies worldwide.

single. I think it's a great idea – I'm in.' If the quick, sure proposal intimated that John was thinking in the moment, an interview with George in the *New Musical Express* on 1 November suggested otherwise. 'In the future,' George said, 'we're going to get an equal-rights thing, so we all have as much on the album.' Furthering the proposition, George told WABC-FM radio. 'It was just over the last year or so we worked something out, which is still a joke really: three songs for me, three songs for Paul, three songs for John, and two for Ringo.' 'The point is nobody's special,' George concluded. 'If Lennon/McCartney are special then Harrison and Starkey are special, too. What I'm saying is that I can be Lennon/McCartney too, but I'd rather be Harrison.'

Here lies the decisive moment in the concept of *Four Sides of The Beatles:* a new record with song allocation divided equally between John, Paul, George and Ringo. At the exact moment John was talking of 'divorce', he was simultaneously offering The Beatles a lifeline and expressing a willingness to record a new album. The suggestion marks the critical point in The Beatles story where history could have irrevocably changed and offers a tangible bridge between the defined past and a wishful future. 'It's the end of The Beatles, maybe how people imagine The Beatles,' George informed Johnny Moran on 30 March 1970:

> The Beatles have never been what people thought they were anyway. So in a way, it's the end of The Beatles like that, but it's not really the end of The Beatles. The Beatles are going to go until they die. I certainly don't want to see the end of The

Beatles. Whatever Paul, John and Ringo would like to do, I'll do it. As long as we can all be free to be individuals at the same time.

A month later, George expanded on the idea on WABC-FM radio. 'All we have to do is accept that we're all individuals and that we all have as much potential as the other. I'm certainly ready to be able to try and work things out with whoever I'm with. But if whoever I'm with is full of hassles then I'm not going to be with him.' While Paul's view on the matter was not expressed on public record, Ringo reassured *NME* readers that all was well within The Beatles camp. 'Everything's fine,' he said on 14 March 1970. 'But I've got things to do, and George has got things to do, and Paul has his solo album to come, and John has his peace thing. We can't do everything at once.'

Attractive as a post-Beatles solo career may be, George saw how both scenarios could coexist. Talking on *Scene and Heard* on 30 March 1970, he said:

Ringo's just completed a great album called *Sentimental Journey*. John's doing a Plastic Ono album with Phil Spector. Paul's doing an album where he's going to play all the instruments himself, which is nice because he couldn't possibly do that in The Beatles – if it was a Beatle album, automatically Paul gets stuck on bass, Ringo gets on the drums. So in a way it's a great relief for us all to be able to work separately at the same time. If I get a chance I'd like to do an album as well, just to get rid of a lot of songs: a George album. I'll try and get that together some time during this summer and I expect by that time we should be ready to do a new Beatle album.

'I've no idea if The Beatles will work together again, or not,' John countered on *Scene and Heard* on 6 February 1970. 'I never really have. It was always open. If somebody didn't feel like it… that's it. It could be a rebirth or death. We'll see what it is. It'll probably be rebirth.' Convinced of renewal, George promoted The Beatles' future relentlessly. 'We've got to a point where we can see each other quite clearly and by allowing each other to be each other, we can become The Beatles again,' he told *Disc* on 5 April 1970. 'We've got unity through diversity because that's what it is – unity through diversity. We still see each other, still make contact. But we had to find ourselves, individually, one day. It was the natural course of events.'

In the meantime, Paul's patience with The Beatles' business affairs and the incompatibility of working with Allen Klein had reached a nadir. Boycotting Apple, Paul retreated to Scotland. As spring approached, and with no signs of protracted disagreements resolving, Paul pressed ahead with a solo project, simply titled *McCartney*. A release date was set but subsequently clashed with the planned issue of *Let It Be*. Paul judged the proposed scheduling delay as a slight against him. As a result, an argument erupted threatening to derail the release of both records. The problem was outlined in a letter to Paul, co-signed by John and George on 31 March 1970. 'It's stupid for Apple to put out two big albums within 7 days of each other,' John wrote. 'Also there's Ringo's and *Hey Jude*.'[12] Further informing Paul that EMI had been advised to press ahead with the release of *Let It Be* on 24 April and hold *McCartney* until 4 June, the despatch ended, 'We're sorry it turned out like this – it's nothing personal. Love John & George. Hare Krishna. A Mantra a Day Keeps MAYA! Away.'

The letter, labelled 'From Us, To You', was left in the Apple office out-tray. Foreseeing the potential impact of the content, Ringo took it upon himself to hand-deliver the message to Paul's London home in St John's Wood. The resulting confrontation was recounted by Paul in an interview with the *Evening Standard* on 21 April 1970. 'Ringo came around to see me with a letter from the others and I called him everything under the sun,' Paul told Ray Connelly. 'But it's all business. I don't want to fall out with Ringo. I like Ringo. I think he's great. We're all talking about peace and love but really we're not feeling peaceful at all. There's no one who's to blame. We were fools to get ourselves in this situation in the first place. But it's not a comfortable situation for me to work in as an artist.' Written in advance of the High Court hearing in 1971, Ringo's account of events was rather more brittle: 'Paul went completely out of control, shouting at me, prodding his fingers towards my face, saying, "I'll finish you now." And, "You'll pay." He told me to put my coat on and get out. I did so.'

Matching Ringo's detailed recollection of events, Paul went for the jugular:

---

12 Released on 26 February 1970, *Hey Jude* compiled ten 'A' and 'B' sides, together with album tracks and slightly altered mixes.

He said, 'Well, on behalf of the board and on behalf of The Beatles and so and so, we think you should do this,' etc. And I was just fed up with that. It was the only time I ever told anyone to GET OUT! It was fairly hostile. But things had got like that by this time. It hadn't actually come to blows, but it was near enough.

Sensitive to a bizarre possibility of a Beatles album competing with a Paul McCartney record, John clarified his position in an interview with *Rolling Stone*. 'There was nothing *against* Paul having an album out. I don't want to fight in the charts! I want to get in while the going's good. It was just an ego game! It would have killed *Let It Be*. Let *Let It Be* breathe!' Compromise was reached – in favour of Paul: on 17 April 1970, *McCartney* was released, followed by *Let It Be* on 8 May.

In his authorized biography, written 25 years, later, Paul revisited the event and defended his headstrong stance. 'I had to do something in order to assert myself because I was just sinking,' he told Barry Miles. 'Linda was very helpful, she was saying, "Look, you don't have to take this crap, you're a grown man, you have every bit as much right..." I was getting pummelled about the head, in my mind anyway.' Whereas in February 1970 – talking on *Scene and Heard* – John spoke with a note of ambiguity – 'All I want for The Beatles is their individual happiness, and whether that's in a collective form or not remains to be seen' – by 1980, regret had replaced doubt: 'I never thought we'd be so stupid, like splitting and arguing, but we were naïve enough to let people come between us and that's what happened.'

If only John had tuned into WABC-FM radio on 1 May 1970 and heeded George's advice:

> We all have to sacrifice a little in order to gain something really big and there is a big gain by recording together, I think musically, financially and spiritually. For the rest of the world, I think that Beatles music is such a big sort of scene that I think that it's the least we could do, to sacrifice three months of the year, at least, just to do an album or two. I think it's very selfish if The Beatles don't record together.

Resolution

Throughout 1969, a tantalizing set of alternative choices were presented to The Beatles, each offering radically different opportunities, and the potential to profoundly alter the course of Beatles history. On Wednesday, 28 May 1969, Glyn Johns presented a finished mix of *Get Back* ready for release, yet, with Michael Lindsay-Hogg's accompanying documentary film of the album's making still incomplete, it was understandably put on hold. Two days later, 'The Ballad of John and Yoko' was issued as The Beatles' twenty-first single and swiftly replaced Tommy Roe's 'Dizzy' at the top of the UK charts. Celebrating a seventeenth number one single, The Beatles took a month's holiday before returning to the studio at the beginning of July to complete *Abbey Road*. Then, on 9 September, a critical meeting took place at Apple to discuss The Beatles' next single. John proposed 'Cold Turkey', a stark lyrical account of heroin addiction. The idea was vetoed. This defining moment triggered a rapid sequence of events leading to John's decision to quit The Beatles, 11 days later.

Hindsight is an intoxicating medicine to remedy the ills of history, but in September 1969, Paul, George and Ringo plainly did not appreciate the depth of John's frustration at being a Beatle. Had they acquiesced and recorded 'Cold Turkey' it would have set in motion a sequence of events conceivably leading to the recording of a new studio album, and consequently saving the band from an unnecessary premature demise. Most immediately, the invitation to attend the Toronto Rock and Roll Revival festival – made a day later, on 10 September – would have given rise to an impromptu Beatles performance. Since the spring of 1969, rumours had circulated of The Beatles returning to the live stage. 'I quite fancy giving some live shows,' John told the *NME*'s Alan Smith on 3 May, 'but Ringo doesn't because he says it'll just be the same when we get on, nothing different. We've got to come to an agreement.'

Between the final North American tour in 1966 and the opportunistic rooftop show on 30 January 1969, The Beatles rarely performed in public. On 9 September 1968, they appeared on *The David Frost Show* performing 'Hey Jude' – albeit with the aid of backing tapes – and 11 days later a promotional video recording of 'Revolution' was shown on *Top of the Pops*. Both engagements were deemed a success and were fondly talked about by The Beatles at Twickenham Studios. In December 1968, John led the star-studded Dirty Macs through an ad-hoc rendition of 'Revolution' and a blazing reading of 'Yer Blues' at *The Rolling Stones Rock and Roll Circus*. The prospect of a Beatles return to the live stage gathered momentum.

Rejecting a return to Hamburg, the Roundhouse in Camden was provisionally booked for three nights, initially for December 1968, and later rescheduled to begin on 18 January 1969. The proposed shows – offering a much-needed end to the *Get Back* project – were duly advertised in the news section of what would be the final issue of *Beatles Monthly* as a 'one colour television show': 'After rehearsals [The Beatles] will give a set of separate "live" performances before invited audiences. All three shows will be recorded on colour videotape and the final television programme will be made up from the best parts of the three.'

The concert never happened but, aware of the lucrative possibilities, the newly employed Allen Klein explored the idea of a Beatles world tour. Again nothing materialized. Itching to play live, Paul recounted his thoughts in an interview with *Melody Maker* in November 1971. 'I wanted to get in a van and do an unadvertised concert at a Saturday night hop at Slough Town Hall or somewhere like that. We'd call ourselves Rikki and the Red Streaks or something and just get up and play. There'd be no press and we'd tell nobody about it. John thought it was a daft idea.'

Paul's ambition was fulfilled a year later, when, on 9 February 1972, his newly formed post-Beatles group, Wings, took to the road in a 12-seat transit van with a rented trailer attached to carry the equipment. With no gigs or hotels booked, the band headed north on the M1 in search of eye-catching destinations.[13] Amused by directions for Ashby-de-la-Zouch, the entourage rolled into the small Derbyshire town hoping to discover a suitable venue to play. With little fitting on offer, locals kindly suggested Nottingham University as a more realistic alternative. Arrangements were hastily made for a lunchtime show in the university ballroom at a ticket price of 40 pence. The performance was a success, and over the next fortnight the band replicated the ad-hoc stratagem of arriving unannounced at ten further locations: York, Hull, Newcastle, Lancaster, Leeds, Sheffield, Manchester, Birmingham, Swansea and Oxford. 'My best playing days were at the Cavern lunchtime sessions,' Paul told *Melody Maker* in 1971:

> We'd go onstage with a cheese roll and a cigarette and we felt
> we had really something going on. The amps used to fuse and
> we'd stop and sing a Sunblest Bread commercial while they were
> repaired. I'd walk off down the street playing my guitar and
> annoying the neighbours. I couldn't do that now, but it's what
> I want to do with this new group.

Facing a daunting wait in Beatles limbo, George suddenly found himself back on the road. On 1 December 1969, having watched the American husband-and-wife duo Delaney & Bonnie in concert at the Royal Albert Hall, London, George then appeared unannounced on stage the following night in Bristol. Post-gig, George readily accepted an invitation to join the touring entourage for the remaining UK and

---

13 The band line-up was Paul (bass), Linda McCartney (keyboards), Denny Laine (guitar), Henry McCullough (guitar) and Denny Seiwell (drums).

European dates. Buoyed by the experience, George returned home with renewed vigour, telling the *NME* that he hoped that The Beatles 'will tour again'. But while John, Paul and George, independently, gravitated towards live performance and the possibility of a Beatles tour, a greater problem was simmering, threatening to curtail their renewed optimism: songwriting.

'You'd come up with a *Magical Mystery Tour*,' John complained to Paul at Apple in September 1969:

> I didn't write any of that except 'Walrus'. I'd accept it and you'd already have five or six songs, so I'd think, 'Fuck it, I can't keep up with that,' so I didn't bother...so for a period if you didn't invite me to be on an album *personally*, if you three didn't say, 'Write some more 'cause we like your work,' I wasn't going to bother.

Opting to listen or perhaps remain tactfully silent, Paul gave space for John to vent his frustrations:

> If you look back on The Beatles' albums you'll find that most times if anybody has got extra time it's you. For no other reason than you worked it like that. Now when we get into a studio I don't want to go through games with you to get space on the album. I don't want to go through a little manoeuvring, or whatever level it's on, to get time.

Shaken by John's vitriol, Paul agreed that he had 'come out stronger' but argued that he had encouraged John to write more songs. 'There was no point turning 'em out,' John countered, 'I couldn't, didn't have the energy to turn 'em out and get 'em on as well.'

Historically, one-upmanship between John and Paul had encouraged them to write better songs and claim the coveted A-side single release. In the early years, John's prolific writing led to a succession of hits, from a 'A Hard Day's Night' and 'I Feel Fine' to 'Ticket to Ride' and 'Help!' But, increasingly, Paul's insatiable competitive appetite resulted in his songs dominating releases: from 'Magical Mystery Tour' and 'Hello Goodbye' in 1967 to 'Lady Madonna' and 'Hey Jude' in 1968. 'When we get into the studio,' John informed Paul, 'I don't care how we do it but I don't want to think about equal time – I just want it known I'm allowed to put four songs on the album...there must be other ways of doing it.'

The solution hit John square on: 'four songs' each on the next record and two for Ringo, 'if he wants them'. It was an incredible proposition – an idea both spectacular and torturous – and provides the greatest of all 'what if...?' moments in The Beatles' illustrious story. What if Paul or George, or even Ringo, had just simply said okay and nodded their approval? Would Beatle fans now have in their possession a record craved for over five decades? It is these pivotal moments in history that offer innumerable and heart-breaking alternative possibilities. Sadly, John's idea was not sufficient to save The Beatles but the temptation to imagine otherwise is irresistible.

Part 2

Four Sides of The Beatles

I do what I like, Paul does what he likes and George does what he likes, and Ringo. You just divide the album time up between ourselves. It's always been that really and the combination of the music is what we call pure Beatles. Like 'It's Getting Better' where we've all written it and we've all turned it into pure Beatle.
John Lennon – *OZ*, 1969

We always regarded ourselves as The Beatles whether we recorded singly or in twos or threes.
Paul McCartney – High Court witness box, 1971

If The Beatles had continued making records, all of the solo stuff that we've done would have been on Beatle albums.
George Harrison – *Undercover*, 1994

If we weren't all together then we'll all be together separately.
Ringo Starr – *Mojo*, 1998

LENNON

1. Instant Karma!
2. Jealous Guy
3. Love
4. Make Love Not War
5. Gimme Some Truth
6. God

McCARTNEY

1. Come and Get It
2. Maybe I'm Amazed
3. Another Day
4. Every Night
5. Junk
6. The Back Seat of My Car

HARRISON

1. What Is Life?
2. My Sweet Lord
3. Not Guilty
4. Wah-Wah
5. Try Some Buy Some
6. All Things Must Pass

STARR

1. It Don't Come Easy
2. I'm the Greatest
3. Early 1970
4. Coochy-Coochy
5. When Every Song Is Sung
6. Suicide

5. The Concept

The year 1969 had been full of contradictions for The Beatles. Of the two albums they had recorded, *Let It Be* and *Abbey Road*, the former sat disregarded with an uncertain future, while the latter had been released to unanimous critical praise. In the singles chart, 'Get Back', 'The Ballad of John and Yoko' and the double-sided release 'Something' and 'Come Together' had afforded The Beatles a trio of hit singles. Behind the scenes, marriages, walk-outs and threats of divorce had dogged the reality of day-to-day life in the group.

It is in this context that the 'what if...?' fantasy of *The Lost Album of The Beatles* comes into play and the proposition of a new record: *Four Sides of The Beatles*. In September 1969 came John's audacious suggestion that The Beatles make a new record as an attempt to save the group from an all-pervasive and suffocating creative malaise. If John's proposition had been accepted, Beatle history as we know it would have irrevocably changed. Instead of *Abbey Road* being their last recorded album, 1970 would have seen a ground-breaking Beatles record take the place of the last gasp, *Let It Be*. It was an idea that been percolating since the recording of the 'White Album'.

In 1968, when The Beatles were choosing a name for the as yet untitled double album, John proposed *A Doll's House*. The title implied a home with many rooms metaphorically matching the eclectic nature of the 30-song set contained within. On a deeper level, the impulse to compartmentalize the record reflected the increasing independence of each of The Beatles and a growing desire to express their musical individuality. Speaking in September 1969 to *OZ* magazine, John said, 'We don't really write together any more. We haven't written together for two years – not really, just occasional bits. I do what I like, Paul does what he likes and George does what he likes. We just divide the album time between ourselves.'

It was a view that George shared in an interview with Howard Smith on WABC-FM radio:

I think this is a good way if we do our own albums. That way we don't have to compromise. I mean, we lose whatever we get from each other – we sacrifice that in order to do a total sort of thing. Because in a way, Paul wants to do his songs his way. He doesn't want to do his songs my way. And I don't want do my songs their way.

By substituting 'our own albums' with 'our own sides', George's fear of losing 'whatever we get from each other' is remedied by the concept of *Four Sides of The Beatles*. It is the ultimate endgame that offers four distinct personalities housed within the reassuring security of a Beatles-labelled product.

At the meeting on 9 September 1969, John made one more stipulation: to divide the publishing credit and effectively end 'the Lennon-and-McCartney myth'. The joint credit dated back to a verbal agreement made between the two writers in 1962, and reflected John and Paul's teenage years when the pair would skip school and hold writing sessions at Paul's house at 20 Forthlin Road, Allerton, or at weekends in the front parlour of Menlove Avenue, much to the annoyance of John's Aunt Mimi – 'John,' she would shout when Paul knocked on the front door, 'Your "little friend" has arrived.' John and Paul wrote as many as a hundred songs together in this period, each one signed off at the top of the page by Paul with the tongue-in-cheek acknowledgement: 'ANOTHER LENNON–MCCARTNEY ORIGINAL'.

The Lennon and McCartney partnership was at the heart of The Beatles success and to a great extent defined the sound, the vision and the commercial appeal of the group. Yet, as the relationship progressed, so too did the collaborative process. Songs were often initiated independently, with John and Paul more frequently coming together later to run ideas past one another. In *Many Years from Now*, Paul said that when he rhymed 'just seventeen' with 'beauty queen' for the opening line of 'I Saw Her Standing There', 'John screamed with laughter and said "You're joking about that line, aren't you?"' Hastily crossed out, 'beauty queen' was replaced by the more ambiguous expression 'you know what I mean'. 'In the Beatle days,' George said in April 1970, 'if someone came in with a song that had a corny line and some of the others got a bit embarrassed by it, we'd say it.' In 1968, when playing 'Hey Jude', Paul pre-empted criticism of the line 'the movement you need is on your shoulder' by saying, 'It's a stupid expression…it sounds like a parrot,' and offering to 'fix it'. 'You won't!' John responded, aghast. 'That's the best line in the song.'

Where John offered light, Paul provided shade. Where Paul oozed melody, John wrote with poetic imagery. 'I was lucky enough to work with John,' Paul told Derek Taylor in the 1990s. 'He was lucky enough to work with me and together we kind of made two sides of a coin. I think John without me lacks something, and I think without him I can be said to lack something.' In March 1967, Hunter Davies, The Beatles' official biographer, witnessed the duo collaborating in a writing session in Paul's music room at Cavendish Avenue as they 'polished-up' 'With a Little Help from My Friends'. Seated at the piano, Paul sang, 'Do you believe in love at first' 'No,' John interrupted, 'it hasn't got the right number of syllables.' Accommodating the suggestion, Paul offered, 'Do you believe in – a – love at first sight?'

John and Paul rehearse at The Cavern Club in Liverpool, 19 February 1963.

Happily tweaking lines and paying close attention to how words scanned with melody, the song was fashioned with microscopic attention to detail. 'What's a rhyme for *time*?' John once asked. '*Yes I'm certain it all happens all the time.* It's got to rhyme with that line.' Sitting quietly reading a magazine in the corner of the room, John's wife Cynthia suggested, 'I just feel fine.' 'No,' John said. 'You never use the word "just". It's meaningless. It's a fill-in-word.' Across the afternoon, John and Paul laughed and fondly reminisced about their days in Hamburg, sang snippets of 'Can't Buy Me Love' and switched instruments from piano to guitar. With the song still incomplete, they telephoned Ringo and organized a recording session at Abbey Road. It was a typical day in John and Paul's creative relationship and one that was repeated many times over successive years.

On other occasions, George and Ringo were involved. 'I was at John's house one day,' George told *Acoustic Guitar*, 'and he was struggling with some tunes. He had loads of bits, maybe three songs that were unfinished, and I made suggestions and helped him to work them together so that they became one finished song: "She Said She Said". The middle part of that record is a different song.' Similarly, in 1966, when Paul arrived at John's house in Weybridge with the essence of 'Eleanor Rigby', contributions were incorporated from a mutual school friend, Pete Shotton, who chipped in with thoughts of 'Father McKenzie' at Eleanor's grave, Ringo piping up with 'darning his socks in the night' and George tying together the theme of the verses with the suggestion 'look at all the lonely people'. Attempting to explain the creative process of songwriting, John told David Sheff in 1980, 'It's hard to describe, even with the clarity of memory, the moment the apple falls. The thing will start moving along at a speed of its own, then you wake up at the end of it and have this whole thing on paper. Who said what to whom as we were writing, I don't know.'

The wish to end the Lennon/McCartney credit was to all intents and purposes decorative. In reality, both writers relied upon one another, and it is this collaborative teamwork which would have transformed the twenty-four selections made for an imaginary *Four Sides of The Beatles*. Added to which, while the majority of the songs selected for the record have arrangements imbedded in our memories from years, if not decades of listening, it cannot be overstated how the chemical charge of John, Paul, George and Ringo playing together would have profoundly changed and indeed enriched their presentation. Yet, rather than hammer home this fact in the forthcoming chapters, I have cautioned against writing '…if Paul had added bass on the track…' or '…imagine if George had played lead guitar here'. That said, as a final note, the reader may justifiably ask whether each song on the proposed record is played with all four Beatles involved. The simple answer is yes. The longer response lies in the group's history where there are many instances of sometimes as few as one Beatle involved in a recording session. For example: Paul recording 'Yesterday' to his own guitar accompaniment with the addition of a string accompaniment; John and Paul playing all the instruments on 'The Ballad of John and Yoko'; Paul and Ringo on 'Why Don't We Do It in the Road?'; or Paul, George and Ringo on 'Maxwell's Silver Hammer' when John was recovering from his motoring accident. 'In short,' Geoff Emerick wrote in his memoir *Here, There and Everywhere*, 'The Beatles had become four individuals. Ever since *Sgt. Pepper* they were always so much better if they weren't all there at the same time...[It] was odd though how that rarely happened when there were two, or even three of them interacting; there was just some kind of bad chemistry when all four of them were in a room together.'

What follows is the record The Beatles would have made had they agreed to make a follow-up to *Abbey Road* – or, at least, my notion of it. Where John proposed a 14-track album, I have expanded the concept to broaden its appeal and second-guess Paul, George and Ringo's development of the idea. Titled *Four Sides of The Beatles*, the four-record set would be a collection of 24 songs, equally divided between the four Beatles, with each side of vinyl devoted to one member of the band. It is an idea that would have revolutionized the formula of the album and, once again, positioned The Beatles as leading innovators in rock and pop history.

6. Side One: Lennon

The year 1969 was a challenging one for John. His growing ambivalence towards The Beatles jarred with an all-consuming relationship with Yoko Ono. The couple married on 20 March, four months after Yoko miscarried the first of three unsuccessful pregnancies. Despite the crushing emotional trauma, the newlyweds embarked on a campaign to promote world peace: planting acorns in Coventry Cathedral; exhibiting experimental films at the Institute of Contemporary Art; staging Bed-ins in Amsterdam and Montreal; and performing as The Plastic Ono Band in Cambridge, London and Toronto.

The schedule was hectic but did little to reactivate John's waning songwriting mojo. When The Beatles arrived at Twickenham Studios, in January 1969, John presented two new songs – 'Don't Let Me Down' and 'Dig a Pony' – and on the third day 'Across the Universe', a song first recorded almost 12 months earlier. Without a lyric sheet to hand, John struggled to remember the words, and Paul stifled a yawn. 'It's another slow one,' John admitted in self-admonishment, 'I know that we'll knock off a couple of fast ones, if I just wasn't so tired when I got in.'

Over the next two days, The Beatles attempted to revive 'Across

Opposite: John at a press conference at Heathrow airport on his return from his honeymoon in Vienna with Yoko Ono, 1 April 1969.

the Universe' but with little enthusiasm. 'Haven't you written anything?' Paul asks, barely suppressing his frustration. 'No,' John says sullenly. 'Haven't you?' Paul repeats despondently. 'We're going to be faced with a crisis, you know.' Then, noticing a microphone dangling above their heads, they soften. 'When I'm up against the wall, Paul,' John smiles, 'you'll find I'm on my best.' 'Yeah, I know, I know,' Paul laughs, 'but I just wish you'd come up with the goods.' Clearly play-acting and stretching his neck up to the microphone, John reassures Paul. 'Look,' he says, 'I think I've got Sunday off.' 'Well, I hope you can deliver,' Paul laughs. John continues, 'I'm hoping for a little rock and roller.' 'Yeah...' Paul says over a wail of feedback piercing across the conversation, 'I was hoping for the same thing myself.'

In February, as The Beatles started work on new tracks, for what would become *Abbey Road*, John offered a clutch of rudimentary ideas, including 'Because', 'Come Together', 'I Want You (She's So Heavy)' as well as 'Mean Mr. Mustard' and 'Polythene Pam' from an older stockpile written in 1968. Struggling from a loss of self-esteem, John attempted to explain his predicament in an interview with Jann Wenner in 1970: 'I got a message on acid that you should destroy your ego, and I did. I was reading that stupid book of Leary's [*The Psychedelic Experience*], and all that shit. I destroyed my ego and I didn't believe I could do anything. I let Paul do what he wanted and say...them all do what he wanted. And I just was nothing. I was shit.'

Helping to rebuild John's confidence, Yoko enriched his life in a blanket of love and emotional support resulting in 'Give Peace a Chance' written in room 1742 of the Queen Elizabeth Hotel in Montreal, Canada, during a Bed-in with Yoko.[1] Yet, having contributed vocals on 'The Continuing Story of Bungalow Bill' and the avant-garde soundscape 'Revolution 9', both from the 'White Album', Yoko had no input on *Abbey Road*. Furthermore, when the *John Lennon/Plastic Ono Band* album was released in autumn 1970, the inner sleeve credited Yoko as 'Wind'.[2] As such, it is reasonable to assume that Yoko would not feature on John's side of a new Beatles record. Nevertheless, the intensity of their relationship would have a profound effect on the music, and Yoko's conceptual influence would be indelibly printed on John's approach.

At the core of John's character was a need for control. Effectively orphaned when he was five years old and raised by his mother's sister, Mimi, John swaggered through his formative teenage years behind a wall of belligerence and aggression. Music was an outlet to channel his pent-up frustrations. From The Quarry Men to The Beatles, John was the gang leader, and as his friendship with Paul developed so, too, did his songwriting eloquence as he gave voice to his inner feelings. Success and adoration did much to soften his edges, but in time, and as Paul's talents also flourished, John the songwriter retreated. Cocooned by an excess of wealth and an inherent laziness, John gradually acceded

---

1   Adopted as an anthem by the peace movement and credited to The Plastic Ono Band, the song peaked at number two in the UK charts a month later. Ironically, as 'Give Peace a Chance' climbed the charts, The Beatles standalone single 'The Ballad of John and Yoko', which had enjoyed a three-week spell at number one, was slipping out of the top ten.

2   A sister release, *Yoko Ono/Plastic Ono Band*, was recorded in October 1970 and released simultaneously with the *John Lennon/Plastic Ono Band* album.

control of The Beatles. 'When I was a Beatle I thought we were the best fucking group in the god-damned world,' John told *Playboy* in 1980. 'And believing that is what made us what we were. But you play me those tracks today and I want to remake every damn one of them...I heard "Lucy in the Sky with Diamonds" on the radio last night. It's abysmal. I mean, it's great, but it wasn't made right.' With the opportunity to make music to his own satisfaction, the John Lennon of late 1969 suggested an artist convincingly re-emerging with the drive and conviction that had defined The Beatles in their early years. At the beginning of the new decade, with the support of Paul, George and Ringo, John's six songs of the new record promised an exhilarating reinvention.

The divided format of *Four Sides of The Beatles* creates the possibility of each Beatle choosing which producer they would work with. The immediate choice for John was George Martin, who had overseen the release of every Beatles record since 1962. In the studio, The Beatles would share their unformed ideas with Martin, where after-arrangement ideas would be addressed: structures modified, additional parts suggested, instrumentation discussed, and harmonies tested. 'We start from scratch,' Martin told Hunter Davies, The Beatles' official biographer, 'thrashing it out in the studio, doing it the hard way.'

But, despite the lavish critical praise heaped on Martin's skill and technical innovation, John was often dismissive of the end product. 'He didn't like "messing about" as he called it,' Martin said in *Anthology* in 1995, 'and he didn't like pretentiousness.' Favouring a more authentic 'old-fashioned' rock sound, John would exclaim,

'The hell with it. Let's blast the living daylights out!' In later years, John claimed a wilfulness to re-record everything The Beatles had ever done. A shocked Martin asked, 'Even "Strawberry Fields?"' 'Especially "Strawberry Fields",' John replied, additionally telling *Rolling Stone*, '[George] is more Paul's style of music than mine.'

Known to dislike the sound of his recorded voice, John would frequently ask for effects to be added in an attempt to mask his natural sound. It can be heard on the vocal distortion applied to 'I Am the Walrus', yet, by the time of the 'White Album' the following year, John was in search of a purer sound. 'I always keep saying I prefer the double album because I'm being myself on it,' John told Jann Wenner in 1970. 'I'm doing it how I like it. Like "I'm So Tired" and all that, is just the guitar. I felt more at ease with *that* than the production. I don't like productions so much.' Ironically, when he came to make his first solo record, post The Beatles, John turned to Phil Spector for help, a producer famed for layering multiple instruments on top of one another. 'I'm fond of Phil's work a lot,' John told BBC radio presenter Andy Peebles:

His personality, I'm not crazy about. I mean he's got tremendous ego. He considers the artist like the film director considers actors, just pieces of garbage...canned goods that you bring on and wheel off. He'd like to bury the artist and so the production is the main thing. But we didn't allow him to do that to us. So on that level it was very good, because we used what we considered is his amazing ear for pop music and sound, without letting it become [deep voice] 'Spector', you know –

thousands of castanets, 'The Wall'. We didn't want 'The Wall of Sound' but we wanted the outside input.

Introducing a minimalistic, raw sound with arrangements stripped of embellishment and unnecessary instrumentation, the debut Plastic Ono Band album, released in December 1970, evoked a 1950s style and attitude. Delivered with just drums, piano, bass and guitar, the record is a compelling suggestion of the direction John would take when he recorded his side of the proposed new Beatles album. The six-song selection on this imagined side – 'Instant Karma!', 'Make Love Not War', 'Gimme Some Truth', 'Love', 'Jealous Guy' and 'God' – reflect John's reawakening as a formidable and unique artist. They are songs which speak of love and new beginnings of political frustration and, in 'God', a devastating end to The Beatles story.

Speaking in 1971 to the *New Musical Express*, John spoke of his musical maturing:

The fact is The Beatles have left school, and we have to get a job. That's made us work – really work harder. I think we're much better than we ever were when we were together. Look at us today. I'd sooner have *RAM*, *John Lennon/Plastic Ono Band*, George's album, and Ringo's single and the movies than *Let It Be* or *Abbey Road*.[3]

3   *RAM* was Paul's second solo album, released in May 1971.

Instant Karma!

On 27 January 1970, John woke up at Tittenhurst Park 'ecstatic, bubbling with excitement and shouting like a kid because he had a great new tune in his head'. When his personal assistant, Anthony Fawcett, took breakfast up to John's bedroom, he observed that 'lyrics seemed to be pouring out of him'. Wrapped in only a bathrobe, John bounded downstairs to the kitchen, sat at the upright piano, and, as Fawcett noted in *One Day at a Time*, sang the 'basic melody over and over again...hammering out the chords'. Thirty minutes later, 'Instant Karma!' was written. With great excitement, John dressed and prepared to travel into central London to record the new composition. Sitting beside Yoko in the back of their chauffeur-driven Mercedes, attention turned to a suitable producer. 'Let's get Phil [Spector] in on the session,' John said. 'He'll get the sound I want.'

In all the excitement, John suddenly remembered that the Apple offices in Mayfair didn't have a piano. The solution was swift and inspired, 'Well,' John said, 'we'll just pick one up on the way.' Les Anthony was instructed to divert across town to 100 New Oxford Street where, on arrival at Alfred Imhof's, and while resolutely seated in the back of the car, John selected a piano from the shop window display. Problem resolved, consideration switched to available musicians for the session. 'John phoned me up,' George Harrison recalled in *Anthology*, 'and said, "I've written this tune and I'm going to record it tonight and have it pressed up and out tomorrow – that's the whole point: Instant Karma!"' Fortuitously, at that moment, George was with Phil Spector and invited the producer to join the session.

A studio was hastily booked at Abbey Road where John and George joined bass player Klaus Voormann and drummer Alan White. Unbeknown to him, John had recently watched White playing in a club with an unsigned band called Griffin. The following morning, White received a phone call asking him to join The Plastic Ono Band. Believing it to be prank call, White put the phone down. Ten minutes later, John called again. 'Can you be at the airport tomorrow?' John said reassuringly. 'I'll send a limo.' Recovering from the shock, White accepted and the next day boarded an outbound flight from London to Canada to perform at the Toronto Rock and Roll Revival festival. Mid-flight, a rehearsal took place where White learned the set by beating the back of a chair with a set of drum sticks. 'I was playing on the seat in front of me,' White told *Music Radar* in 2009, 'and John said to me, "Now, remember, Alan, the way Carl Perkins played ['Blue Suede Shoes'], there's an extra beat after the line *well there's a one for the money – da-da-duh*!" John was very conscious of details like that.' The first White saw of a real kit was walking out on stage later that evening: 'I took the whole thing in my stride. It wasn't until years later that I went, "Wow, what an amazing thing to have happened!"'

Ironically, if 'Instant Karma!' had been recorded by The Beatles, Ringo would have been unavailable for the session. Unlike Paul, who lived a few minutes' walk away from Abbey Road, and where a quick phone call from John was all that was needed for his writing partner to pop down to the studio,[4] Ringo was in Los Angeles appearing as a guest on *Rowan & Martin's Laugh-In* delivering a set of satirical one-liners at the end of the primetime show.[5] In his absence, John asked Alan White to play on the record, giving the instruction to 'break the meter of the song' and 'disrupt the rhythmic flow of the verses'. White responded accordingly. The effect was a jarring two-bar drum fill in the second and third verses of the song, making for a strange syncopated shift in the beat.

When it came to the lead vocal, John again was clear in his direction, as he recounted in an interview with *Rolling Stone*. '[Spector] said, "How do you want it?" 'I said, "You know, 1950s, but now." And he said, "Right," and boom, I did it in just about three goes.' The delivery was gritty and crackled with attitude as John's voice soared over the uplifting chorus line 'We all shine on', before landing softly for the balancing simile 'like the moons, the stars and the sun'. Skilfully voiced between sung notes and speech – known in German opera as *Sprechstimme* – the economical melody was reminiscent of 'Lucy in the Sky with Diamonds'. But where in 1967 the chorus of The Beatles' song glowed from the ornate melodic tone

---

4 Like John, Paul was prone to impatience. In 1967, during the making of *Sgt. Pepper's Lonely Hearts Club Band*, Paul asked Mike Leander to write an orchestral score for 'She's Leaving Home' when George Martin was not available at Paul's immediate request.

5 Ringo's script included lines such as 'There is no truth in the rumour that my latest picture *The Magic Christian* is about Billy Graham doing card tricks', 'You can be certain that a man with a banana in his ear does not want you to notice his feet', and 'You know, if your President doesn't want instant analysis of his speeches, he shouldn't be giving speeches that can be instantly analysed.'

of Paul's complementary vocal harmony, 'Instant Karma!' relied on a plainer three-note lead line. To add richness to the song, long-serving roadie Mal Evans was tasked with rounding up a group of would-be vocalists from the nearby Revolver Club. Accordingly procured, the drunken rabble arranged themselves around a microphone at Abbey Road where they were coerced and conducted by George Harrison for the singalong chorus.

John had first heard the phrase 'instant karma' from Melinda Kendall – the wife of Tony Cox – when he and Yoko stayed with the couple in Denmark in December 1969.[6] Popular as an in-phrase in the late 1960s, karma connected the belief in a past and future life. Advancing the concept, John made an association between karma as a spiritual philosophy, and *instant* television commercials advertising the latest 'must-have' product. 'It was like the idea of *instant* coffee,' he told journalist David Sheff, 'presenting something in a new form.'

The lyrics of 'Instant Karma!' read like spoken dialogue, similar to those of 'The Ballad of John and Yoko' in which John described the events surrounding his wedding to Yoko. 'I want records to be like newspapers,' John told David Wigg in February 1970:

> I'd like them to come out at least once a week, or twice a week. With ['Instant Karma!'] we wrote it in the morning, recorded and re-mixed it and got it out in a week, here and in the States, which was pretty fast and moving. I write songs about what's

---

6   Cox and Ono were married in 1962 and had a daughter, Kyoko. They divorced in January 1969.

happening to me at that moment and I want it to be out at that moment. I don't care what name goes on it.

There was much about 'Instant Karma!' that made it right for The Beatles. The introduction featured a piano striking three distinct rising notes – E, G and A – appropriated from one of John's favourite records, 'Some Other Guy', a song embedded into the group's history when it was filmed by Granada Television during a midday session at the Cavern Club on Wednesday, 22 August, 1962.[7] The black-and-white footage shows all four Beatles wearing white shirts, neatly knotted ties and black tank-tops. Standing side by side, symmetrically posed, John and Paul bawl out the raunchy lead vocal: John, stage left, Rickenbacker guitar thrust out facing a dank brick wall; Paul, centre stage, his Hofner bass pointing in the direction of George, who is set back in shadow. Three days earlier, Ringo Starr had replaced Pete Best as The Beatles drummer and before the show a disgruntled faction of Cavern faithfuls vented their disapproval. During a backstage melee, George was punched in the face and can be seen in the film footage nursing a black eye. When The Beatles launched into 'Some Other Guy', shouts of 'Pete forever, Ringo never' could be heard.

When he appeared as a guest DJ on WNEW-FM New York on 28 September 1974, John was keen to share the connection between the past and the present. 'This is an American record that nobody

---

7   Written by Jerry Leiber, Mike Stoller and Richard Barrett, 'Some Other Guy' was recorded by Barrett in 1962. Shortly after, the Liverpool group The Big Three covered the song, earning a place on John Lennon's jukebox.

I know over here seems to have ever heard of it,' John told host Dennis Schulitz. 'It's called "Some Other Guy" by Ritchie Barrett. There are some strange bootlegs of The Beatles singing it rather crappily from The Cavern somewhere, way back in '61...you'll notice the intro is slightly like "Instant Karma!"'

At 4am on Wednesday, 28 January 1970, less than 24 hours after the song's conception, 'Instant Karma!' was completed. By any measure, it had been a breath-taking act of creation. Finishing a rough mix of the song, Phil Spector marked the tape box 'Do Not Use'. 'To hell with it,' John retorted. 'Issue it. It'll do. Who will know?' Ten days later, 'Instant Karma!' entered the UK chart at number seven.[8]

'PLAY LOUD' read the instruction on the paper label.

---

8   Billed as Lennon/Ono with The Plastic Ono Band, the following week 'Instant Karma!' climbed to number five. A fortnight later, when the record slipped down a position, The Beatles' twenty-third, and final, single, 'Let It Be' entered the chart at number two.

Jealous Guy

It was one of John Lennon's most beautiful songs, melodically rich and lyrically universal in its sentiment and depth of feeling. Yet the journey of 'Jealous Guy' from its inception in 1968 to its recording on John's second solo album, *Imagine*, in 1971 is one of both inner artistic struggle and outer violent brutality.

In February 1968, The Beatles retreated to India to be inducted into the Eastern philosophy of Transcendental Meditation. Breathing in the peaceful air and the beauty of the landscape, one may imagine the breeze sweet with the sound of Paul writing 'Mother Nature's Son' conjuring images of 'mountain streams and fields of grass' as John was singing of 'desert skies' and 'mountain ranges'. '"Mother Nature's Son" was from a lecture of Maharishi where he was talking about nature,' John told David Sheff in 1980, 'and I had a piece called "I'm Just a Child of Nature", which turned into "Jealous Guy" years later. Both inspired from the same lecture by Maharishi.'

The Beatles had intended to visit Rishikesh – the location of Maharishi Mahesh Yogi's ashram – six months earlier, having spent a weekend at a seminar of the Maharishi's in Bangor, Wales, only for the excursion to be cut short when it was announced that Brian Epstein had died. Further distracted by the making of the television film *Magical Mystery Tour*, The Beatles embraced their rescheduled visit to India as a welcome escape from the ensuing critical drubbing. But what should have been a time of enlightened relaxation soon soured. After ten days in India, Ringo's supply of Heinz baked beans ran out, prompting his early return to England. A fortnight later, Paul followed him, rejuvenated by a short 'holiday'. Keen to penetrate his otherworldliness, John volunteered to take a ride in a helicopter in the hope that the Maharishi might 'slip him the answer'. But heavenly aspirations were brought down to earth when the Maharishi was accused of subjecting the actress Mia Farrow to unwanted attention. Feeling deceived, John packed his bags and left, with a mystified George in tow.[9]

In the last week of May, The Beatles regrouped at George's home, Kinfauns, in Esher, to record ideas for what was to become the 'White Album'. Twenty-seven demos were put down on an Ampex four-track reel-to-reel tape recorder. Among them, 15 songs contributed by John[10] including 'Sexy Sadie' – questioning the validity of Maharishi's cosmic knowing[11] – and 'Child of Nature'. But, despite its outward charm and beguiling melody, 'Child of Nature' was not revisited during the subsequent album sessions, perhaps in preference to Paul's 'Mother's Nature's Son', with which it shared a strong thematic likeness.

On 2 January 1969, the first day of the *Get Back* sessions, John

9   In his 1970 *Rolling Stone* interview, John claimed he was told that the
    Maharishi had attempted to 'rape Mia Farrow...and a few other women'. John
    and George confronted the Maharishi and told him they were leaving. 'Why?'
    the Maharishi asked. 'Well, if you're so cosmic,' John replied, 'you'll know why.'

10 'Dear Prudence', 'Glass Onion', 'The Continuing Story of Bungalow Bill',
    'Happiness Is a Warm Gun', 'I'm So Tired', 'Julia' ,'Yer Blues', 'Everybody's Got
    Something to Hide Except Me and My Monkey', 'Sexy Sadie', 'Revolution', 'Cry
    Baby Cry', 'Mean Mr. Mustard', 'Polythene Pam', 'What's the New Mary Jane'.

11 When it was first written, John sang, 'Maharishi, what have you done', but later
    changed it to 'Sexy Sadie what have you done...you made a fool of everyone.'

reintroduced 'Child of Nature' with a slightly altered lyric, switching the location from 'Rishikesh' to 'on the road to Marrakesh' in an attempt to distance himself from the contentious experience in India. Familiar with the song, George strummed along, adding vocal harmonies and picking out guitar lines in the chorus. Unconvinced, John questioned the song's suitability for the intended upcoming live show. 'We'll probably write some fast ones here, together, all of us,' he said dismissively.

Two weeks later, with The Beatles now relocated at Apple and an impressive stock of songs mounting, including Paul's upbeat collection of 'Two of Us', 'Get Back' and 'I've Got a Feeling', attention turned to John's negligible contribution. 'Do you have anything more you're writing?' Michael Lindsay-Hogg asks. 'You're writing all the time, aren't you, John?' George Martin answers on his behalf, barely disguising his scepticism. 'Yes,' John replies, biting on a slice of buttered toast. 'With a decent band, like Billy [Preston], I'd do "On the Road to Marrakesh," which is a sweet number, baby, a sweet number. I was going to do a big Thirties orchestra bit, but I don't think I've got the energy.'

The following day, with John having suggested that, 'if we get a repertoire that's heavy then we can really get into the ballads', The Beatles play through a version of 'Child of Nature', which, uninspired, peters out after the second chorus. 'It'd be nice if you could play Hawaiian guitar in that, George,' John suggests. 'Where is it?' George asks. 'I couldn't find the proper lead to go with it,' John says. Three days later, with Paul absent at a meeting, John says that he'd 'like to learn "On the Road to Marrakesh"'. 'Just try and gig it,' he says, turning to

Billy Preston sitting at the organ. 'I want it fruity at the beginning.' Shouting out the chords, John sings through the song backed by Ringo and Preston's swirling chords. 'If you can play Hawaiian it'd be great,' John says mid-song. 'There's too many chords, probably, to do it. I was trying to think of ways we could do it like a fruity old band, for that part. It's probably just voices, isn't it?' 'Just keep doing it,' Preston responds. 'Okay,' John says. But after several incomplete attempts interest in the song wanes. 'That's it, really,' John says, with a note of resignation in his voice.

'The words were silly,' John explained to Hilary Henson for the BBC's *Woman's Hour* on 28 May 1971. 'I sang it to Yoko, Phil Spector and a few people and they always winced. I decided to change it – and with Yoko's help, I did.' Rewriting the song in 1971 as 'Jealous Guy', John presented a sublime meditation on the nature of jealousy, and, in doing so, confronted a deep-rooted weakness in his character. 'I don't believe these tight-skinned people who are never jealous,' John told Henson, during the making of the record:

> The more relationships you have, the more you learn about other people. When you actually are in love with somebody you tend to be jealous and want to own them and possess them one hundred per cent, which I do. I love Yoko. I want to possess her completely. I don't want to stifle her. That's the danger; that you want to possess them to death.

The 'danger' alluded to was in part a reflection of John's growing acceptance of his violent temperament and the need to address his unsavoury past. In December 1959, while studying at Liverpool College of Art, John accused his then girlfriend, Cynthia Powell, of dancing with another man. Losing his temper, he hit her. 'I was just hysterical,' John told Hunter Davies, The Beatles' official biographer. 'That was the trouble. I was jealous of anyone she [Cynthia] had anything to do with. I demanded absolute trust from her, just because I wasn't trustworthy myself. I was neurotic, taking out all my frustrations on her.'

John begged her forgiveness, and Cynthia accepted his promise to never hit her again. As she wrote in her memoir, 'John was true to his word...he was never again physically violent to me.' Nevertheless, a year later, while attending a college dance with fellow student Thelma Pickles, John took her upstairs to the art room to find a quiet place to have sex. 'I told John I was uneasy about doing it in a place like that especially with other people there,' Pickles revealed to Mark Lewisohn in 2010. 'He wasn't happy with my attitude. When I insisted on going, and got up to leave, he became rough and whacked me one – his fist connected somewhere between my shoulder and my head, around my neck.'

In an interview with the *Hartford Courant*, on 26 November 1972, John attempted to explain his intolerant behaviour. 'Not only did we dress like James Dean and walk around like that but we acted out those cinematic charades. The he-man was supposed to smack a girl, make her succumb in tears and then make love. Most of the guys I knew in Liverpool thought that's how you do it.' Further explaining himself and the meaning behind 'Jealous Guy', John told *Playboy* in 1980:

I was a very jealous, possessive guy and the lyrics explained that pretty clearly. All that *I used to be cruel to my woman, I beat her and kept her apart from the things that she loved* was me. Any woman. I was a hitter. I am a violent man who has learned not to be violent and regrets his violence. It's partly to do with childhood. A very insecure male who wants to put his woman in a little box and lock the key and just bring her out when he feels like playing with her.

Sadly, The Beatles never recorded 'Jealous Guy' but it would have fitted perfectly within the group's canon of powerful ballads, as many written by John are conventionally attributed to Paul. Alongside such gems as 'In My Life' and 'You've Got To Hide Your Love Away', John had a rare ability to write words as if in private conversation with the listener. But for all its melodic sweetness and stately orchestral sweeps, 'Jealous Guy' is a reminder of male oppression and the need for equity in sexual relationships.

Love

A palindrome is a word or phrase that reads the same backwards as forwards, like H-A-N-N-A-H or R-A-C-E-C-A-R. Incorporating the linguistic structure into his writing, many of John Lennon's songs have inexact symmetrically reversed phrases creating playful, if not predictable, patterns like 'all you need is love – love is all you need' or 'hold on John – John hold on'. But while the device lent many of John's songs a stylistic charm, any deeper meaning was perhaps wanting.

'Love' – written in 1970 – was an exception. Eschewing random wordplay, John adopted the technique to offer adroit verbal luminosity. In each of the song's three verses, 'love' is variously described by either a noun or an adjective and then reversed to complete the phrase: for example 'Love is real / Real is love' and 'Love is touch / 'Touch is love'. The device was simple but affecting.

Fittingly, the melody of 'Love' was equally concise and wrapped the words in a tight impermeable embrace. In the first line of the song, three notes – F sharp, A and C sharp – climb the major scale accompanied by the words 'Love is real'. The melody then rises over two further notes, B and C sharp, before dropping down to an A to complement the reversed phrase 'Real is love'. Ingeniously, both lines are perfectly balanced: three notes; three words.

The second line of the lyric – 'Love is feeling' – is sung over four notes to accentuate the additional syllable in the last word 'feel-ing'. It is this interlocking of single words with single notes that provides the key to 'Love's' enduring appeal. 'It's like a child's song,' John told *Rolling Stone* magazine. 'The idea came like a child's song and I wanted to keep it so a child could understand it. I like the melody and the words and everything. It's a beautiful melody and I'm not even known for writing melody,' he added with a note of false modesty.

In 1970, John recorded two versions of 'Love' on a home tape recorder accompanying himself on guitar. The first recording was played in the key of E flat with a capo on the first fret of the guitar augmented by an added tremolo effect. The second version, set a key lower, was plaintive and unadorned. At this point, as a Beatle, John would have taken the song to Paul to firm up the arrangement or alternatively tested its worth in the studio aided by the involvement of George and Ringo. Even with a song of such apparent simplicity, the engagement of The Beatles would have dramatically altered the direction of the song's presentation. When you consider, for example, Paul and George's expressive backing vocals in the middle eight of 'Girl' or the startling minimalism of Ringo's hi-hat introducing the verses of 'All I've Got to Do', we can only imagine how 'Love' may have been stretched and pulled as a Beatles performance.[12] But, as it was, John's first attempts at recording the song featured just one Beatle, Ringo, with Klaus Voormann on bass. After a handful of takes, the traditional band approach was aborted with John finally suggesting to Phil Spector that he should play piano. Uncertain, Spector improvised, but to little effect.

'We'll probably get a feel for it,' John said, but despite his encouragement further unsatisfactory takes followed. Listening from the control room, Yoko suggested that the song was being played too fast. 'I know,' John says. 'I need a fucking strap. I can't just stand there. I can't relax here stood up here like a fuckin' nightclub singer. I feel like the guest show on Johnny Cash like this. Okay, we'll try and do it slower.' Suddenly, in a flash of inspiration, Spector experiments with an unassuming arpeggio pattern reminiscent of the Romantic style of Debussy or Chopin. The innovation frees the music and inspires John to deliver a beautiful and delicate vocal. Released on the *Plastic Ono Band* album – and posthumously as a single, coupled with 'Gimme

---

12 After recording the song 'Girl' for *Rubber Soul* in November 1965, John later admitted that the apparently innocuous backing vocals were actually Paul and George singing *tit, tit, tit, tit*.

Some Truth' in 1982 – there are few songs in John's canon of work, or indeed in either Paul's or George's selected tracks for this album, that are as exposing or effortless in their beauty and honesty.

No doubt, there may be many readers challenging the inclusion of 'Love' and arguing, rather, for 'Oh My Love'. Dating back to 1968, a home recording of 'Oh My Love', played on a nylon-string acoustic guitar, reveals John exploring the direction of the song while struggling to rhythmically and lyrically identify its meaning. Flirting with concepts of emotionally 'shivering' and 'a very strong heart beat gone too', the 90-second extract ends with John saying, 'It's just a bit hard to go through it all.' Three years later, in 1971, John recorded a sublime and refined version of the song during the *Imagine* sessions, augmented by an exquisite guitar part, picked by George on a sunburst Gibson Les Paul. The reading of the song is beautiful and, like 'Love', unmasked John as a deeply felt romantic balladeer.

Yet, unfathomably, in the five decades since its release, 'Love' has rarely been listed or indeed discussed in polls of all-time great songs. It may be argued that the omission is understandable or even just. But, returning to an earlier theme, perhaps the song's potential was never fully realized. Is 'Love' an example of what was lost without The Beatles involvement? Or maybe, in the same way that George Martin endowed many Beatle ballads with a striking originality that crossed classical approaches with a pop sensibility – as can be heard on 'Yesterday', 'Eleanor Rigby' or the harpsichord arrangement on 'Because' – was 'Love', with its understated production, shorn of its promise? And perhaps, like the arrangement of 'Oh My Love' –

recorded a year later – the inclusion of a Beatle would have nourished the possibility of 'Love'. These are questions that time can never answer, but it was a charge that John found himself defending even to the last year of his life. '"Imagine", "Love" and those Plastic Ono Band songs stand up to any song that was written when I was a Beatle,' John told *Playboy* in 1980. 'Now, it may take you twenty or thirty years to appreciate that, but the fact is, if you check those songs out, you will see that it is as good as any fucking stuff that was ever done.'

Make Love Not War

On 11 February 1970, Tony Cox was on the set of *Top of the Pops* shooting footage for a proposed documentary – *3 Days in the Life* – about the day-to-day activities of John and Yoko. The film shows John picking up an acoustic guitar during the rehearsal for a performance of 'Instant Karma!' and tinkering with an idea for a new song. In the next scene, Yoko is seen lying on a bed in a hotel room while John strums a guitar repeating the phrase 'I want you to make love not war.' Written while still a Beatle, 'Make Love Not War' offered John an opportunity to comment on the escalating conflict in Vietnam, where previously Brian Epstein's managerial control had advised against making political statements. Yet, the song, which would three years later materialize as the lead track on John's third solo album, *Mind Games*, was almost lost to posterity as a victim of creative frustration and political disillusionment.

'Make Love Not War' was a counterculture slogan dating back to the mid-1960s and popularized within the peace movement by left-wing revolutionary organizations opposed to the conflict in Vietnam. On 12 December 1967, a 56-year-old Ronald Reagan, then Senator for California and later the fortieth US president, drew attention to the phrase to express concern about the youth of America. 'The last bunch of pickets were carrying signs that said "Make Love Not War",' Reagan told *CBS News*. 'The only trouble was they didn't look like they were capable of doing either.'

Reagan's blithe aside did little more than confirm to peace activists the Establishment's 'out of touch' lack of concern for the rising death toll in South-east Asia. Outraged by the continued scale of US aggression, John and Yoko vigorously campaigned for an end to the conflict. In June 1969, the couple, propped up in bed wearing only pyjamas, held a week-long Bed-In at the Queen Elizabeth Hotel in Canada where guests were invited to discuss and debate political issues of the day. Confronted by a hostile audience, the self-titled 'commercial for peace' was lambasted as naive by a sceptical media. Aggrieved by the cynicism, John composed 'Give Peace a Chance'. 'I wanted to write something that would take over "We Shall Overcome",' he told *Rolling Stone*. 'I don't know why that's the one they always sang. I thought, "Why isn't somebody writing one for the people now?" That's what my job and our job is.'

'Give Peace a Chance' proved to be an instant success and was promptly adopted by the peace movement. In November 1969, when half a million people attended an anti-Vietnam protest in Washington, DC, the crowd en masse chanted the song's infectious chorus, 'All we are saying is give peace a chance.'

Overcome with emotion, John declared, 'It was one of the biggest moments of my life.'

Lifted by this achievement, John focused his attention on writing a new song – 'Make Love Not War'. Written on acoustic guitar, the idea built on a descending pattern pivoting around an opening C major chord, after which the music follows the downward bass notes on the fifth string of the guitar: first a half-tone drop to B, then down through A, G, F, a half-tone fall to E and D, before neatly arriving back at the starting chord, C. The cyclical sequence has a tremendous emotional pull, and is infused with a sense of yearning that carries the listener through a tumbling sensation familiar from many Beatles songs: from the luscious piano runs in 'Hello Goodbye' and 'Lady Madonna' or the 'English garden' section of 'I Am the Walrus' to the sublime guitar cadences of 'Dear Prudence', 'Cry Baby Cry' and the verses of 'While My Guitar Gently Weeps'. As such, 'Make Love Not War' would have been a perfect song for The Beatles to record, with its infectious melody and anthemic chorus.

Yet, estranged from his writing partner, Paul, John struggled to complete the idea. In December 1970, on what would become the first of many subsequent occasions, John revisited the song. Recording directly into a domestic cassette recorder John sang 'I want you to make love not war' with a dreamy lure over a simple piano accompaniment. After repeating the phrase twice over, John introduces a new passage, 'Love is the answer', followed by an immediate self-conscious rebuff, 'You've heard it before – oh yeah.' Looping the two sections, John then hits a creative impasse.

At a further point on the cassette, John is heard improvising a new idea, labelled on the tape box as 'I Promise', with a chord sequence that bears an overt resemblance to 'Oh! Darling' – written by Paul – from The Beatles album *Abbey Road*. Hammering out the chords, John makes a sudden connection and links this song to 'Make Love Not War' by integrating 'Love is the answer' as a connecting passage. The recording is a revealing insight into the fragmentary nature of songwriting and demonstrates how two independent themes can often be attached to create a third, new idea. The Beatles regularly assimilated incomplete ideas to finish one another's songs. For example, when John needed a middle eight for 'A Day in the Life', Paul offered a half-finished idea cataloguing a mundane morning routine of falling out of bed and dragging 'a comb across my head'. Likewise, for 'I've Got a Feeling' John added the overlapping passage 'everybody had a hard year' to complement and expand Paul's existing verses and chorus. It was this practice that repeatedly transformed a single vision into a collective endeavour and elevated an abundance of Beatle compositions to incredible levels of originality.

What Paul, or even George, would have added to 'Make Love Not War' we will never know, but John had the essence of something very exciting. In 1971, during sessions for his second solo album, *Imagine*, 'Make Love Not War' was revisited. But in the year since its inception the song had advanced little. Taking a break, John is filmed drinking tea in his home-cum-studio, seated at a large wooden kitchen table with Yoko, George and Phil Spector. Handwritten notes are being prepared for a forthcoming press conference. Grinning, John sings to George, 'I want you to *mach Liebe nicht Krieg*'. George leans forwards and repeats the phrase. Turning to Yoko, she says. 'Okay,' and passes a piece of card on which John writes out the slogan 'Make Love Not War'. 'What was the French one?' he asks. *'Faites l'amour pas la guerre,'* Spector replies. 'Is that just *your* French,' John questions. 'I don't want to be coming on the air saying "Not Love New War", you know!'

In 1973, when John returned to the recording studio, the world landscape had radically transformed, most significantly in the retreat of American troops from Vietnam following the Paris Peace Accords. Freed from political anxiety, John reappraised 'Make Love Not War'. Maintaining the same chord sequence and melody from two years earlier, John conjured a new set of words to reflect the new social climate: 'pushing the barriers...planting seeds... chanting the mantra'.

'"Make Love Not War" was such a cliché that you couldn't say it anymore,' John told *Playboy* in 1980, 'so I wrote it obscurely, but it's all the same story. In the early Seventies, everybody was starting to say the Sixties was a joke, it didn't mean anything; those love-and-peaceniks were idiots.' Rewritten as 'Mind Games', the newly written lyrics explored themes expressed by Robert Masters and Jean Houston in their book *Mind Games: The Guide to Inner Space*. 'We all have to face the reality of being nasty human beings who are born evil and everything's gonna be lousy and rotten so boo-hoo-hoo,' John told David Sheff. '"We had fun in the Sixties," they said, "but the others took it away from us and spoiled it all for us." And I was trying to say: "No, just keep doin' it."'

John relaxes at producer Lou Adler's home in Beverly Hills, the day after the US release of *Mind Games*, 3 November 1973.

In November 1973, 'Mind Games' was completed and issued as a single, securing John a minor hit single on both sides of the Atlantic.[13] Reflecting back on the track, John explained the inspiration behind the music to BBC Radio 1 DJ Andy Peebles. 'That was a fun track because the voice is in stereo and the seeming orchestra on it is just me playing three notes with a slide guitar. And the middle eight is reggae. Trying to explain to American musicians what reggae was in 1973 was pretty hard...they didn't know what reggae was then.'

---

13 'Mind Games' was the first official John Lennon solo release. Previous releases had been either been credited to John Lennon and Yoko Ono or The Plastic Ono Band. The single reached number 26 in the UK chart and number 18 in the US.

Ironically, six months earlier, Paul had enjoyed a smash hit with the James Bond film theme 'Live and Let Die', in which the middle section of the song incorporated a distinctly Jamaica-influenced off-beat. 'I sat down at the piano and worked something out,' Paul said in 1973. 'Linda wrote the middle reggae bit of the song. We rehearsed it as a band, recorded it and then left it up to George Martin, who produced it with us.'

That John and Paul both adopted elements of reggae in their music within months of one another – albeit one writing about peace and the other about a man of war with a licence to kill – is perhaps coincidental. But viewed charitably, and with a touch of fancy, it was as if Lennon and McCartney were in conversation – independently writing, but in synch.

Gimme Some Truth

On 3 January 1969 – The Beatles' second day at Twickenham Studios – George prepares to introduce a new song ('All Things Must Pass'), when John interrupts him and says, 'I've got one. "Gimme Some Truth".' '"Gimme Some Truth,"' Paul says, *'me, mine, politician.'* 'We can finish that,' John continues, 'remember your *hangman* bit?' 'Yeah!' Paul says rolling the words around his tongue. *'No freaked out yellow bellied son of Gary Cooper.'*

Written a year earlier, when The Beatles were on retreat in India, 'Gimme Some Truth' had languished among a pile of unfinished songs discarded during the 'White Album' sessions. At Twickenham, John plucks the song's opening chords as Paul recalls random phrases – 'selling dope…ain't got a hope…it's just money for rope'. Sung in a high-pitched single note and uncertain of the exact words, Paul fills out the melody with shapeless sounds. 'Money for rope,' John adds in a low harmony, prompting Paul to repeat the line an octave higher.

'It started in D, didn't it?' Paul says. 'Yeah,' John answers. Paul sings the melody, but struggles with John's suggested key. 'Yours was in E, wasn't it?' 'No, it wasn't,' John replies. 'Oh yeah,' Paul says, plucking the bottom string of the bass guitar. 'It was in D and E. My bit was in E.' 'No, it wasn't,' John says again. 'Maybe we had capos then?' Paul suggests. 'Oh yeah,' John says, pleased to have resolved the confusion. Mis-pitching at first, Paul then settles on a high note and softly sings the opening line. Second time round, John joins in and the combination of the two voices in unison is exhilarating, Paul adding attack and urgency to John's monaural melody. Then, frustratingly, just as the song begins to take shape, George finishes tuning his guitar and the rehearsal moves in a new direction.

Four days later, 'Gimme Some Truth' is a given a brief reprise during an attempt to reintroduce another of John's older songs, 'Across the Universe'. 'The only trouble about the slow ones,' Paul complains, 'is it takes the mood down learning them.' 'I'm sick and tired of hearing things,' George sings. 'It's another one ['Gimme Some Truth']', John says, acknowledging Paul's concern. 'It's a pity that they're all so similar 'cause it would have been nice that *hypocrite's* one.'

Uncertain how to move forward, John improvises: first singing 'everyone knows it's a case of the blues' and then 'money for rope'. Joining in, Paul then asks, 'Do you know the other bits?' 'My bits

I know,' John says. Together they sing 'all I want is the truth'. 'We should change it there,' John calls out. They repeat the section, with John subtly adapting the words from 'give me' to 'just gimme some truth' and then for no apparent reason they abruptly stop. 'That's just as exciting as the other one,' John ruefully concludes. And that was it: over two days, half a week apart; in little more than two-and-a-half minutes The Beatles playing 'Gimme Some Truth'. Seventeen days later, on 20 January 1969, Richard Nixon was inaugurated as the 37th US president. Unbeknown to John, Nixon's victory would have a life-changing effect on him. It would not only determine his future application for American citizenship in the following decade but significantly influence the lyrics for 'Gimme Some Truth' before its release on *Imagine* in 1971. In his inaugural address, Nixon offered hope and optimism:

> For the first time, because the people of the world want peace, and the leaders of the world are afraid of war, the times are on the side of peace. We see the hope of tomorrow in the youth of today. I know America's youth. I believe in them. We can be proud that they are better educated, more committed, more passionately driven by conscience than any generation in our history.

The reality was anything but. In the coming years, Nixon would be found guilty of obstruction of justice and criminal abuse of power. And among the White House documents, files on John Lennon would be found, central to which was an unlikely meeting between the president and Elvis Presley.

Invited to the Oval Office on 21 December 1970, Presley arrived with a warning. 'The Beatles,' he informed the president, 'have been a real force for anti-American spirit.' Privy to the White House transcripts, Paul shared his sense of betrayal in *Anthology*: 'Elvis actually tried to shop us!' Accused of taking drugs, Paul was outraged. 'The great joke is [Elvis] was caught on the toilet full of them!' Equally incensed at the possibility of being banished from the country, Ringo added, 'He was very big with the FBI.'

Thwarted at every turn to establish a home in New York with Yoko and secure US citizenship, John vented his frustration in song. In the two years since he had worked on 'Gimme Some Truth' at Twickenham, the political temperature in the US had dramatically risen. Against the backdrop of a burgeoning Civil Rights movement and anti-Vietnam counterculture demonstrations, Nixon's leadership had plunged into chaos. Stood at the microphone, John spat out a venomous diatribe aimed at 'Tricky Dicky...pig-headed politicians'...and 'uptight, short-sighted, narrow-minded hypocrites'.[14] Backed by a menacing guitar arpeggio, George Harrison delivered an electrifying slide guitar part, which John described in an interview with *Crawdaddy* as a 'sharp solo with his steel finger', adding, 'he's not too proud of it but I like it'. Little remained of Paul's high harmonies practised at the *Get Back* sessions, but John magnanimously credited his former writing

---

14 Often believed to be a reference to the Watergate Scandal, the nickname 'Tricky Dicky' was first coined by Helen Gahagan Douglas – a former Broadway star – to label the untrustworthy character of candidate Richard Nixon during the 1950 US Senate race.

partner 'with a middle eight written with Paul – he's getting half the money anyway and vice versa'.

It was a teasing glimpse of what may have been. Dark and brooding, the song sounded laboured, as if it was being pulled reluctantly up a muddy slope – the tempo sluggish, the bass plodding. Having come so close to being a Beatles song, it missed their input. 'The only reason Ringo wasn't on it,' John explained to *NME*'s Alan Smith in 1972, 'was because he was abroad, making his movie. So then the three of us would have been on, but then it wouldn't have been The Beatles. It would have been Plastic Ono because I would have the final say.' Further explaining the power dynamic of The Beatles, John added, 'There would be no decision making by George or Ringo, other than if I liked an idea I'd take it – which is what happened with The Beatles – but then it was more diplomatic.'

Reviewing 'Gimme Some Truth' in the *New Musical Express*, Alan Smith wrote, 'Side Two opens with a "2001" touch...but then evolving into a long Lennon statement of the things and the values he's come to reject – a device you may recall from the last album. In this he talks of earning *money for rope*, *money for dope*, and says he's *sick and tired* of "neurotic...psychotic".' But perhaps, the most telling comment came in the record's accompanying sleeve notes. 'I like the overall sound on this track,' John wrote, 'tho' I'm not sure I'd go out and buy it.'

God

As a declaration of independence, the lyrics of 'God' could not have been more explicit. The song was not only a categorical rejection of myth and false prophets but, in five crushing words – 'I don't believe in Beatles' – a brutal demolition of John's past. Drawing a comparison between John's damning indictment of The Beatles and Paul's previous statement issued with *McCartney*, journalist Paul Gambaccini observed, 'Where Paul's press release is the end of the physical Beatles, "God" is the end of the state of mind that is The Beatles.'

What had driven John to denounce his legacy can, in part, be traced back to an involvement with Dr Arthur Janov and the practice of psychotherapy. Janov was the author of *The Primal Scream* – published in 1969 – which set out a methodology to release childhood trauma through so-called primal therapy. In March 1970, John and Yoko invited Janov to their home in Ascot to undergo treatment. 'In the therapy you really feel every painful moment of your life,' John explained to the underground newspaper *Red Mole*. 'It's excruciating: you are forced to realise that your pain, the kind that makes you wake up afraid with your heart pounding, is really yours and not the result of somebody up in the sky. It's the result of your parents and your environment.'

In Janov's care, patients were encouraged to scream and rid the body of its suppressed pain. Bawling was not unfamiliar to John. In 1968, he had asked session engineer Richard Lush to drop in screams at the end of 'Everybody's Got Something to Hide Except for Me and My Monkey', and in 1969, guttural wrenches and shrieks provide an uncomfortable soundtrack to the end coda of 'Cold Turkey'. John's experimentation owed much to the influence of Yoko's uninhibited singing style and one that he increasingly adopted in the early years of their relationship.

Eager to embrace Janov's methods, John and Yoko travelled to Los Angeles in May 1970 to continue their induction into primal therapy at the Primal Institute in Bel Air, Los Angeles. It was here, while in Janov's safekeeping, that John made his first demo recording of 'God'. Utilizing a commonly used 1950s-style doo-wop chord progression, the song's opening stanza was an incredible and deeply profound statement: 'God is a concept / By which we measure our pain'. Inspired to repeat the phrase twice over, John then introduced a list of subjects, each prefaced with the phrase 'I don't believe in...': first, belief systems – the Bible, tarot; then, leaders – Hitler, Jesus, Kennedy, Buddha; next, practices – mantra, Gita, yoga; and, finally, gods – kings, Elvis, Zimmerman[15] and, completing the litany of denunciations, 'Beatles'. Satisfied with the recording, John signed off in mock-preacher spoken word: 'Hallelujah! Eureka brother! I got the news. It came to me in the night.'

Returning to England to record the debut Plastic Ono Band album, John was accompanied in the studio by Ringo on drums, Klaus Voormann on bass and Billy Preston on keyboards. 'Somebody's pinched "God",' John says, riffling through a sheet of lyrics. Then finding them, he quips, 'God is alive and living in the Eiffel Tower!' The first take of 'God' bristles with a country rock feel, the music

---

15 Robert Zimmerman is the birth name of Bob Dylan.

fluid, becoming increasingly dramatic as John imbues it with a soulful vocal. The track is transformed when John switches from guitar to piano, adding a tense dynamic to Preston's gospel-influenced playing style. 'Incredible!' Ringo exulted in 2008 on the TV documentary series *Classic Albums*. 'Billy Preston never put his hands in the wrong place, never...and I've known him since he was sixteen.'

The act of two former Beatles – John and Ringo – playing on a track condemning their erstwhile band is both electrifying and powerfully shocking. The rejection – 'I don't believe in Beatles' – portentously stripped of the definite article, 'The' – has naturally been the subject of intense critical debate in the ensuing decades. 'Like a lot of the words,' John told *Rolling Stone* in December 1970, 'they just came out of my mouth. I was going to leave a gap and say, "Just fill in your own, for whoever you don't believe in," it just got out of hand.' He then added, 'The dream's over. I'm not just talking about The Beatles, I'm talking about the generation thing. It was a dream. That's all. I don't believe in the dream anymore.' Two months later – on 21 January 1971 – John embellished his thoughts in an interview with Tariq Ali and Robin Blackburn for *Red Mole*. 'Most people channel their pain into God or masturbation or some dream of making it. [I started] facing up to reality instead of always looking for some kind of Heaven.'

Alongside being one of the greatest self-sabotaging lyrics in rock history, the notion of The Beatles recording a song which rejected their very existence is utterly compelling. It not only offered an extraordinary final statement but left the devastating suggestion that, even as The Beatles were taking a final bow, they were disowning all that they had created before.

PAUL McCARTNEY

 Apple Records

Distributed by Capitol Records Distributing Corp.

7. Side Two: McCartney

There are few artists with the vision and musical ability of Paul McCartney. His unerring compositional understanding and indefatigable innovation led The Beatles into areas previously unexplored in popular music. Seizing upon basic ideas, Paul transformed not only his own songs but those of John, George and Ringo to exceptional levels. When John presented 'Don't Let Me Down' to The Beatles at Twickenham Studios in January 1969, the simple two-chord vamp was converted into a hard-edged screaming ballad. Across hours of recorded audio, Paul is heard orchestrating the arrangement and developing ambitious counter-instrumental lines to underpin John's straighter approach.

Similarly, George's understated sketch of 'Something', first heard by The Beatles during the 'White Album' sessions in 1968, was dramatically invigorated over several months in the summer of 1969 into a majestic paean to love. Key to its transformation was a sharp tightening of the song's structure and a mesmeric bass line, played by Paul, oscillating between elaborate lead lines and subtle interplay, enriching the song's rhythm with grace and perpetual motion. On the reverse of *Abbey Road*, the exhilarating collage of songs – 'You Never Give Me Your Money', 'Sun King', 'Mean Mr. Mustard', 'Polythene Pam', 'She Came in through the Bathroom Window', 'Golden

Opposite: Capital Records publicity shot of Paul, 1972.

Slumbers', 'Carry That Weight' and 'The End' – is further evidence of Paul's peerless command of contemporary music offering a tour de force of the musical imagination.

Yet, after the breakup of The Beatles, and somewhat unfathomably, Paul's solo recordings, under his own name or with Wings, rarely displayed the levels of heightened brilliance that defined his 1960s output. That is not to say that he did not create exceptional records – one only has to think of 'Maybe I'm Amazed', 'Live and Let Die', 'My Love', 'Jet' or 'Band On The Run' – but the singular highs were outnumbered by a slew of mediocrity. Put simply: Paul lost his touch, or rather, he was diminished by the loss of the collaborative input of his former bandmates.

Understandably, Paul wanted to break from the past. But alchemy conjured collectively – the unquantifiable chemical charge of a unique set of individuals playing music together – cannot be easily replicated by one musician or by a set of session players. Reflecting on his different approach to writing and recording in the 1970s, Paul told journalist Paul Du Noyer, 'I tried to avoid any Beatle clichés so the songs became a little more episodic.'

Notwithstanding the fact that Wings was formed in 1971, the new band was nonetheless clearly a vehicle for, and beholden to, Paul as leader. Creating a new musical identity, beyond the democratic sound that a group demands, was one thing, but the change felt merely self-indulgent. In doing so, Paul crossed a creative boundary. In January 1963, when Paul introduced a new song 'A World without Love' to The Beatles, everyone laughed. 'And that was it,' Paul explained at a press conference in Milwaukee, adding with an air of humility, 'The funny first line always used to please John. *Please lock me away...* "Yes, okay!"' Freed from John's witty judgement and the constraints of group compromise, Paul's exploration of a singular vision as a solo artist suffered from artistic hubris.

Key to The Beatles' success was the relationship between John and Paul. And despite their co-dependence waning over successive years, a mutual respect for one another's songwriting remained critical to the music they produced. When the partnership splintered, Paul was left working without an equal for the first time in his career. Bereft of John to question, to inspire, to mock or to challenge, Paul succumbed to his own creative whim. 'We missed the collaborative thing, of John saying, "Don't do that", or "Do that". Sparking each other off,' Paul told Paul Du Noyer. 'For a while I was certainly very conscious of it.'

Furthermore, George Martin's input had indelibly marked many of Paul's greatest achievements: from 'Eleanor Rigby' and 'Your Mother Should Know' to the three-part clarinet arrangement on 'When I'm Sixty-Four'. Quoted in *The Beatles Recording Sessions*, Geoff Emerick said, of 'Here, There and Everywhere', that 'George's real expertise was in vocal harmony work, there's no doubt about it. That's his forte, grooming and working out those great harmonies.' Typically modest, Martin added, 'The harmonies are very simple, just basic triads which the boys hummed behind and found very easy to do. There's nothing very clever, no counterpoint, just moving block harmonies. Very simple to do...but very effective.' Martin told official Beatles biographer Hunter Davies:

If Paul has written a song, he comes into the studio with it in his head. It's very hard for him to give it to us and for us to get it. When we suggest something, it might not be what he wants because he hasn't got it in his head. So it takes a long time. Nobody knows what the tunes sound like till we've recorded them then listened to them.

Interviewed in 2012 for the re-release of Paul's second solo album, *RAM*, Martin was keen to set the record straight:

After *Let It Be*, I never thought I could work with the band again, but Paul persuaded me to take on the final album, *Abbey Road*, and everything worked out fine. Paul had such a vivid imagination he could easily have done the scoring himself if he had a little instruction. I urged him to take some lessons, but he said to me truthfully, 'Why should I when I have you?'

Nevertheless, on hearing the finished *Let It Be* album in 1970 – remixed by Phil Spector – Paul was incensed, expressed frankly in a letter to Allen Klein. Forbidding anyone 'to add to or subtract from a recording of one of my songs without my permission', Paul outlined how he had considered orchestrating 'The Long and Winding Road' himself but had 'decided against it'.

The letter ended with four numbered stipulations: '1. Strings, horns, voices and all added noises to be reduced in volume. 2. Vocal and Beatle instrumentation to be brought up in volume. 3. Harp to be removed completely at the end of the song and original piano notes substituted. 4. Don't ever do it again.'[1]

When recording *RAM*, in September 1970, Paul turned to his erstwhile collaborator. Despite being uncredited on the finished record, George Martin wrote orchestral scores for 'Long Haired Lady', 'The Back Seat of My Car' and 'Uncle Albert / Admiral Halsey' – Paul's first number one single in the US. It was a working relationship that would endure over many decades and is sufficient reason to assume that Martin would have been Paul's first choice as producer had The Beatles recorded a new record after *Abbey Road*.

Following John's 'divorce' declaration, in late October 1969 Paul retreated with his wife, Linda, and their new-born daughter, Mary, to High Park Farm in the hills above Campbeltown, a remote district in the Kintyre Peninsula of Scotland.[2] Stunned by the precipitous decay of The Beatles and the toxic atmosphere at Apple, Paul's mental health rapidly deteriorated. In an interview with *Melody Maker*, Paul said, 'I felt, "What am I going to do?" I needed at least a month to think a bit. I went into a period of what everyone called being a recluse, a hermit in isolation.'

Falling into a deep well of despair, Paul reflected on the breakup of The Beatles and his subsequent battle with depression in an

---

1 Many of these suggestions formed the basis of *The Beatles...Naked* released in 2003 presenting *Let It Be* stripped of its additional arrangements. Ironically, 'The Long and Winding Road' string arrangement was originally recorded on April Fool's Day, 1970, scored by Richard Hewson. Hewson had written the horn and string arrangements on Mary Hopkin's first album – written and produced by Paul – and in June 1971 he orchestrated an instrumental version of Paul's second solo album, *RAM*, retitled *Thrillington*.

2 Paul purchased the property in December 1967.

interview with *Playboy* in April 1984. 'It was a barrelling, empty feeling that just rolled across my soul. I really was done in for the first time in my life. Until then I was a kind of cocky sod. It was the first time I'd had a major blow to my confidence.' Examining further the period in *Many Years from Now,* Paul noted, 'I was going through a bad time what I suspect was almost a nervous breakdown.

Paul, Linda and their dog Martha at High Park Farm, Scotland, February 1971.

I remember lying awake at nights shaking.' On one occasion, Paul recalled not being able to lift his head from his pillow. 'I thought, Jesus, if I don't do this I'll suffocate.'

Redundant, Paul wallowed in self-pity: not shaving, staying in bed and drinking whisky in the morning. 'I felt I'd outlived my usefulness,' he told Barry Miles. 'This was the overall feeling: that it was good while I was in The Beatles, I was useful and I could play bass for their songs, I could write songs for them to sing and for me to sing, and we could make records of them. But the minute I wasn't with The Beatles any more it became really very difficult.'

Encouraged by Linda, Paul found solace recording crude demos – including 'The Lovely Linda', 'Oo You', 'Momma Miss America', 'Valentine's Day' and 'That Would Be Something' – in a makeshift studio built within the crumbling farmhouse surrounded by poultry and roaming sheep. Slowly rediscovering himself through music, Paul also arranged 'Stardust' for Ringo's album of cover versions, *Sentimental Journey*, and contributed an extract for The Beatles Fan Club Christmas Single.

In December 1969, Paul returned to London and continued recording on a Studer 4-track machine set up in his home in Cavendish Avenue – and later at Morgan Studios under the pseudonym Billy Martin – collecting enough songs for a solo record. Released in April 1970, *McCartney* entered the US charts at number one and the UK charts at number two where it stayed in the top ten for 18 consecutive weeks.[3] But, despite its commercial success,

---

3   McCartney was denied the number one position by Simon & Garfunkel's farewell album *Bridge Over Troubled Water*.

McCartney was clearly a work-in-progress with barely a handful of the 13 tracks complete – '"The Lovely Linda" was recorded to test the machine,' Paul wrote in the album's accompanying press release. 'The song is a trailer to the full song which will be recorded in the future.' As an artistic statement in response to his leaving The Beatles, it was wanting.

Elsewhere on *McCartney*, more accomplished tracks teased at what could have been, as George Harrison noted in a radio broadcast with George Smith in May 1970:

> 'That Would Be Something' and 'Maybe I'm Amazed' I think are great and everything else I think is fair…and the others just don't do anything for me because I can hear other people play better drums and guitars and things. The arrangements of some of these songs like 'Teddy Boy' and 'Junk' with a little bit more arrangement they could've sounded better.

Cutting to the quick, John lambasted the record with characteristic bluntness. 'I thought Paul's was rubbish,' he said in *Rolling Stone* in 1970. 'I think he'll make a better one, when he's frightened into it.' Conveying a weight of unsatisfied high critical expectation, Chris Charlesworth wrote in *Melody Maker*, 'I expected [Paul's] solo albums to be better than those of his three former colleagues. Unfortunately this is not the case. His first solo effort, with the exception of one track ("Maybe I'm Amazed") completely lacked the McCartney magic.'

Nevertheless, Paul was not short of outstanding songs at his disposal. And as we know, with the involvement of the other Beatles, Paul's creativity thrived. It is also worth remembering, at this juncture two of Paul's greatest songwriting achievements – 'Let It Be' and 'The Long And Winding Road' – lay dormant in The Beatles archive. Although both songs carried the distinct air of a solo performance they also served as a reminder: that in 1970, Paul needed The Beatles as much as John, George and Ringo needed Paul.

Come and Get It

It took one hour to record: 2.30 to 3.30 pm. Paul in Abbey Road with Studio Two to himself. 'Red light,' Paul says, sitting at the piano. 'Demo, take one,' engineer Phil McDonald responds. Four beautifully crisp chords ring out from the piano, and Paul sings the opening verse, 'If you want it, here it is...' 'Okay,' he says at the end of the take. 'Give us it on headphones and I'll track it.' Building up a rhythm track, Paul overdubs a second vocal while shaking a pair of maracas, then adds drums, and finally a bass guitar. As the clock ticks down towards the hour, the song is recorded, mixed and pressed to acetate disc. And during the 60 minutes it takes to complete the process, John Lennon sits upstairs in the control room. Silent. Not one word is exchanged between the two Beatles. Why, has remained a mystery ever since.

Three days earlier, on Monday, 21 July 1969, The Beatles recorded 'Come Together' in the same EMI studio: John at the microphone, tambourine in hand, Paul on bass, George playing electric guitar, and Ringo drums. It was John's first song contribution to *Abbey Road* since his discharge from hospital three weeks earlier. After six attempts, a satisfactory backing track was committed to tape and the following day overdubs were added to the basic rhythm. But Paul was disappointed, as he revealed in a candid interview with the *Evening Standard* in 1970. 'I would have liked to sing harmony with John and I think John would have liked me to, but I was too embarrassed to ask him.'

The admission is as confusing as it is startling. Firstly, Paul did sing backing vocals on 'Come Together': harmonizing the last phrase of the second verse – 'Walrus gumboot…Ono sideboard…spinal cracker' – and in later verses and in the chorus adding texture to John's lead vocal. Secondly, sparing a memory lapse, that notion that Paul was 'too embarrassed' to contribute backing vocals is baffling. John and Paul freely sang on one another's songs, neither seeking nor asking permission. It was how they operated. In January 1969, when The Beatles rehearsed 'Don't Let Me Down' at Twickenham, Paul instinctively sang harmony over John's vocal lead. Similarly, when Paul took the lead on 'Two of Us' John intuitively sang a pitch lower to complement Paul's mid-range delivery.

Nevertheless, on 24 July, Paul recorded 'Come and Get It' without John's involvement. Soon after, George and Ringo arrived ready to work on John's new composition 'Here Comes the Sun King' – later divided into two separate songs, 'Sun King' and 'Mean Mr. Mustard'. As the customary tea and toast were ordered, Paul relaxed reading an interview in *Disc and Music Echo* about the Welsh four-piece Badfinger.[4] Grumbling about the band, guitar

---

4 Badfinger were originally signed to Apple Records in July 1968 as The Iveys, but their first release, 'Maybe Tomorrow', made no impact on the national chart.

player, Ron Griffiths, told the paper that they had received little more than tea, coffee and cigarettes from the record company promotions department since signing to Apple. Suddenly, Paul had an idea. Running out of the studio and jumping into his yellow mini, he drove four miles north from Abbey Road to Badfinger's shared flat in Golders Green. Arriving 20 minutes later, Paul knocked on the door and, handing over an acetate of 'Come and Get It', blurted out: 'Here's your next single!'

From its opening chords Paul's demo recording of 'Come and Get It' pulsated with optimism, every beat in every bar accented with metronomic precision. The brightness of the sound was as uplifting as it was infectious. Propelled by its rhythmic accompaniment, the song swirls around three major chords – E, A and B. Then at the end of the verse a half-tone climb subtly lifts the song from B to C major and into a bridge section. Unexpectedly, a minor chord sounds, momentarily darkening the mood until a half-tone lifts the song from E minor to F major. The musical divergence resolved, the song gracefully returns to its introductory chord, E major. It is classic McCartney: the song allowed to flow on a seductive downstream augmented with delicate twists and turns and driven by a constant forward rhythm, in this instance, played by maracas shaken in double time.

The inspiration for the song came to Paul at an unexpected hour. 'I was lying in bed trying to get to sleep,' he told Graeme Thomson for *The Word* in October 2005, 'and this song kept coming. I thought, "No, go to sleep, you've done enough work for the day *ding ding ding ding – if you want it here it is come and get it*. Oh, okay!' Lying by his side, Linda, then Paul's girlfriend, drifted off to sleep. 'I've got an idea for a song,' Paul murmured in her ear. 'I went downstairs and just whispered it into my tape recorder, very quietly so as not to wake her. I knew it was a very catchy song.'

Understandably, Badfinger jumped at the opportunity to record 'Come and Get It', and nine days after Paul's unannounced arrival at their home the band met for a Saturday-morning session at Abbey Road. 'I said to Badfinger, "'It's got to be exactly like this demo because it had a great feeling on it,"' Paul recounted in *Anthology*. 'They actually wanted to put their own variations on, but I said, "No, this really is the right way." They listened to me – I was producing, after all – and they were good.'

The record was issued in a black-and-white sleeve with a photograph of a crowd made up of repeated images of the members of Badfinger, and the accompanying text read: 'Come and Get It' from the film *Magic Christian*.[5] Released in December 1969, it swiftly rose up the charts, peaking at number four in the UK and number seven in the US.

'Come and Get It' would have been a tempting choice for The Beatles to record after the success of *Abbey Road*. Indeed, with its easy singalong appeal, it would have been a strong contender as a follow-up to the double A-side single of 'Something' and 'Come Together'. Although initially given to Badfinger, historically it was not uncommon for songs written by The Beatles to be first released

---

5   The writing credit on the vinyl disc read 'Paul McCartney'. Excluding the film soundtrack *The Family Way* (1966) composed by Paul, and John and Yoko's solo releases – *Unfinished Music No. 1: Two Virgins* (1968), *Unfinished Music No. 2: Life with the Lions* (1969), *Wedding Album* (1969) – it was the first time a song written by either John or Paul was not acknowledged as a 'Lennon/McCartney' original.

by other artists. In 1963, Billy J Kramer had a hit with Lennon and McCartney's 'I Call Your Name' before The Beatles cut their own version for the *Long Tall Sally* EP. Likewise, The Rolling Stones covered 'I Wanna Be Your Man' in 1963 several weeks before Ringo sang the lead vocal on *With The Beatles*. In 1969, Joe Cocker recorded George Harrison's song 'Something' – predating The Beatles version on *Abbey Road* – for his second solo album, the eponymously titled *Joe Cocker!* Also in 1969, 'Two of Us' – written by Paul and first rehearsed by The Beatles at Twickenham – was given to the New York trio Mortimer under its working title, 'On Our Way Home',[6] before the original version was eventually heard on *Let It Be* in 1970.

In 1996, a remixed recording of 'Come and Get It' was issued on *Anthology 3* credited to The Beatles. It had taken 27 years, and although the record featured only Paul, it was nonetheless an exciting recognition of what could have been.

Another Day

On 9 January 1969, Paul and Linda arrived early at Twickenham Studios and fell into conversation with Michael Lindsay-Hogg. The film director recounted the story of a book – *My Father and Myself* by J R Ackerley – about a gay man whose father kept two households: one with his wife and children; and a second with a mistress and their three illegitimate children. The infidelity, Lindsay-Hogg concluded, was only discovered when the man died. 'I better go and put in some piano

6   It was scheduled for the summer, but Apple unexpectedly cancelled the release.

practice,' Paul responded, chuckling and politely excusing himself from the small talk. 'Oh!' replied Lindsay-Hogg. 'We can film it.' 'Don't tell me!' Paul exclaimed with feigned annoyance. 'No,' Lindsay-Hogg admonished himself. 'Candidly, so you're not noticing.'

Sitting down at a German-made Blüthner grand piano with matching black leather seat, Paul quietly sang about a woman dressing, wetting her hair and wrapping 'a towel around her'. Clad in stockings and a raincoat she steps 'into shoes'. In the next verse, the woman is at work where she drinks coffee and 'finds it hard to stay awake'. Occupied by the domestically tinged narrative, Paul repeats the verses accompanying his melody with plain, unadorned chords. Uncertain of the song's direction, he extemporizes but is soon unsatisfied and switches back to the verse ending the song with an emphatic chord, an elongated bluesy flourish, with echoes of 'Lady Madonna'. Finally, he slides the back of his hand down the length of the keyboard, right to left, to generate a cacophony of harmonics. Two years later, the as-yet-unnamed song will become Paul's debut solo single, 'Another Day'.

A fortnight later, with The Beatles now decamped in the basement studio in Savile Row, Paul picks out 'Another Day' on an acoustic guitar. Playing a basic backbeat, Ringo embellishes the verses with characteristic drum rolls and rumbling toms, offering the merest hint of a rhythmical approach until Paul stops to tune his guitar. Even at this rudimentary stage, 'Another Day' has enough elements to suggest its potential as a Beatles prototype. Its beguiling vocal melody and floating rhythm with light pushes and pulls are all distinctly in place; as was often the case with The Beatles, a simple idea could quickly develop in rehearsal, stretching the possibility of a song until the feel was right. Indeed, 'Two of Us' did just that, undergoing a dramatic transition from a rolling thunderous electric rhythm – later adopted for 'Get Back' – to a lilting acoustic duet. Needless to say, neither John nor George would stamp their identity on 'Another Day', and by the time Paul completed the song, The Beatles were no longer together. It was a missed opportunity.

On 12 October 1970 – six months after the official breakup of The Beatles – Paul was in Columbia Studios, New York, with a newly assembled cast of musicians.[7] In the 21 months since playing 'Another Day' at Twickenham with Ringo, the arrangement of the song had developed to incorporate a bridge section – played in three-quarter time – and an improved set of words focusing on the mundanity of everyday working life. The song's female protagonist takes a 'morning bath' to reflect on her sadness brought on by the idealized ache of a romantic relationship for 'the man of her dreams' who comes to her apartment but 'leaves the next day'. Seeking guidance, the woman 'posts another letter to the *Sound of Five*'.[8] 'I liked the idea of writing songs about ordinary people and day-to-day lives,' Paul recounted in the documentary *Wingspan*. '"Another Day" was one of them. We all get up in the morning and do our usual stuff yet, somehow, even through it all, there are often magic moments...and it was a hit which, at that time, was especially pleasing.'

---

7   David Spinozza: acoustic and electric guitar. Denny Seiwell: drums and percussion. Linda McCartney: backing vocals. Paul McCartney: acoustic and electric guitars, bass and percussion.

8   A reference to a popular radio show of the time in which a panel of experts offered advice to listener's problems.

Released on the opening day of the High Court case to dissolve The Beatles – *James Paul McCartney v John Ono Lennon, George Harrison, Richard Starkey and Apple Corps Limited* – 'Another Day' was portentously credited to 'Mr and Mrs McCartney'. Yet, Linda's contribution to the record is difficult to decipher. Notwithstanding the possibility that she contributed additional words or melody, on record Linda's input is limited to subtly enhancing the overall wash of Paul's lead vocal with 'oohs' and 'ahs'. For all their sweetness, the celebrated harmonies of the Fab Four they are not. Elsewhere, an intoned pseudo-slide guitar part, poignantly conjuring the ghost of George Harrison, falls short of lending 'Another Day' some of the Beatles sparkle.

History has commonly judged 'Another Day' as lightweight, as lacking the punch of a Beatles record. Despite being convinced of the song's merits, Dixon Van Winkle, the studio assistant on 'Another Day', believes that the version issued was a mistake. 'We were sitting in Studio A2 one day listening to the takes and Paul asked me to pick the single,' Van Winkle told *Mix* in 2004:

I had definite feelings about the record and was in love with 'Another Day'. Paul said, 'Okay. "Another Day" it is.' I mixed the track and David Crawford cut about 100 copies of it in a back room at A&R for the radio stations. The next day, when I heard it on the air, I realised it was a disaster. We got carried away with the bass part, and when it hit the radio station's compressor, it pumped like crazy. I learned that lesson real quick! But we never remixed the song, and Paul never said anything about it.

In February 1971 'Another Day' reached number five in the US charts, and in the UK was twice denied the number one spot by first Mungo Jerry's 'Baby Jump' and a fortnight later by T. Rex's 'Hot Love'.[9] Immune to the success of 'Another Day', and consumed by an escalating war of words, John Lennon wrote 'How Do You Sleep' accusing Paul of being 'just another day'. The feud between the two former writing partners was bitter and did little to improve the quality of their standing, or indeed songwriting. But, perhaps more affected by John's righteous vitriol than he was prepared to share in interviews, Paul did not perform 'Another Day' until 1993. By which time John Lennon had been dead for 13 years.

Maybe I'm Amazed

Addressing the audience at the Fillmore East, New York, on 10 November 1970, Rod Stewart announced, 'All right, here's one you may well know and if you don't know it, I really don't know where you've been.' Backed by The Faces, Stewart leads the band into a raunchy rendition of Paul McCartney's 'Maybe I'm Amazed', a song they have been playing since it was first released six months earlier. The dual vocal approach of Stewart and bass player Ronnie Lane is robust and spirited and unsurprisingly brings to mind the dynamic style of Lennon and McCartney. Voicing the opening with a reserved tenderness, Lane makes way in the second verse for Stewart's soaring gutsy throttle. From behind the drum kit, Kenny Jones pounds at the rhythm, Ronnie

---

9   On 7 March, 'Another Day' climbed the chart to number two, one place above 'My Sweet Lord' by George Harrison, a former number one record.

Wood weaves guitar lines between the beat, and keyboard player Ian McLagan punctuates the melody with crescendos and gospel-styled chords. Mid-song, Lane and Wood come together at the microphone to harmonize – again inducing images of Lennon and McCartney – and lead the band into an extended instrumental passage. Abruptly the music stops: 'Baby won't you to try to understand', Stewart sings in the suspended atmosphere. It's blues rock at its best – heavier and broodier than many of its ilk but unmistakably indebted to 'Helter Skelter', 'Yer Blues' and The Beatles' past glories.

Four decades on, Wood is sceptical of The Faces version. 'Nowhere near as good as Paul played it,' he told Sky Arts viewers on *The Ronnie Wood Show* in 2012. Explaining how they'd been turned onto the track when they were in a garage on a beach in Los Angeles, Wood then announced the evening's special guest. 'Anything special about "Maybe I'm Amazed"?' Wood asks Paul McCartney. 'It was when I'd just met Linda,' Paul explains. 'So it was the story of our romance. It was me thinking...how amazed I was! All the little insecurities: *you hung me on the line* or *you pulled me out of time...maybe I'm afraid of the way I leave you*, all the little things that can happen in a relationship.'

Conceived during a tumultuous period, 'Maybe I'm Amazed' owes much to Paul's retreat to Scotland and his time of deep self-reflection as he pondered John's decision to quit The Beatles. Supported by Linda, Paul channelled his fears into song with unbridled honesty. Unlike John, who readily expressed his inner feelings, Paul favoured situations or characters as a device to convey his emotions – a common technique among songwriters to protect themselves and keep sensitive subject matters at arm's length.

Thinking back to 1965, Paul revealed to Barry Miles that the lyrics of 'We Can Work It Out' 'might have been personal', adding that songwriting 'is often a good way to talk to someone or to work your own thoughts out. It saves you going to a psychiatrist, you allow yourself to say what you might not say in person.' Four years later, Paul wrote 'Let It Be' to face the death of his mother albeit masked by the biblical figure of 'Mother Mary'. 'I had a dream I saw my mum,' Paul explained in *Many Years from Now*. 'She said, "It'll be all right." I'm not sure if she used the words *let it be* but that was the gist of her advice. So that got me writing the song. I literally started off *Mother Mary*, which was her name...'

Balancing tragedy and wistfulness, 'Maybe I'm Amazed' was a wrought, heartfelt commitment to love, animalistic in its despair and tender in its emotional surrender. Its supplication to one woman – Linda – is written not in seduction or romance, but rather as an admission of a man's anguish: deep in dejection and in need of solace. The opening verse, which at first speaks of both being 'amazed' and 'frightened' by love, is replaced by the writer questioning his mental fragility and loneliness: 'won't you help me to understand?' Resting on a C major chord, the first verse climaxes with a dramatic 11-note bass chromatic run. Played on the left hand, the unexpected flourish is as startling as it is memorable – repeated three times throughout the song – and theatrically intensifying the music with dazzling effect.

Technically, despite the final note of the ascending figure lowering the key of the song by a tone, the melodramatic sequence has the opposite effect, seemingly heightening the emotion of the music. Accompanied by the introduction of drums, it furthermore and ingeniously sets the second verse on a sudden raised platform. As the intensity of the song builds, Paul screams out the melody bringing to mind his great performances from the past from 'Long Tall Sally' to 'Oh! Darling' as the bass takes centre stage, augmenting the song with sophisticated flourishes and daring runs. Then, as the track nears its closing bars, the bass signs off with a stunning glissando evoking 'I Want You (She's So Heavy)', the closing track of side one of *Abbey Road*.

Paul introduced the chords of 'Maybe I'm Amazed' and its chromatic rising phrase during a jam with George and Ringo in London on 3 January 1970. At what would be The Beatles' penultimate recording session, the three Beatles met at Abbey Road to record 'I Me Mine' at the behest of film director Michael Lindsay-Hogg. During a loose improvisation, Paul is briefly heard picking out the chords of 'Maybe I'm Amazed' on the piano before being distracted by George returning to the 12-bar ad-lib. After a second and final day of recording – the following day – the fleeting possibility of The Beatles playing Paul's new song passes. A month later, on 22 February 1970, Paul returned to Abbey Road to record 'Maybe I'm Amazed' on 8-track in Studio Two.[10] In the world of missed opportunities, a mere seven weeks stood between the solo recording of 'Maybe I'm Amazed' and George's curiosity being piqued to play along with Paul over a long-forgotten blues improvisation.

---

10 During the same session Paul recorded 'Every Night', which alongside 'Maybe I'm Amazed' would also appear on his debut solo album, *McCartney*.

Believing The Beatles to be a spent force, Paul approached 'Maybe I'm Amazed' by adopting an approach similar to that of 'Come and Get It' and layering all the instruments in turn – piano, organ, drums, bass and guitars – before adding vocals and additional backing from Linda. On 19 April 1970, just ten days after The Beatles' split hit the headlines, a promotional video for 'Maybe I'm Amazed' was exclusively aired on ITV,[11] featuring a montage of family photographs taken by Linda and directed by David Putnam. Then, surprisingly, no further promotion of the song followed. 'At the time,' Paul told broadcaster Paul Gambaccini, 'we thought "Maybe I'm Amazed" was a good track and maybe we should do that as a single, which it probably should have been. But we never did.'

Seven years later, as disco fever spread across both sides of the Atlantic and punk rock exploded as a subculture out of London and New York, 'Maybe I'm Amazed' was issued as a single to promote the triple album *Wings over America*. In February 1977, celebrating a critically acclaimed world tour – the set list of which included five Beatles songs: 'Lady Madonna', 'The Long and Winding Road', 'I've Just Seen a Face', 'Blackbird' and 'Yesterday' – Paul's live version of 'Maybe I'm Amazed' peaked at number ten on the *Billboard* chart. It is this version, coupled with a recording performed by Wings in autumn 1974 at Abbey Road for the film *One Hand Clapping*, which offers the best insight as to how The Beatles may have interpreted 'Maybe I'm Amazed'. Invigorated by a new band, Paul feeds off the fresh interplay and delivers the song with renewed fervour. Introducing the song as

---

11 Broadcast in the US on *The Ed Sullivan Show*.

'a piano tune that goes back a few albums', Paul pitches and scratches at the top end of his vocal range before nodding to 23-year-old Jimmy McCulloch to let rip at the guitar solo.

'"Maybe I'm Amazed",' declared Richard Williams in *Melody Maker*, 'would have been a classic had it been included on, say, *Abbey Road*.' It is difficult to disagree. It was a gem among an array of dazzling jewels. Recorded by The Beatles, it would have been destined to become not only an all-time classic but an odds-on favourite to be their eighteenth number one single.

Paul before his performance on the Wings over America tour at Madison Square Garden, New York City, 24 May 1976.

Every Night

'Every Night' was another Paul McCartney composition dating back to the *Get Back* sessions and introduced to The Beatles on their second day at Apple on 21 January 1969. The morning session began in a convivial atmosphere to the sounds of a piano being tuned and John, Paul, George and Ringo reading articles from the morning papers to one another. Responding to circulating rumours that he had walked out on The Beatles 11 days earlier, after a fight with John, George scoffs, 'The Apple wagon again hits the road.'

Picking up their instruments, The Beatles warm up with short versions of Eddie Cochran's 'Somethin' Else', The Lovin' Spoonful's 'Daydream' and the country music standard 'You Are My Sunshine'. Distracted by another headline – 'Beatle George May Face French jail' – John reads out a reported incident from May 1968 when George allegedly assaulted a French photographer (M. Charles Bebert) as he and Ringo left a nightclub at the Cannes Film Festival. 'If he does not appear in court,' John says, mimicking the style of an American television reporter, 'George Harrison will be given an immediate jail sentence. French law provides that the defendant must appear in court in person or face a sentence of two years.'[12] 'I don't think we need a press department,' Paul laughs. 'We don't!' John says, 'Or we want a silent one...a conceptual press department... NO COMMENT!' he shouts out as the tape cuts out.

When the sound returns, The Beatles are rehearsing 'Every Night'.

---

12 George was found guilty on 20 January and fined 1,000 francs.

Singing off-mic, Paul strums an E chord accompanied by harmonies from John and a steady backbeat played by Ringo. Introducing an A major chord, Paul pushes his vocal up a register, seeking out melody while simultaneously playing a succession of ascending bass notes. Dropping back down to E, the music slips into a slow dirge before petering out over a wail of feedback doubled by Paul holding a sung note over a monotone drone. 'O-KAY!' John yells, now mimicking an American cowboy. And with a '1, 2, 3' he counts in 'Dig a Pony'.

Three days later – on Friday, 24 January – the four Beatles gather in the control room of Apple to listen to the first playback recording of 'Get Back'. Enthused by what they hear, they return to the live room to work on John's guitar solo. Idly strumming a guitar, Paul plays through a set of his acoustic songs, 'Two of Us', 'Her Majesty' – backed by John, George and Ringo – and a new song, 'There You Go, Eddie', written by Paul a year earlier. Hunter Davies recalled in 1985:

> I remember one tune [Paul] played for me in Portugal, which he had written on the lavatory (he rarely went there without his guitar), which was called 'There You Go Eddie'. Just a short verse, and I don't think he ever completed it. He had discovered that my first Christian name is Edward, something I've always kept quiet.

Although clearly in an embryonic stage, there is much to suggest that 'There You Go, Eddie' could have become something special. Delivering the chorus line in light falsetto, Paul drops his voice for the verses and sings of pretending to be 'in with the in-crowd' before revealing Eddie 'is a dog'. 'It's a song about a dog!' John exclaims. Tickled by the idea, John suggests 'There you go, Bernard' and then, almost immediately after, 'There you go, Nigel'. Incorporating both ideas, Paul carries the song through another round, signing off with 'There you go, Mimi', a reference perhaps to John's Aunt Mimi. Sadly, no more came of the song, but 'There You Go, Eddie' offered a glimpse of an alternative reality and is therefore a contender for the proposed *Four Sides of The Beatles*. Continuing his acoustic medley, Paul once again plays 'Every Night', prompting John to ask, 'What key you in?' 'E,' Paul says, quickening the song's tempo. 'E seven,' George qualifies. Without a defined lyric sheet, Paul mixes random words and phrases – 'out of my head'; 'pillow for your head' – accompanied by an amorphous slide guitar part courtesy of John. 'It should just go on straight,' John suggests, singing a light harmony over Paul's lower vocal.

After five months of continuous rehearsing and recording, The Beatles took a much-needed break. Flying to Greece on 16 May, Paul spent a month in the small village of Benitses on the island of Corfu with Linda and her six-year-old daughter, Heather. It was here Paul finished writing 'Every Night'. Latterly describing the song as a 'blues', Paul wrote about a man balancing the lure of hedonism to 'get out of my head' against the comforting appeal of staying at home to 'be with you'. First heard by the general public a year later on *McCartney* – in the wake of The Beatles breakup – the former sanguine narrative read more like someone emerging from debilitating depression. Yet, in an interview, given on 15 May 1969 for the BBC Radio Merseyside show *Light and Local*, Paul openly shared his feelings on a range of subjects from marriage to 'high finance' and, in doing so, gave an insight into his state of mind at the time and the challenges facing The Beatles. 'When we started off as Beatles we knew nothing about the business side of it,' Paul told Roy Corlett. 'Sometimes you can get a bit carved up. I still can't stand business. The four of us are really just a rock band but we've got to think when we sign a contract, "What does it mean?" It's growing up. You've got to do it one time in your life.' Asked about Beatlemania, Paul referenced the capacity performances at Shea Stadium – in 1965 and 1966 – 'Those things are fantastic at the time, but then you think to yourself, "What more can we do? They're my three best friends. They're good lads!"'

As with many of the songs on *McCartney*, 'Every Night' promised more than it delivered. The recording opens with an acoustic guitar panned to the right and a snare drum marking the first beat of each bar, on the left. The crack of the snare hits loud and then incrementally diminishes on each successive strike. It was a Beatles trick stretching as far back as 1963 where Paul can be heard instructing Ringo during the recording of 'I Want to Hold Your Hand': 'The first one attack... the second one not quite so loud.' The close attention to detail was not in itself unusual, but like an artist applying a darker shade to the edges of a painting to emphasize its outer profile, Paul revelled in finer artful tones. Nonetheless, working alone and bereft of a thriving collective atmosphere, Paul struggled to inject the spirit 'Every Night' required. Reflecting on his working relationship with John, Paul told Roy Corlett, 'We are a good combination because if I'm left on my own I'll write songs that are a bit sloppy, which I like. I'm a bit more sentimental, on the surface. John'll write harder songs. But if we come together then you get a bit of each. It's a nice combination.'

In 1979, Paul performed 'Every Night' at the Concerts for the People of Kampuchea where, backed by Wings and joined on vocals by Denny Laine, a former member of The Moody Blues, he delivered the song with renewed vigour. The additional harmonies provided a perfect foil for Paul, while inevitably inviting comparison with John Lennon and what he would have given to the song a decade earlier. In 1991, 'Every Night' was again revived by Paul, on this occasion for *MTV Unplugged*, and with it the introduction of a new arrangement: mid-song the instruments gave way to a chorus of voices singing three-part harmony. The fresh approach perhaps suggested that 'Every Night' – unlike the half a dozen other Beatle songs performed that evening[13] – was still in search of a definitive arrangement.

---

13 The other songs were: 'Here, There and Everywhere', 'We Can Work It Out', 'I've Just Seen a Face', 'She's a Woman', 'And I Love Her', 'Blackbird' and 'I Lost My Little Girl' – one of the first songs Paul wrote and briefly revived by The Beatles during the *Get Back* sessions.

Junk

In American slang 'junk' refers to narcotic drugs, especially heroin. First used during the 'White Album' sessions in 1968, John charted his battle with the drug in song: first as a user – 'I need a fix 'cause I'm going down; – and then, as described in 'Cold Turkey' in withdrawal – 'temperature's rising, fever is high'. Never shy of discussing their drug intake, The Beatles populated their music with references to marijuana and LSD.[14] Heroin, on the other hand, remained a taboo subject until after the breakup. 'Heroin,' John told Jann Wenner in December 1970. 'It just was not too much fun. I never injected it or anything. We sniffed a little when we were in real pain.'

Written during The Beatles' stay in India in 1968, 'Junk' lyrically adhered to the dictionary definition of its title – discarded articles of little or no use or value – itemizing 'handle bars', 'army boots' and 'candlesticks' among a list of unrelated everyday paraphernalia. The Beatles' official biographer, Hunter Davies, recalls Paul playing the song, variously referred to as 'Jubilee' and 'Junk in the Yard', to a room full of friends. 'He paused in the middle of singing a line about *broken hearted jubilee mug* to say wasn't *jubilee* a lovely word to sing.' Revelling in the playfulness of the written word, Paul then shifted the lyrical perspective in the bridge section from inanimate to personified objects: *Buy! buy! / Says the sign in the shop window. / Why? why? / Says the junk in the yard.*

---

14 LSD was made illegal in the UK in October 1966 and in October 1968 in the US.

A 16-second rendition of 'Junk', recorded on 9 January 1969 at Twickenham, captures a hilarious exchange between John and Paul exhibiting both their shared sense of humour and playful love of language. Momentarily breaking into a jaunty rendition of 'Teddy Boy', Paul says, 'Remember that one?' 'Yeah,' John replies. '...And "Junk"?' Paul says, singing 'epsilon' – the fifth letter of the Greek alphabet – and then in French 'il y a le temps de partir'. The nonsensical phrase sparks John's imagination and prompts them both to trade a mixture of indecipherable and random words in mock European accents: 'Je partais pour...elephant...parachute.' Listening, bemused, George strums the song's chords.

Foreign language wordplay was an amusing sideshow in The Beatles' music and led to a handful of anomalies: the German-issued single 'Sie liebt dich' ('She Loves You') and 'Komm, gib mir deine Hand' ('I Want to Hold Your Hand') in 1964; Paul's seduction of 'Michelle' – 'sont les mots qui vont très bien ensemble' – in 1965; and the etymological challenges in 'Sun King' on *Abbey Road*. John told Tony McArthur on Radio Luxembourg:

> When we came to sing it, we started joking, singing *cuando para mucho*. Paul knew a few Spanish words from school, so we just strung any Spanish words that sounded vaguely like something. And we got *chicka ferdi* in, that's a Liverpool expression. It doesn't mean anything, just like na, na, na, na-nah. The one we missed...we should have had *para-noia* but we forgot all about it.

Questioned a year later whether any of the songs on *McCartney* were originally written with The Beatles in mind, Paul replied in the album press release that 'Junk' 'was intended for *Abbey Road* but something happened'. In fact, 'Junk' was originally among the set of songs demoed in May 1968 for the 'White Album', with Paul accompanying himself on acoustic guitar. A high harmony vocal was then overdubbed on the demo, recorded at George Harrison's house, and a lead guitar part which picked out the vocal melody. As the tape ends, John is heard remarking ambiguously off-mic, 'I sing that middle eight.'

After the song was overlooked for the double album release, *Abbey Road* and *Let It Be*, Paul recorded 'Junk' for *McCartney*, both as a vocal version and an instrumental track – 'Singalong-Junk'. The album's press release explained their differences. 'This was take 1, for the vocal version, which was take 2, and a shorter version,' Paul wrote. 'Guitars, and piano and bass, were put on at home, and the rest added at Morgan Studios. The strings are Mellotron, and they were done at the same time as the electric guitar, bass drum, and sizzle cymbal.' Adding an additional 30 seconds to the running length, 'Singalong-Junk' was richer in sound with plaintive acoustic guitars replaced by a succession of interchanging instruments repeating and duplicating the song's central motif.

A year later, in 1971, George Martin orchestrated a version of 'Junk' for Cilla Black.[15] The arrangement was sparse and, like Paul's

---

15 Having started her working life as a cloakroom attendant at the Cavern Club in Liverpool, Black went on to have a successful recording career as a solo artist, including the 1964 number one singles 'Anyone Who Had a Heart' and 'You're My World' and in 1968 the top ten hit 'Step Inside Love' written for her by Paul.

recording on *McCartney*, featured an acoustic guitar at its centre. Martin's notable production addition was a wind-like sound effect, played on a keyboard, fading in and out of the mix. Two decades later, in January 1991, Paul performed 'Singalong-Junk' on *MTV Unplugged* for the first time with a full band arrangement, featuring Linda on keyboards, Hamish Stuart, formerly of the Average White Band, on bass, Paul Wickens on piano, Blair Cunningham on drums, and one-time Pretenders' member Robbie McIntosh on guitar. The instrumental take – broadcast over the end credits of the show – was in the main faithful to the original recording. Nevertheless, faced with a deceptively plain melody, the musicians somewhat inevitably succumbed to virtuoso inflections, which, although irresistible to play, suspended the soporific air of the piece. Unnecessary embellishment, or 'showboating' as it is commonly referred to, was a temptation The Beatles doggedly resisted. Across their catalogue of over two hundred recorded songs, a listener would be hard pushed to find evidence of unwarranted technical skill, unnecessary passing notes or self-indulgent showmanship. Serving the song was a benchmark of The Beatles' approach and is precious for its rarity in popular music.

In contrast to the other selections proposed across this new Beatles album, 'Junk' was a reflective song that was neither confessional, like many of John's, spiritually yearning as with George's contributions, or good-time rocking like Ringo's. Rather, 'Junk' offered a beguiling melody infused with images and a sense of nostalgia for an unspecified place of innocence.

The Back Seat of My Car

Dating back to 1968, 'The Back Seat of My Car' was written by Paul for his then girlfriend, Maggie McGivern. 'They flew to Sardinia,' Philp Norman wrote in *Paul McCartney: The Biography*, 'spending five days in a beach-side hotel and living in swimsuits, T-shirts and flip-flops' as Paul conjured images 'looking back to illicit drives in his Aston Martin with Maggie'.

The song was too late to be considered for inclusion on the 'White Album', so Paul returned to it on Tuesday, 14 January 1969 at Twickenham. Arriving early, as he often did, Paul used the quiet of the hour to extemporize on the piano and develop new ideas. Warming up with renditions of 'Martha My Dear', Jesse Fuller's 'San Francisco Bay Blues', The Rolling Stones' 'Lady Jane', the unreleased 'Oh, Baby I Love You' and the newly written 'The Day I Went Back to School', which, as he informs Paul Bow (clapper loader), 'I had the idea this morning.' While Paul is tinkering on the piano, Ringo arrives and together they improvise an up-tempo 12-bar blues, later titled 'I Bought a Piano the Other Day' and credited to Lennon/McCartney/Starkey. Ringo pounds out a double time rhythm,at the top end of the keyboard. 'Well, that's me finished!' he puffs. Playing on, Paul sings 'Woman', a song written in 1964 for Peter & Gordon under the pseudonym 'Bernard Webb',[16] and a work-in-progress, 'The Back Seat of My Car'. The song has progressed little in the past year, requiring Paul to blend half-formed sentences over a distinct melody

---

16 Not to be confused with the song of the same title released by Lennon in 1980.

stretching from low vocal notes to high falsetto leaps. At intervals, Paul mimics the sound of a drum kit to suggest arrangement ideas while simultaneously emphasizing individual chords to mark rhythmical changes. Drawn to the upper register melody and inserting American-inflected colloquialisms – 'Gee, it's getting late'; 'speeding down the highway' – Glyn Johns exclaims, 'It's like The Beach Boys!' 'That's just a little skip off,' Paul casually replies before being called away to take a phone call.

Unaware of 'The Back Seat of My Car' until 1971, when the song was sequenced as the closing track on Paul's second solo album, *RAM*, John was enraged when he heard the record. Studying its content, John interpreted many of Paul's lyrics as direct and personal attacks on himself and Yoko. The view was reinforced by the album cover, which depicted two beetles copulating – the suggestion of both lyrics and image being that Paul was being 'fucked over' by his former bandmates.

Coming 12 months after the split of The Beatles in a year defined by acrimony and high-profile public spats, John identified a set of thinly veiled swipes: from 'I thought you was my friend but you let me down' in 'Three Legs'; to the introductory salutation 'piss off', disguised as 'piece of cake', in 'Too Many People'. '*Too many people* going what?' John fumed in his unwritten notes for the *Imagine* album. 'Missed our lucky what? *Can't be wrong* huh! I mean Yoko, me and other friends can't all be hearing things.'

In defence, Paul told *Playboy* in 1984:

There was one tiny little reference to John in the whole thing. He'd been doing a lot of preaching and it got up my nose a little bit. In one song, I wrote *too many people preaching practices*. That was a little dig at John and Yoko. There wasn't anything else on it that was about them. Oh, there was you *took your lucky break and broke it in two*.

Five years later – in 1989 – Paul expanded on the issue. 'I felt John and Yoko were telling everyone what to do and I felt we didn't *need* to be told what to do,' he told journalist Paul Du Noyer. 'The whole tenor of The Beatles thing had been, like each to his own. Freedom. Suddenly, it was, "You should do this." It was the wagging finger. I got pissed off with it. So that one ['Back Seat of My Car'] got to be a thing about them.' Barely hiding his contempt, John attempted to channel his anger with an attempted objective reading of Paul's first two records: 'The first time I heard it, I thought *RAM* was awful,' he told *Hit Parader* in February 1972:

And then the second time, ahem, I fixed the record player a bit and it sounded better. I enjoyed a couple like 'My Dog It's Got Three Legs' or something, and the intro to 'Uncle Albert'. *McCartney* was better because at least there were some tunes on it like 'Junk'. I liked the little bit about *hands across the water* but it just tripped off all the time. That's what he was getting into on the back of *Abbey Road*. There were all the bits at the beginning like *too many people going underground* – that was Yoko and me – and *you took your lucky break* that was considering we had a lucky break to be with him.

Launching a counterattack, John penned 'How Do You Sleep?' – an idea conceived in 1969 as a rhythm with 'a heavy beat' – as a platform from which to admonish Paul with a venomous verbal lashing: accusing his former writing partner of being 'dead'; of living with sycophants; and making 'muzak to my ears'. Allen Klein remembers cautioning John during the writing of the song while paradoxically suggesting an alternative cutting lyric. 'There was a line that goes *the only thing you did was yesterday* and the line that followed was *and you probably pinched that bitch anyway*. I thought it was too strong, not worthy of John, so I suggested *since you've gone you're just another day*. And he loved it,' Klein told *Playboy* in 1971.

If 'How Do You Sleep?' was not recrimination enough, the artwork of *Imagine* – John's second solo album – took a further swipe at Paul. Parodying the front cover of *RAM*, which showed Paul clutching the horns of a ram standing passively in a pen, *Imagine* included a free black-and-white photograph of John dressed in white trousers, white shirt and a knitted tank top, knees half bent, arms fully stretched, holding the ears of a pig while looking inquisitively up to the camera. 'Some people don't see the funny side of it at all. Too bad. What am I supposed to do, make you laugh?' John rallied in the notes to *Imagine*, adding in reference to 'How Do You Sleep?', 'It's what you might call an "angry letter" only sung, get it?' Further damnation came when a film of the making of *Imagine* revealed John in the studio singing, 'How do you sleep, you cunt?', aided and abetted by a slashing guitar part played by George, and by banter between the two former Beatles dismissing Paul as 'Beatle Head'.

'I think the truth, as a lot of people have said,' Paul commented with dignified restraint, 'is that we were missing each other.' Musically, it was difficult not to disagree. Despite its enduring appeal, 'The Back Seat of My Car' sorely missed The Beatles' creative input. Left to his own devices, Paul let the structure of the song meander, leaving lazy rhymes – 'lights are pretty / Mexico City' – uncontested. '"Back Seat of My Car" goes off a bit,' Paul admitted to Paul Du Noyer. Yet, the song's concluding line, 'We believe that we can't be wrong', far from John's paranoid reading of Paul's intended meaning, provided an anthemic finale to the paramour tale of hot-headed passion in the face of adult hostility. '"Back Seat of My Car" is the ultimate teenage song,' Paul told *Billboard* in 2001. 'It's very romantic *we can make it to Mexico City*. That's a really teenage song, with the stereotypical parent who doesn't agree, and the two lovers are going to take on the world *we believe that we can't be wrong*. I always like the underdog. And obviously *back seat* is snogging, making love."

Released as a single in August 1971, on the back of a number one album, 'The Back Seat of My Car – backed by 'Heart of the Country' – surprisingly made little impact on the national chart, peaking at a lowly number 39. In the US, the alternative choice of 'Uncle Albert/Admiral Halsey' – coupled with 'Too Many People' – topped the Billboard charts. Nevertheless, bringing *RAM* to a close, 'The Back Seat of My Car' was astutely positioned to leave listeners on an exhilarating high. Adding to the luscious orchestral backing, recorded by the New York Philharmonic Orchestra and conducted by Paul, the end of the song is framed by the music cutting to a half-time rhythm, carried by just guitar and bass. Out of the coiling holdup, Paul suddenly unleashes an almighty scream and with it the band crash in to play the end coda. It is a thrilling moment: triumphalist and jubilant and one of the best vocal moments of Paul's career. 'Another instantly recognisable McCartney melody' was Chris Charlesworth's admiring summary in *Melody Maker*. 'Slow, tuneful, building up to a dramatic ending. A likely song for others to cover.'

8. Side Three: Harrison

Four years after the breakup, George Harrison was still resentful of his – and Ringo's – lowly status within The Beatles. 'An attitude came over John and Paul,' George told Alan Freeman on Radio 1 in December 1974, 'of "We're the grooves and you two just watch it."' At the heart of George's grievance was the issue of songwriting. In 1962, John and Paul made a verbal agreement to equally credit their works – as Lennon & McCartney – and, critically, to exclude George from the arrangement. Keen to avert recrimination, Brian Epstein suggested a compromise: recommending that George sing an equal amount of songs on stage. Accordingly, lead vocal duties were divided proportionally between John, Paul and George but, as recording artists, the songs of Lennon and McCartney continued to dominate.

Initially, the arrangement worked without complaint. But in time, as George began to write, his songs received little enthusiasm. In 1963, George's first attempt at writing, 'Don't Bother Me', was recorded for *With The Beatles*, but in the same year a second song – 'You Know What to Do' – was rejected for *A Hard Day's Night*, in favour of 13 Lennon and McCartney originals. Increasingly derided or judged below par, George's offerings were relegated to one or two songs per album. 'They'd been writing since we were at school,' George grumbled

Opposite: George in the grounds of his home, Friar Park, Henley-on-Thames, 1975.

more than two decades later in The Beatles *Anthology*. 'They'd written all or most of their bad songs before we got into the recording studio. I had to come from nowhere and start writing and to have something at least quality enough to put in the record with all their wondrous hits.'

Unlike either John or Paul who would freely use one another as songwriting sounding boards, George worked alone and when he did seek help was often humiliatingly belittled. Asked for assistance on 'Taxman' in 1966, John begrudgingly offered George 'a few one-liners' as he admitted to *Playboy* in 1980. 'He came to me because Paul wouldn't have helped him at that period. I didn't want to do it. I thought, "Oh, no, don't tell me I have to work on George's stuff." It took me years to come around to George and to start considering him as an equal or anything.'

In the same year – 1966 – The Beatles stopped touring and, whether by design or coincidence, George's songwriting flourished. Over the next three years, he wrote a string of songs which in time have come to be considered as ground-breaking or, in some cases, classics: in 1967, 'Within You, Without You'; in 1968, 'The Inner Light' and 'While My Guitar Gently Weeps'; and in 1969, 'Something' and 'Here Comes the Sun'.[1] In fact – as Mark

---

1   In 2020, 'Here Comes the Sun' was declared as the number one most downloaded and streamed Beatles song by the Official Charts Company. The remaining songs in the top ten were: 'All You Need Is Love' (10), 'Yesterday' (9), 'In My Life' (8), 'Blackbird' (7), 'Help' (6), 'Twist and Shout' (5), 'Come Together' (4), 'Hey Jude' (3) and 'Let It Be' (2). All of these were Lennon/McCartney originals with the exception of 'Twist and Shout' (written by Phil Medley and Bert Berns). Only one other George Harrison composition – 'While My Guitar Gently Weeps' (13) – made the top 60.

Lewisohn noted in his 2019 lecture 'Hornsey Road' – of the 180 songs written in the first six years of The Beatles' recording career, George contributed 21. In the seventh year – 1969 – George wrote more than 30. Among the showcasing of material at Twickenham, George innocently asked, 'Shall we do other people's tunes as well?' 'I don't know any,' John replied wickedly. 'I don't like anybody else's,' Paul added. 'I can only just bear doing your songs,' John added flatly, addressing George, 'never mind strangers'.'

On 7 January 1969, George broached the issue in a conversation with Paul at Twickenham Studios. 'What I was saying about the songs…I've got about twenty songs from 1948…was because I knew very well the moment I bring them in the studio [blows a raspberry] it's

George reading Bob Dylan's *Don't Look Back* at Apple, London, 1968.

gone. Slowly, now, I can bring a couple out because I can get it more like it should have been then.' Over the next fortnight George introduced a handful of new works, including 'All Things Must Pass', 'Isn't It a Pity', 'Hear Me Lord', 'Old Brown Shoe', 'Window, Window', 'I Me Mine' and 'For You Blue', which were received with an unpredictable mixture of willing engagement or muted neglect. George raised the subject with John on 29 January. 'I've got so many songs that I've got my quota for the next ten years,' George said. 'I'd just like to, maybe, do an album of songs.' 'On your own?' John asked. 'Yeah,' George nodded. 'It would be nice to mainly get them all out the way. And secondly, just to hear what all mine are like together.' Foreseeing a compromise, John suggests, 'If we put out an LP and it was all The Beatles together but George is doing an album.' 'Yeah,' George concurs:

> But it would be nice if any of us can do separate things like that as well. That way it also preserves The Beatle bit of it, more. All these songs of mine. I can give to people who can do them good, but I suddenly realised, 'Fuck all that, I'm just going to do me for a bit.' With all these tunes, I could just do 'em in a week, at the most. I could record them all, remixed and everything because they're all very simple. I don't think they need much.

Three weeks later on his twenty-sixth birthday – 25 February – George set the idea in motion. Taking advantage of downtime at Abbey Road, and with only an engineer present, George recorded three songs, each one differing in its approach: 'Old Brown Shoe' was an elaborate arrangement featuring piano, vocals and guitars; a tender reading of 'All Things Must Pass' was performed on electric guitar; and 'Something' recorded in one take, also on electric guitar, featured an extended heartfelt middle vocal passage.[2]

Long overshadowed by the compositions of Lennon and McCartney, the songs of George Harrison breathed new life into The Beatles' oeuvre and increasingly attracted attention from a host of established artists – Shirley Bassey, Richie Havens, Johnny Mathis, Frank Sinatra, Nina Simone and Dionne Warwick, to name but a few – while critically being recognized for their depth of feeling and universal themes. 'Out of the new records from Apple,' George reflected in May 1970, 'I've done "Let It Be" with Paul; "Instant Karma!" with John; "Ain't That Cute" for Doris Troy; the record with Jackie Lomax; an album with Billy Preston; the records with Radha Krishna Temple, and now possibly a single with Ringo. And maybe, if I get a chance, I'll get round to do something for myself.'

'His talents have developed over the years,' John told *Rolling Stone* in December 1970:

> He was working with two fucking brilliant songwriters and he learned a lot from us. I wouldn't have minded being George, the invisible man, and learning what he learned. And maybe it was hard sometimes for him, because Paul and I are such egomaniacs, but that's the game. I don't consider my talents fantastic compared with the fuckin' universe, but I consider George's less.

2   All three recordings can be heard on *The Beatles Anthology 3*.

Ignorant of John's arrogance, George launched his solo career with an ambitious three-album set. Many of the songs had been written while George was a Beatle and highlighted the strength of material that would have been available to the band after *Abbey Road*.

Slimmed down from the 17 tracks on *All Things Must Pass* – not including the final disc of band jams – George's side of a new Beatles record would have presented an abundance of riches. The six songs selected for *Four Sides of The Beatles* brim with energy and vitality. Yet, resultantly, many alternate choices would be side-lined, not least the epic 'Let It Down', the majestic 'Beware of Darkness' and the entrancing 'I'd Have You Anytime' – the last, co-written with Bob Dylan, carrying with it the tantalizing prospect of a much admired peer collaborating with The Beatles.

Nevertheless, *All Things Must Pass* was a dramatic statement showcasing an array of songs, musical styles and guest musicians including Ringo, Peter Frampton, Billy Preston, Dave Mason, Ginger Baker, members of Badfinger and Procol Harum, and Eric Clapton. Phil Spector, moreover, was asked to co-produce the record, but consequently many of the songs were swamped in a wash of reverb and overindulgent multi-tracking. Gone was the subtlety of arrangement which George Martin had brought to George's songs in The Beatles – from the orchestral sweeps on 'Piggies', 'Savoy Truffle', 'Something' and 'Here Comes the Sun' to the lone cello on 'Blue Jay Way'.

Martin was considered John and Paul's man, and perhaps wishing to avoid The Beatles' fragmentary working practice, George had developed an impressive ability to work independently behind the studio desk while also producing records for many other artists.

Indeed, throughout the 1970s and early 1980s, George would produce a further seven of his own records – *Living in the Material World*, *Dark Horse*, *Extra Texture*, *Thirty Three & 1/3*, *George Harrison*, *Somewhere in England* and *Gone Troppo* – and was clearly intent on controlling the artistic output of his own work. In 2006, George Martin wrote the orchestration to a solo recording of 'While My Guitar Gently Weeps' for Cirque du Soleil's theatrical production *Love*.[3] The reimagining of the 'White Album' studio outtake was a posthumous tribute to George, who died in 2001, and beautifully captured in sound a relationship that had struggled to blossom three decades earlier.

Presented in a triple gate-fold box set, the black-and-white cover of *All Things Must Pass* depicted George – dressed in Wellington boots and a straw hat – sitting in a field surrounded by four stone dwarfs. 'Like the *McCartney* album,' Alan Smith wrote in the *New Musical Express*, 'all I can say is that *All Things Must Pass* stands head and shoulders above just about any other solo album released this year but there's still something missing!' Alluding to the 'soft rhythms of a dream' and the 'profound beauty of the lyricism', Smith tempered his review with a cautionary note: 'Its brilliance has been overshadowed by its average.'

Regardless, *All Things Must Pass* was rapturously received by the buying public and enjoyed an eight-week tenure at number one on the UK chart. Yet, despite the record's cross-Atlantic acclaim, George

---

3 *Love* was an ambitious collaboration, using the songs of The Beatles in a staged theatrical production. The show premiered at the Mirage Hotel, Las Vegas, on 30 June 2006.

George listening to his first solo album with former Beatles promoter Peter Bennett and producer Phil Spector, New York, 31 October 1970.

yearned for a Beatles reunion. After receiving an acetate of Paul's debut single, 'Another Day', George compiled a would-be next Beatles album. 'He took me over to Eric Clapton's house one day,' musician Leon Russell recalled in conversation with author Graeme Thomson. 'And on the way George played me what sounded like a series of Beatles songs. He had taken one song out of all their solo records and put them together. And it sounded just like a Beatles record. He thought that was amazing. And I did too.'

What Is Life?

In 1943, the physicist Erwin Schrödinger gave a lecture in Dublin and posed the question, 'How can the events in space and time which take place within the spatial boundary of a living organism be accounted for by physics and chemistry?' His findings were published a year later as *What Is Life? The Physical Aspect of the Living Cell*. Perhaps unaware of Schrödinger's existential study, George Harrison was similarly also searching for a meaning to life beyond the physical world. Spiritual quest increasingly dominated George's songwriting and privately offered solace from the rancour and protracted breakup of The Beatles: not so much a withdrawal from the demands of everyday existence but submission to a celestial alternative.

Written in 1969, 'What Is Life?' was as exuberant as it was ambiguous: 'Tell me, who am I without you by my side?' Whether intended as a paean to earthly love – George's wife, Pattie – or devotion to a spiritual being – God – George's lyrics spoke of an all-consuming love 'there for you, any time of day'. 'I wrote it very quickly,' George recorded in his biography *I Me Mine*, 'fifteen minutes or half an hour maybe, on my way to Olympic Studios where I was producing one of Billy [Preston's] albums.' Arriving at the session, George reasoned that a catchy pop song would be ill-suited 'while Billy was playing his funky stuff' and judiciously decided to record the song for himself.

Laid down at Abbey Road between May and October 1970 for *All Things Must Pass*, 'What Is Life?' exploded with a pulsating fuzz guitar riff – reminiscent of 'Think for Yourself' from The Beatles

1965 album *Rubber Soul* – and a blazing horn section. Propelled by a subtle snare roll on the first beat of every bar, the frantic arrangement was further accentuated by a bank of acoustic guitars and dazzling lead lines weaved by Eric Clapton around the song's central riff. Backed by a studio band, including Billy Preston and Badfinger's Pete Ham, Tom Evans and Joey Molland, much of the instrumental subtlety and rumbustious string arrangement – scored by John Barham[4] – was nevertheless submerged behind an ambitious production. Seeking instruction, George sent an early mix of 'What Is Life?' to Phil Spector who – according to Klaus Voormann – had initially attended sessions 'completely drunk', subsequently fallen over backwards in the control room, broken his arm, and 'sort of disappeared', though he was actually convalescing in Los Angeles. Replying on 19 August 1970, Spector assured George that the 'band track was fine', advising 'this needs a good performance by you and proper background voice. It should be done at Trident Studios if further tracks are necessary.'

A discarded mix of 'What Is Life?' recorded at Trident Studios – discovered when *All Things Must Pass* was remastered three decades later – revealed, as Spector recommended, further attempts to expand the cacophony of sound. 'I tried having this piccolo trumpet player like the guy who played on "Penny Lane",' George told *Billboard* magazine in December 2000. 'It wasn't actually the

---

4   In 1967, George wrote 'Blue Jay Way' based upon a piano piece by John
    Barham, derived from Raga Marwa. In 1970, Barham wrote choral
    arrangements for 'The Long and Winding Road' and 'Across the Universe'.
    In 1971, Barham worked with John Lennon on 'Jealous Guy'.

same bloke but I wanted that sound. So I had an oboe and a piccolo trumpet and I had this part for them all written out but they couldn't play it the same; they couldn't do this kind of "hush" phrase, and they played it very staccato like a classical player.'

In January 1971, George secured his first UK number one single when 'What Is Life?' was released as a double A-side with 'My Sweet Lord'.[5] In contrast to the more overt pop songs on *Four Sides of The Beatles* – John's 'Instant Karma!', Paul's 'Come and Get It' and Ringo's 'It Don't Come Easy' – 'What Is Life?' was an all-guns-blazing surrender to commerciality. Marrying infectious melody and a pounding Motown-esque rhythm, the song unashamedly revived the spirit of the Swinging Sixties. Albums thrive on hit singles and where latterly Beatle A-sides had been mid-paced – 'Come Together', 'Hey Jude' or even 'Get Back' – 'What Is Life?' echoed the urgency and joyous nature of The Beatles' earliest releases from 'Please Please Me' and 'She Loves You' through to 'Paperback Writer' and 'Day Tripper'.

'What Is Life?' was a celebration of sound and spirit, and, as successful songs often do, acted as an open-armed invitation to listeners to indulge and explore deeper the soul of George Harrison. The bidding was in the form of a philosophical question, but what lay beyond the veiled call was a world of answers openly encouraging audiences to embrace devoutness.

---

5   In the US, 'What Is Life?' was coupled with 'Apple Scruffs', also from *All Things Must Pass*, and peaked at number ten on the Billboard chart.

My Sweet Lord

Written as a song of praise to a higher being, 'My Sweet Lord' has transcended the decades to become one of George Harrison's most successful compositions. In 1971, 'My Sweet Lord' was a number one record on both sides of the Atlantic and, in the UK, the biggest-selling single of the year. Yet, despite its spiritual invocation, the ownership of the song has been tainted by lawsuits and claims of copyright infringement.

On 1 December 1969, George attended a concert given by the American husband-and-wife duo Delaney & Bonnie at the Royal Albert Hall. At the after-show party, George asked, 'Would you mind if I joined the band?' The following night – at Colston Hall, Bristol[6] – George appeared on stage as an unannounced guest and after the show accepted an invitation to join the tour for the remainder of the UK and European dates. It would be the first time George had been on the road since touring with The Beatles in 1966, and also provided the inspiration for 'My Sweet Lord'.

Delaney Bramlett claims to remember the moment the song was conceived mid-tour, as he explained in 2000 to author Marc Shapiro:

> George came up to me one night after a show and said, 'You write a lot of gospel songs. I'd like to know what inspires you to do that.' I told him that I get things from the Bible: from what a preacher may say; or just the feelings I felt toward God. George

---

6   In September 2020, the Grade II listed building was renamed Bristol Beacon.

said, 'Can you give me a for instance?' So I grabbed my guitar and started playing The Chiffons melody from 'He's So Fine' and then sang the words *my sweet Lord, oh my Lord, oh my Lord, I just wanna be with you*. Then I said, 'Then you praise the Lord in your own way.' As it happened Rita Coolidge, who was on the tour, and my wife at the time – Bonnie – were sitting there and so I told them that when we got to this one part they should sing *Hallelujah*. They did. George said okay and that was the end of it.

Also touring with the band was Billy Preston, who, in an interview for the film documentary *George Harrison: Living in the Material World*, recalled, 'We had a piano in the dressing room and the discussion was "How do you write a gospel song?" So I started playing some gospel changes. And I don't know if it was Delaney or Bonnie but one of them started *oh my lord*. They went on and we went *Hallelujah*.'[7]

A year later, Delaney Bramlett heard 'My Sweet Lord' on the radio and was shocked. 'I immediately called George up,' as he explained to Marc Shapiro, 'and told him that I didn't mean for him to use the melody of "He's So Fine". He said, "Well, it's not exactly the same."' Bramlett further claimed that George not only offered to credit him on the next print of the record but also admitted that, to 'a large extent', he, Bramlett, had written the song. Nevertheless, Bramlett decided against pursuing ownership rights and unclaimed royalties.

---

7   Recorded in January 1970, Preston's recording of 'My Sweet Lord' was released on his fifth solo album, *Encouraging Words*, in September 1970.

Quoted in *The Beatles: Off the Record*, George's version of events directly contradicted Bramlett's account: 'I remember Eric [Clapton] and Delaney & Bonnie were doing interviews with somebody in either Copenhagen or Gothenburg, somewhere in Sweden,' George said, 'and I was so thrilled with "Oh Happy Day" by The Edwin Hawkins Singers. It really just knocked me out, the idea of that song and I just felt a great feeling of the Lord. So I thought, "I'll write another 'Oh Happy Day'," which became "My Sweet Lord".'

On 10 February 1971 – with 'My Sweet Lord' now topping the charts in 16 countries – Bright Tunes Music filed a complaint against Harrisongs Music claiming 'My Sweet Lord' infringed the copyright of The Chiffons' 'He's So Fine'. In an attempt to resolve the dispute out of court, George's manager, Allen Klein, moved to buy Bright Tunes, but was initially rejected. Klein's later successful bid in 1973 – on behalf of George – was nonetheless unable to prevent five years of protracted negotiations. In September 1976, the case was finally brought before a court, where 'My Sweet Lord' was subjected to scientific deconstruction, as George explained. 'The plaintiff had huge charts made up with the three notes from Motif A [G, E and D] and five notes from Motif B [G, A, C, A and C] drawn on them and they talked about these for about three days, to the point where I started to believe that maybe they did own those notes.'

During the proceedings, a slew of witnesses were called to the stand, among them Delaney Bramlett. 'I received a call from George and his lawyers,' Bramlett told Marc Shapiro. 'They wanted me to fly to New York to testify on his behalf. But I had a previous engagement so they got in touch with Bonnie [Bramlett], and she went and testified. And the irony was that even though Bonnie was sitting there with George and me that night, the judge considered her testimony hearsay and wouldn't allow it.'[8]

In September 1976, Judge Richard Owen, a composer himself, found George guilty of 'subconscious plagiarism' and later awarded damages of $1,599,987 of the earnings from 'My Sweet Lord' to Bright Tunes. With regard to Harrison's use of the music of 'He's So Fine', Judge Owen said, 'I do not believe he did so deliberately. Nevertheless, it is clear that "My Sweet Lord" is the very same song as "He's So Fine" with different words, and Harrison had access to "He's So Fine". This is, under the law, infringement of copyright, and is no less so even though subconsciously accomplished.' George noted in *I Me Mine*:

I wasn't consciously aware of the similarity when I wrote the song, but once it started to get a lot of airplay, people started

8   On 7 January 2015, Bonnie Bramlett posted an online response to Delaney Bramlett's claim to have co-written 'My Sweet Lord', suggesting that her former husband's memory was 'somewhat clouded'. 'I have the original paperwork regarding the trial,' she wrote. 'In the documented statement, May 1977, Delaney is quoted as saying that a good example of some gospel music that he, Bonnie and Bobby Whitlock would sing would be something like "O Happy Day" ... [George] had begun writing his own gospel song upstairs after a show. ... Delaney says he likes it. They all began to jam, George began to vamp ...singing *my sweet Lord* and *Hallelujah* ... Billy Preston started to play (the chords George had worked out), band members start playing tambourines. He says although the song was simple he didn't think George would have or could have written it without him. (Delaney was prone to saying that about everybody.) He states, and I quote. "At no time did it cross my mind that evening that the song George had started sounded like any other song I knew."'

talking about it, and it was then I thought, 'Why didn't I realize?' It would have been very easy to change a note here or there and not affect the feeling of the record. I don't feel guilty or bad about it, in fact it saved many a heroin addict's life. I know the motive behind writing the song in the first place and its effect far exceeded the legal hassle.

George concluded, 'As far as I'm concerned, "My Sweet Lord" was a hit because of the sound and its simplicity.' It was a view upheld by two of his former bandmates. 'George was very unlucky,' Ringo told Ray Coleman of *Melody Maker* in October 1976:

> There's no doubt that the tune is similar but how many songs have been written with other melodies in mind? George's version is much heavier than The Chiffons' – he might have done it with the original in the back of his mind, but he's just very unlucky that someone wanted to make it a test case in court. If I'd written "He's So Fine", I guess I'd have sued if I'd wanted some money.

Talking to *Playboy* in 1980, John said, '[George] walked right into it. He knew what he was doing. He must have known. He's smarter than that...George could have changed a few bars in that song and nobody could have ever touched him, but he just let it go and paid the price. Maybe he thought God would just sort of let him off.'

Had The Beatles recorded 'My Sweet Lord', the controversial 'few bars' referred to by both John and George would have been most likely challenged. There are multiple examples of songs, written by any one of the four Beatles, that were either dropped or adapted to avoid similarity to previously recorded tracks. They range from John saying of 'Not a Second Time' that 'the chords at the end are like Mahler's Fifth Symphony' to adapting lines from Chuck Berry's 'You Can Catch Me' for 'Come Together', and from Paul subtly shifting the piano introduction of Humphrey Lyttelton's 'Bad Penny Blues' for the opening to 'Lady Madonna' to George unashamedly lifting the first line of James Taylor's 'Something in the Way She Moves' for 'Something' and then months later comparing elements of 'I've Got a Feeling' to Otis Redding's 'Hard to Handle' and 'Get Back' to The Four Tops' 'Reach Out (I'll Be There)'.

Originally recorded in the summer of 1970, 'My Sweet Lord' employed an array of musicians to create a great wash of instrumentation, including two drummers – Ringo and Jim Gordon – a bass player, two pianos, five acoustic guitars and a tambourine player. 'It sounds like one huge guitar!' George exclaimed, who for his own part, played a distinctive bottle-neck guitar figure.[9] Having learned 'slide' during the Delaney & Bonnie tour, George would dedicate a lifetime to mastering the technique, releasing within him an emotional musical language wonderfully eloquent in its vocabulary.

Emboldened by the expressive recording, George added a Sanskrit prayer within the mix of 'My Sweet Lord', successfully secreting Eastern spiritualism into the fulcrum of Western popular culture.

---

9   Slide guitar is typically played by sliding a bottle neck placed over a finger on the left hand up or down the guitar fret board while the right hand picks notes across the strings.

It was an audacious act. 'I was just thinking of a way to combine *Hallelujah*,' George told Radio 1's Anne Nightingale on 1 February 1977, 'and then suddenly shove *Hare Krishna* in and catch them before they realised.' Writing in *I Me Mine*, George expanded on the process. 'Many people fear the words "Lord" and "God" – but at the same time I thought, "Nobody's *saying* it; I wish somebody else was doing it." I came to believe in the importance that if you feel something strong enough then you should say it.'

Not Guilty

'The lyrics are a bit passé all about upsetting "Apple carts" and what was happening at the time,' George told *Rolling Stone* in 1979. 'Paul-John-Apple Rishikesh-Indian friends, etc.' Written in 1968, 'Not Guilty' confronted George's growing frustrations within The Beatles. 'Me getting pissed off at Lennon and McCartney for the grief I was catching during the making of the "White Album",' he told *Billboard* in 2000. 'I said I wasn't guilty of getting in the way of their careers. I said I wasn't guilty of leading them astray in our all going to Rishikesh to see the Maharishi. I was sticking up for myself.' Infamously recorded in 102 takes – over four working days in August 1968 – 'Not Guilty' was never released by The Beatles and unfathomably remained in the EMI vaults for almost 30 years until it was given a posthumous issue on *Anthology 3* in 1996.

In the summer of 1968, The Beatles were at the top of their game. In the week prior to working on 'Not Guilty', they recorded the seven-minute single 'Hey Jude' in an impressive 25 takes before George

Martin arranged a score – played by a 36-piece orchestra – and then mixed the song to mono and stereo, ready for release. The next day – Wednesday, 7 August – attention turned to 'Not Guilty'. In an epic session – 8.45pm to 5.30am – John, Paul, George and Ringo concentrated on the song's introduction over 18 takes, capturing the basic rhythm of guitar, bass, electric piano and drums. There followed a further 27 attempts to record the basic rhythm track, of which only five takes were complete, until John remarked: 'I don't mind if we keep on doing it but I don't think it's going anywhere.'

Adding to the technical demand of the song, a newly conceived six-bar passage, played in 3/8 time, was incorporated at the end of the guitar solo. It was not uncommon for The Beatles to switch time signatures mid-song. In 1965 – at George's suggestion – the middle eight of 'We Can Work It Out' changed from common time to a waltz pattern over John and Paul singing 'fussing and fighting, my friend' and then 'ask you once again'. Likewise, 'She Said She Said', from the 1966 album *Revolver*, interchanged three-bar counts neatly within its four-bar verses. But whereas the rhythmic changes seamlessly segued within both earlier recordings, they were problematic in 'Not Guilty', breaking the meter of the song and challenging the musicians to master its artful demands.

On the second day of recording – 8 August – 50 more takes of 'Not Guilty' were attempted as John switched from electric piano to acoustic harpsichord,[10] prompting him to say, 'I think that's the best so far, on average, like!' By the end of another all-night session, take 99 was

10 Although often credited to Chris Thomas (engineer/producer), he denied this in a podcast conversation with Robert Rodriguez in December 2018.

identified as the 'best'. The following day, Friday, additional bass and drum parts and a lead guitar were overdubbed, requiring additional demands, as described by engineer Brian Gibson in *The Complete Beatles Recording Sessions*. 'George asked us to put his guitar amplifier at one end of the echo chambers with a microphone at the other end to pick up the output,' Gibson said. 'He sat playing the guitar in the studio control room with a line plugged through to the chamber.'

When the band returned to the track after a weekend break, focus turned to George's lead vocal, which, as engineer Ken Scott recounted in *The Complete Beatles Recording Sessions*, was not without its challenges. 'George had this idea that he wanted to do it in the control room with the speakers blasting so that he got more of an on-stage feel. So we had to monitor through headphones, setting the monitor speakers at a level where he felt comfortable and it wouldn't completely blast out his vocal.' The engineer was working through the night, struggling to cope with the increased audio levels, and remembers saying when John arrived, 'Bloody hell, the way you lot are carrying on you'll be wanting to record everything in the room next door!' Scott continues: '"That's a great idea!" John replied. "Let's try it on the next number." The next number was "Yer Blues" and we literally had to set it all up – them and the instruments – in this *minute* room...it worked out great!'

The same could not be said for 'Not Guilty'. Although included as one of 23 demos recorded at Esher in May 1968 – alongside two more of George's songs, 'Sour Milk Sea'[11] and 'Circles'[12] – 'Not Guilty' was

---

11 Recorded by Jackie Lomax in June 1968 and released two months later on Apple, the record featured Paul on bass, Ringo on drums and George as producer.
12 Recorded for George's 1982 album *Gone Troppo*.

excluded from the final cut of the 'White Album'. Compared to other, less distinguished tracks on the double set, namely John's experimental soundscape 'Revolution 9', Paul's 54-second filler 'Wild Honey Pie' and Ringo's 'Don't Pass Me By', it is hardly surprising that George lost interest in the song. 'I forgot all about "Not Guilty"' until a year ago, when I found this old demo,' he told *Rolling Stone* in 1979. 'I like the tune a lot; it would make a great tune for Peggy Lee or someone.'

Re-recorded for the eponymous album *George Harrison*, the new version of 'Not Guilty' – befitting the late-1970s mainstream mood – was much softer than The Beatles' arrangement. Tempered by a Fender Rhodes electric piano, played by former Spencer Davis Group and Traffic member Steve Winwood, the troublesome waltz section was unsurprisingly vanquished.

In 2018, 'Not Guilty' was heard for the first time in its full arrangement on the 'White Album' 50th anniversary release including for the first time the opening line of the second verse, 'Getting underneath your feet', and a reinstated guitar solo both omitted from the previous *Anthology 3* collection. Still fresh, half a decade later, take 102 of 'Not Guilty' brimmed with attitude and excitement – from Paul's deep bass line and Ringo's resourceful snare rolls to John's rhythmic harpsichord strokes and George's dramatic overdriven guitar riff. As three songs demonstrated – 'One After 909' (March 1963), 'You Know My Name (Look Up the Number)' (May 1967) and 'Across the Universe' (February 1968) – The Beatles were not averse to reviving past songs in 1969. As George's subtle wordplay suggested – 'like you heard me said' – 'Not Guilty' is one of the best examples in this collection of what could have been.

Wah-Wah

'You're giving me a wah-wah,' George Harrison wailed on Friday, 10 January 1969, after walking out on The Beatles. Following a heated discussion with John over lunch at Twickenham Studios, George went home and wrote 'Wah-Wah'. 'It had given me a wah-wah,' he told *Crawdaddy* in February 1977. 'I had such a headache with that whole argument.'

Within the lexicon of rock 'n' roll, 'wah' has an inarticulate history – in 1956, Bo Diddley sang of the mythical town 'Diddy Wah Diddy', and in 1964, Manfred Mann had a transatlantic number one with 'Do Wah Diddy Diddy' – but in the *Oxford English Dictionary*, the two-part definition of 'wah-wah' invites a more exact insight into George's mindset and songwriting: '1. a musical effect achieved on brass instruments by manipulation of a mute and on an electric guitar by means of a pedal controlling output from the amplifier. 2. The sound of a baby's crying; a noise resembling this.'

Initially, John and George's bust-up remained private, but on 16 January 1969, the story reached the desk of show business reporter Michael Housego at the *Daily Sketch*. 'Two Beatles Row in TV Studio. George drives home after "tiff" with John', page three of the paper declared. 'Rehearsals for a Beatles TV spectacular broke up at the weekend – after a row between John Lennon and George Harrison. And last night the recordings were called off again.' Quoting a Beatles spokesman, Housego continued, 'There was a bit of bother among the group in the studio,' to which 'A friend added, "It was just a personal tiff, I don't know what started it."'

Returning to rehearsals, to start recording, on 21 January – relocated to Savile Row – John and George discussed a follow-up article in the *Daily Sketch*, also written by Michael Housego, under the heading 'The End of a Beautiful Friendship?' 'It says swung "a few vicious phrases at each other,"' George reads. 'Untrue.' Jumping out of his seat, John goads George into a mock fight. 'There's only one guy I'd like to get,' John scoffs, 'and that's Housego.' George continues to read aloud: '"It may have been the first time reports of such an 'argument' hit the news pages but it wasn't the first time it had happened by a long way. On one occasion for certain they traded a few punches."' Looking over George's shoulder, John reads out from the offending piece:

> Drugs, divorce, and a slipping image: I've known The Beatles long enough and close enough not to accept a total split. But I also know they have been drifting apart as buddies, seeking strange new thrills, and frankly, getting on each other's nerves. It's only the suddenness of their decline from the status of 'boys next door' to the category of 'weirdies' that has left most people agog.

Describing a past 'rosy garden' of show business peaks, Housego describes The Beatles as 'fed up', going 'their own private way' and becoming 'less reliant on each other for guidance and comradeship'. Concluding the article, Housego is predictably condemning, 'I can say definitely that as a friendly foursome, tied irrevocably to each other's pigtails, it's all over. They will never be exactly the same again.'

Incensed, George spoke out: 'There was no punch-up. We just fell out,' he told the *Daily Mail*. And to the *Daily Express*: 'There's no truth in it. We are still good friends.' 'I was there when it was supposed to have taken place,' Ringo added. 'It's quite untrue.'

Where the detail of the argument may have been inaccurately reported, it was nonetheless evident that there had been a breakdown in communication. In part exacerbated by the omnipotent presence of Yoko, and John's willingness to defer to her opinions and increasingly remain silent in Beatle meetings, George was also frustrated by an age-old rub with Paul. 'I got tired of being with The Beatles,' he told Howard Smith on WABC-FM radio, 'because musically it was like being in a bag and they wouldn't let me out the bag, which was mainly Paul at that time. It never came to blows but I thought, "What's the point of this? I'm quite capable of being relatively happy on my own and I'm not able to be happy in this situation."'

Substantiating George's disquiet, Ringo wrote in his affidavit to the High Court, 'Paul is the greatest bass player in the world. He is also determined. He goes on and on to see if he can get his own way. While that may be a virtue, it did mean that musical disagreements inevitably rose from time to time.' Acknowledging his tendency to talk down to George, Paul admitted in *Anthology* in 1995, 'If you've known a guy when he's thirteen and you're fourteen it's hard to think of him as a grown-up.' Raising an eyebrow, George responded, 'Paul was always nine months older than me. Even now, after all these years, he's still nine months older!'

Perhaps for obvious reasons, 'Wah-Wah' was never introduced

to The Beatles. But when George started work on a solo album in May 1970, 'Wah-Wah' was presented in the early hours of the first recording session after a successful take of 'All Things Must Pass'. With Ringo behind the drum kit, 'Wah-Wah' pulsated with an incessant two-chord rhythm driven by George's guitar riff, a jubilant brass arrangement, and the biting lyrical accusation 'You made me such a big star'. Complemented by the virtuoso musicianship of Eric Clapton on guitar, Billy Preston on organ, and Bobby Keys and Jim Price on saxophone and trumpet, respectively, rarely had a George Harrison song sounded so bold and thrilling.

'It was sounding really nice,' George was quoted in Martin Scorsese's film *George Harrison: Living in the Material World*. 'All these nice acoustics and piano and no echo on anything. We did it for hours until Phil Spector had it right in the control room. Then we went in and listened to it, and I just thought, "I hate it. It's horrible."' 'The sound in your headphones was reasonably dry, but in the control room to hear the playback, the sound was loud and incredible,' bass player Klaus Voormann told *Mojo* in 2014. 'I loved it but George didn't: "What are you doing to my song!"' Coated in a wash of reverb, Spector's production nullified the nuanced performances 'in which horns sound like guitars and vice versa', asserted *Rolling Stone*, a 'grand cacophony of sound!'

On 1 August 1971, George opened both his sets at the Concert for Bangladesh at Madison Square Garden with 'Wah-Wah'. Dressed in a white suit and playing a matching white Fender Telecaster, George thrilled the audience with renditions of 'While My Guitar Gently Weeps', 'Here Comes the Sun' and 'Something'. In the weeks leading up to the event, there was much anticipation of a Beatles reunion. When Ringo was announced on stage, suddenly the incredible became possible. But, as Yoko described in the sleeve notes to the *John Lennon Anthology* in 1998, it was never going to be. After receiving a phone call from George, John hung up, visibly upset. 'He's saying, "Join the Bangladesh concert…Dylan is coming too." I'm not going.' When Yoko attempted to persuade him that it was for charity and together they could do their own thing, John became angry. 'I thought he was being big-headed about it,' Yoko said, announcing that in that case, she would go alone. 'John flipped out: "You want to be a performing flea, go ahead!" John left the room in a huff. I heard much later that George told John to come alone without me. Was that the real reason John did not want to do the show? I guess I will never know.'

'I was asked to play and I didn't,' Paul told *Melody Maker* in 1971:

Klein called a press conference and told everyone I had refused to do so for the Pakistani refugees – that's what he called them. It wasn't so. I said to George the reason I couldn't do it was because it would mean that all the world's press would scream that The Beatles had got back together again, and I know that it would have made Klein very happy. It would have been an historical event and Klein would have taken the credit. If it wasn't for Klein I might have had second thoughts about it.

Try Some Buy Some

In January 1970, when Phil Spector was hired to work on the *Get Back* tapes, it was agreed that Apple Records would also sign his wife, Ronnie Spector, to the label. A former member of The Ronettes, she was desperate to record again having being forced to withdraw from the music industry by her husband when, five years earlier, 'River Deep, Mountain High' – recorded by Ike & Tina Turner and produced by Phil Spector – failed to make a notable impact on the US chart.[13] In an interview with Phil Symes of *Disc and Music Echo* in May 1971, Ronnie Spector said:

> I stopped singing when I married Phil because he retired and being his wife I had to do the same. Phil didn't want to carry on in the business because he didn't respect it any more. For four years Phil and I completely detached ourselves from everyone in the business and settled down in California. I was so bored and missed the stage so much I nearly had a nervous breakdown.[14]

On 2 February 1971, George invited Ronnie to Abbey Road to record a song that he had written during the *All Things Must Pass* sessions a year earlier. '"Try Some Buy Some" was written on the organ,' George explained in his memoir *I Me Mine*, 'and as I don't know the instrument well enough I got into all these complications.'

---

13 It was a number three in the UK.

14 A survivor of psychological and physical abuse, Ronnie Spector eventually escaped from her husband in 1972.

Attempting to play a contrary motion pattern – E major to B seven and A minor to D major, requiring the left hand to play descending bass notes as the right hand forms ascending shapes – George was beaten by the 'weird chords…I couldn't play both parts at the same time and I had a friend write it down for me.'

Seated at the piano, Ronnie listened to the song but understandably was not impressed. 'The first verse didn't exactly grab me,' she wrote in her biography *Be My Baby*. 'Exactly what he was trying to *try* and *buy* wasn't exactly clear. Religion? Drugs? Sex? I was mystified. And the more George sang, the more confused I got.' When the song finished, George asked Ronnie for her opinion. 'I thought it was terrible,' she wrote. 'All I knew for sure was that this was not *something in the way she moves*.' 'Wow!' Ronnie said to George. 'You sure took a different approach with that one!'

Despite Ronnie's reservations, 'Try Some Buy Some' was recorded over two days – 2 and 3 February 1971 – with Phil Spector producing. Recorded as a duet, the result was stunning. Ronnie's sensual tone introduces the song, making way for George's yearning baritone to deliver the second half of the verse. Over a waltz rhythm, with a subtle accent on the first beat of every bar, George and Ronnie then harmonize over a floating chorus backed by a luscious string arrangement – written and arranged by John Barham – lifting the song to a higher level of cinematic expanse. Reversing the structure, the second verse leads with George's voice before Ronnie sings with amatorious desire: 'And when it seemed I would / Always be lonely / I opened my eyes and saw you.'

Understandably, the years of enforced absence had changed Ronnie's voice. Encouraging her to 'hit the high notes', Phil Spector was quick to dismiss her use of vibrato.[15] 'It's Sixties,' he admonished his wife. 'This is 1971.' 'It took me a long time to learn the song as it was hard to understand,' Ronnie told *Disc and Music Echo*. 'I love the record. It's completely different for me; it's more of a music thing than vocal.' In 1999, Ronnie told *Alternative Press*, 'The record was done to make me happy, and it did. It might not have been made for the right reasons, but it's a good record.' David Bowie agreed, telling Radio 1 listeners that the recording was 'absolutely incredible'.[16]

Similarly impressed by the recording, John Lennon asked Phil Spector in 1971 to replicate the mandolin part – played in double time – on 'Try Some Buy Some' with acoustic guitars for The Plastic Ono Band Christmas record 'Happy Xmas (War Is Over)'. 'If you want to do some comparison shopping,' John told BBC Radio 1 presenter Andy Peebles, 'listen to the track that George made with Ronnie Spector, you'll hear the idea for the backing there, which is what we did.'[17]

---

15 Defined as a rapid slight variation in pitch, vibrato is a technique common in classical music but in popular music it is often besmirched as a substitute for purity of sound. In 1965, when Paul McCartney recorded 'Yesterday', he requested the accompanying string quartet to play without vibrato, thereby causing much consternation.

16 During the 1990s, David Bowie segued elements of 'Try Some Buy Some' into 'The Jean Genie' on his Sound + Vision tour. Recording the song in 2003 for the album *Reality*, Bowie said, 'For me it was a Ronnie Spector song. It never really occurred to me that I was actually covering a George Harrison song...it's rather fitting and quite lovely that it is an unwitting tribute to George.' George Harrison had died on 29 November 2001.

17 Four years later, and evidently still smitten with the track, John incorporated the

In 1973, George recorded his own version of 'Try Some Buy Some' for his second solo album, *Living in the Material World*. Using the original backing track, albeit slowed down, George sang of an awakening beyond the trappings of the material world: 'Not a thing did I have [...] Till I called on your love.' 'Even though the words are mundane,' he noted in *I Me Mine*, 'if the attitude is directed back at the source then it becomes more spiritual for me and has more meaning.'

All Things Must Pass

Enriched from a winter sojourn spent producing Jackie Lomax in Los Angeles and 'hanging out' with Bob Dylan and The Band in Woodstock, George Harrison returned to England in January 1969, renewed and full of optimism.[18] Armed with a clutch of new songs, he arrived at Twickenham Studios keen to share his new ideas. Over six days, spread across the calendar month, The Beatles would dedicate many hours to rehearsing and arranging 'All Things Must Pass'. Yet, for all the time and effort invested, the song was never recorded. However, what remains from the hours of audio archive is a fascinating insight into The Beatles' working practice and a clear suggestion of how one of George's finest compositions almost became a Beatles classic.

---

descending melody of 'Try Some Buy Some' into the string arrangement of his 1975 hit '#9 Dream'.

18 In 1966, The Band backed Bob Dylan on a world tour, and the following year they recorded a collection of songs together, later issued as *The Basement Tapes*. In 1968, The Band recorded the influential album *Music from Big Pink*.

Introducing the song on 3 January, George played through 'All Things Must Pass' on the electric guitar and encouraged Ringo to add a basic rhythm. 'Because there's no solo or anything complicated,' George explained. 'It's purely just rhythmical and vocal.' Leaving John to set up a Lowrey organ, George called out the chord changes. 'Just play it through,' Paul suggests, 'and I'll try and follow you.' 'What key's it in?' John asks. 'E,' George replies. Attempting a run-though, George stops mid-song, aware that John is struggling to keep up. 'Maybe you should just play it a few times on the guitar so you know where the changes are,' George suggests. 'What does it do all the time?' John asks. George demonstrates the sequence of rising chords, and at first John picks out the notes but then again queries the key of the song. 'I know what it is until I do a chord...it's really A flat minor,' he says.

Having resolved the technicalities, they play through the song again, and Paul softly sings an octave harmony over the chorus as he feels his way into the arrangement. 'Really I should play this on acoustic guitar,' George says, thinking out aloud. 'Yes,' Paul replies. 'So how am I going to do that on the famous TV show?' he adds doubtfully, mindful of the fact that The Beatles are rehearsing for a live performance and not making a record. 'Do you fancy doing it just on your own with an acoustic?' Paul asks. 'That would work, but it's a bit of a thing for you to do.' Undecided, the rehearsal presses on, as John, Paul and Ringo familiarize themselves with the different segments of the song. Suddenly, there is an unexpected howl of feedback. 'Fuckin' hell!' George screams. 'Electric shocks! I just got a belt, man! Really,

I just got an electric shock!' 'If this boy dies,' Paul laughs, 'you're gonna cop it!'

'When I wrote "All Things Must Pass",' George commented in *I Me Mine*, 'I was trying to do a Robbie Robertson-Band sort of tune.' The ego-less approach of The Band – working as a collective, exploring ideas and swapping instruments until the right player was found for each song – had in the past few months greatly impressed George. 'There's some players who can play 10,000 notes a second but it doesn't mean anything,' he said in an interview for the *Classic Albums* series. 'I always thought Robbie [Robertson] was that type of guitarist, who was more concerned with the overall song and structure than his own personal prowess.'

Lyrically, George had appropriated verse from 'Prayers for Preparations – Homage to Lao Tse' from Timothy Leary's *Psychedelic Prayers after the Tao Te Ching* (1966) to inform the song's title and opening stanza:[19] 'A sunrise does not last all morning / a cloudburst does not last all day / all things pass.' Elaborating further, George told *Billboard* in 2000: 'I got [the title] from Richard Alpert/Baba Ram Dass. When you read of philosophy or spiritual things, it's a pretty widely used phrase. It was written in Woodstock trying to capture the "religious" and "country feel" of "The Weight". When I heard that song in my head I always heard Levon Helm singing it!'[20]

---

19 George also used the works of Tao, as collected in *Lamps of Fire: From the Scriptures and Wisdom of the World*, edited by Juan Mascaró (1961), as the source for 'The Inner Light', recorded by The Beatles in 1968 and released as the B-side of 'Lady Madonna'.

20 Levon Helm was the drummer and one of the vocalists in The Band.

'We're pretending to be The Band for this one,' George gleefully informed The Beatles. 'After it says *being that grey* I'd like the backing group, The Raelettes,' George chuckles, referencing Ray Charles's backing group, 'to sing *all things must pass away* and I'll join in.' 'Okay, do that bit then,' Paul says, testing the idea. Then, instructing John, Paul adds, 'If John sings what you're singing and I sing harmony that will be The Raelettes!'

Distracted, John has discovered a pitch bender facility on the organ. George seizes the moment to tell everybody about Garth Hudson. 'This guy, who Paul is looking a bit like, in The Band is the organist. He's really fantastic.' Illustrating how the organ effect can be best employed, George tells John, 'It sounds a bit like a synthesiser because the notes bend.' Enthused, John experiments with the sound as Paul and George practise harmony ideas. 'It's one of those, it's easy...' Paul says as George interrupts him, 'It's just getting to know it.' Nodding, Paul continues, 'There's so much you can do in it because it's so easy.' When they play though the song again, John unexpectedly adds a high vocal in harmony with Paul. The impact of all the voices together is glorious and rousing, enriching the sound with a classic three-part Beatles swell of sound, until John breaks off with a typical oblique quip. 'In the beginning was the word. The word was scribble. And they scribbled.'

Keen to build on the positive atmosphere, Paul says, 'Go through it from the beginning again because we're sort of glossing over bits we're not getting right...and stop us whenever it doesn't go right.' 'It's sounding alright,' George says. 'Or if you can think of any riffs then try and sing them,' Paul adds. 'As long as you know the chords and the changes and you're not playing anything wrong it's fine,' George qualifies. 'It's just a matter of the more you know it the more you can feel how to do it.'

'Just to get it,' Paul proposes, adopting a pragmatic approach, 'do everything really mechanical and then we can get it all good after that.' At the end of the second chorus, Paul stops to address a mistake. 'Okay. Now there's where it goes, isn't it? Just tell us what you're doing there because I expected you to go...' Illustrating his point, Paul sings an alternative chorus melody, provoking a wry observation from John, 'It's getting like...gospel,' he says. Across further three-part harmonies, Paul tries interjecting 'all things must pass' over the verse, inviting more comparison from John. 'It sounds like...' 'The Chambers Sisters,' Paul fills in.[21] 'Yeah,' John agrees. 'It's a hell of a long breath.' 'That idea would be good if you carry it on where I come in,' George says, 'then you can get a quick breath.'

Working in short bursts, The Beatles jump from one song to another and, despite the seemingly ad-hoc approach to rehearsing, George is clearly pleased with the progress and the effortless collaborative ease which begins to shape 'All Things Must Pass'. The following week, further improvements and modifications help to refine the song both instrumentally and structurally. With the band relocated to Savile Row, almost three weeks after last working on the song, Paul sings the opening line, 'Sunlight doesn't last all morning'.

---

21 This is likely a reference to the American gospel quartet The Chambers Brothers, whose psychedelic 'Time Has Come Today' was a landmark Billboard hit in 1968.

On the second line, John takes over: 'A cloudburst doesn't last all day'. 'That's it!' says George admiringly. 'Yes!' John replies, as all three vocalists harmonize on the concluding and prescient lyric, 'It's not always going to be this way'.[22]

---

22 When George recorded 'All Things Must Pass' a year later, the verse ended 'It's not always going to be this grey.'

9. Side Four: Starr

After The Beatles split in April 1970, the prospect of Ringo Starr becoming a successful solo artist was at best questionable and, in reality, improbable. Ringo was first and foremost a drummer. And although most Beatle albums since 1963 had featured a song with Ringo as a vocalist,[1] the motivation for their inclusion was essentially a matter of novelty rather than artistic merit. After claiming his first songwriting acknowledgement in 1965 for 'What Goes On' – featured on *Rubber Soul* and credited to Lennon–McCartney–Starkey – Ringo was asked at a press conference at Capitol Records Tower in Los Angeles in August 1966 how much he had contributed to the song's writing. 'About five words,' he

---

1 'Boys' (*Please, Please Me*, 1963), 'I Wanna Be Your Man' (*With The Beatles*, 1963), 'Honey Don't' (*Beatles for Sale*, 1964), 'Act Naturally' (*Help!*, 1965), 'What Goes On' (*Rubber Soul*, 1965), 'Yellow Submarine' (*Revolver*, 1966; *Yellow Submarine*, 1969), 'With a Little Help from My Friends' (*Sgt. Pepper*, 1967), 'Don't Pass Me By' and 'Good Night' (*The Beatles*, 1968), 'Octopus's Garden' (*Abbey Road*, 1969). Ringo did not feature as a lead vocalist on *A Hard Day's Night* (1964) or *Let It Be* (1970). In 1967, 'Flying' – an instrumental track recorded for the *Magical Mystery Tour* EP – was credited to Lennon–McCartney–Harrison–Starr.

Opposite: Ringo attending the premiere of *The Godfather* in London, 23 August 1972.

said, adding drolly, 'And I haven't done a thing since.'

Two years later – in July 1968 – Ringo recorded his first solo composition for The Beatles' 'White Album'. 'I wrote "Don't Pass Me By" when I was sitting round at home,' Ringo told *Anthology*:

> I only play three chords. I was fiddling with the piano – I just bang away – and then if a melody comes and some words, I just have to keep going. That's how it happened: I was just sitting at home alone and 'Don't Pass Me By' arrived. We played it with a country attitude. It was great to get my first song down, one that I had written. It was a very exciting time for me and everyone was really helpful.

In fact, Ringo had written 'Don't Pass Me By' six years earlier. After joining The Beatles in August 1962, he played the song to John, Paul and George only for it to be greeted with mild hysterics and denounced as a rewrite of a Jerry Lee Lewis B-side. Two years later, in the course of a Beatles seven-day tour of New Zealand, John and Paul sang a verse of 'Don't Pass Me By' on a local radio interview. 'It was going to be a country and western,' Ringo explained, 'but Paul and John singing it with that blues feeling, knocked me out.' A month later, on 14 July 1964, presenter Brian Matthew asked Ringo on the inaugural edition of the BBC Radio music programme *Top Gear* how his songwriting 'was coming along'. 'I've written a good one,' Ringo says, 'but no one seems to want to record it.' 'No!' George interjects. 'Oh, Paul may record one,' Ringo qualifies, much to Paul's horror. 'NO!' he shrieks. 'YES! PAUL!' Ringo insists. 'YOU PROMISED!'

'Okay,' Paul laughs. 'The thing is I was doing the tune for you to sing.' Regaining his composure, Ringo continues, 'No, I don't want to sing it. You sing it.' At which point, Paul croons in a cod-American accent, 'Don't pass me by, don't make me cry, don't make me blue, baby', adding, 'It's sensational!' Impressed, Matthew countered, 'He's the Dylan Thomas of Liverpool!'

Recorded on 22 July 1968 – under the working title 'Ringo's Tune' and then 'This Is Some Friendly' – 'Don't Pass Me By' began with a classical score. 'It was for John that I did an off-the-wall introduction because we hadn't a clue what to do with Ringo's song,' George Martin said. 'In the event, the intro was too bizarre for us to use and the score was scrapped.' Asked by the BBCs Kenny Everett during the session what he thought of Ringo's song, John joked, 'I think it's the most wonderful thing I've ever heard since Nilsson's "River Deep, Mountain Dew."'

The following year, Ringo added a second composition to his catalogue, 'Octopus's Garden', featured on The Beatles last recorded album, *Abbey Road*. 'It's lovely,' George said upon its release.[2] 'I think it's a really great song because on the surface, it's just like a daft kid's song, but the lyrics are great.' Then, considering the lyrics, George added an unexpected level of his subterranean analysis. 'For me, I find very deep meaning in the lyrics, which Ringo probably doesn't

---

2 'Octopus's Garden' was introduced to The Beatles in January 1969 at Twickenham where George helped Ringo to write the song. In May 2008, Ringo told Dave Stewart on the HBO programme *Off the Record*: 'I was great at a verse and a chorus, or two verses and a chorus. I could never, like, finish them. [George] would round them off for me. I would give them to him and he'd put in the passing chords and there would be, like, ten chords and I'd be like a genius!'

see, but all the thing like *resting our head on the sea bed* and *we'll be warm beneath the storm* which is really great. Because it's like this level is a storm, and if you get sort of deep in your consciousness, it's very peaceful. So Ringo's writing his cosmic songs without noticing.'

In 2006, 'Octopus's Garden' formed part of Cirque du Soleil's theatrical production *Love* augmented by an orchestral score lifted from 'Good Night', a song originally written by John for Ringo to sing on the 'White Album'. Alongside two other recordings, 'Yellow Submarine' (1966) and 'With a Little Help from My Friends' (1967) – both sung by Ringo – the short vignette was recognition of an

Ringo with George Martin filming the television tribute show *With a Little Help from My Friends*, Leeds, 14 December 1969.

enduring public affection for Ringo's idiosyncratic singing style. Yet, as characterful and charming as his voice was, Ringo was manifestly a musician – and one of the world's greatest drummers.

Being left-handed, Ringo played drums with a 'reverse' stroke enriching many Beatle recordings with a distinct and unusual signature. From the thunderous beat in 'Rain' or the battalion rolls on 'Strawberry Fields Forever', Ringo's rhythmic contribution never competed for attention. Rather the generosity of his playing enabled songs to breathe, allowing space for melody and arrangements to come to the fore. Capable when necessary of grounding a rhythm with a solid backbeat, Ringo's unique style was more often felt in the sensitive and inventive use of toms and cymbals. It can be heard across countless Beatles records from 'In My Life' and 'Hello Goodbye' to 'A Day in the Life' and 'Something'. The isolated drum track on the *Abbey Road* medley – made available on the video game *The Beatles: Rock Band* – is a tour de force and lesson in creative musicianship. And, in 'The End' is a breath-taking masterclass of solo percussion, providing a link between the extended song sequence with duelling guitars and the album's dramatic finale.

As The Beatles contemplated their next move – and accepting that The Beatles would make another record after *Abbey Road* – Ringo was in need of songs. In late 1969, John, Paul and George between them had an abundance of material to spare. If they each offered one song to Ringo, his contribution to *Four Sides of The Beatles* would have been a revelation. Far from being a consolatory collection, Ringo's side of the record would be an assembly of rollicking up-tempo feel-good numbers stretching the artistic palette of the four-sided disc.

As it was, in October 1969 – a month after the release of *Abbey Road* – Ringo compiled an assortment of pre-war standards. 'I got an idea to record an album of songs that I had been brought up with,' Ringo said in *Anthology*. 'There was a pub on the album cover. My family used to go to that pub and all my mum's friends and the family would come back to our place, and at the parties everybody sang those songs. They were my first musical influences, so for want of a better idea I thought I'd do that.'

Enlisting the help of George Martin, Ringo compiled a list of songs to record and then sent out invitations to a handpicked selection of arrangers with the simple instruction, 'Just go in a studio with whatever musicians you want – and please send us the tapes.' Quincy Jones, Elmer Bernstein, Richard Perry, Oliver Nelson, Chico O'Farrill, Maurice Gibb, Ron Goodwin, Klaus Voormann, Les Reed, Johnnie Dankworth and Paul McCartney all responded positively to the request and over a six-month period worked with Ringo to record a set of 12 songs, ranging from Cole Porter's 'Night and Day' and Hoagy Carmichael and Mitchell Parish's 'Stardust' to 'Dream' by Johnny Mercer and 'Have I Told You Lately That I Love You?' by Scott Wiseman.

Released in March 1970, *Sentimental Journey* spent a healthy six weeks on the UK album charts, peaking at number seven, and reached 22 in the US. It received a mixed and sometimes peevish critical response, however. 'Ringo can't sing,' John Gabree wrote in *High Fidelity*. 'Some of the tiredest junk ever written.' '*Sentimental Journey* may be horrendous,' Greil Marcus wrote in *Rolling Stone*, 'but at least it's classy.' Assessing the album at the end of the year in conjunction with John, Paul and George's solo records, Geoffrey Cannon wrote in *The Guardian*:

> A couple of years back, reviewing the 'White Album',
> I suggested that the magnetism of The Beatles could be seen
> in terms of the temperament of each man corresponding with
> the four elements (Harrison, fire; Starr, earth; Lennon, water;
> McCartney, air), and also the four humours. So that, working
> together, they could work for any listener, whatever his nature
> and mood. It would follow that, separate, their temperament
> would clearly be very different each from the others.

Castigating *Sentimental Journey* as a 'bread gig', Cannon concluded, 'Listening to them all, all through, it's difficult to believe that they were made by four men who once formed a band together. I hear no important points of connection.'

Six months after the release of *Sentimental Journey*, Ringo recorded a second album in Nashville – *Beaucoups of Blues* – consisting of 12 country and western cover versions. It flopped. Nevertheless, throughout the 1970s, Ringo put out a clutch of successful albums. But, in truth, his ability to sustain a listener's attention over the length of an LP was left wanting. 'I used to wish that I could write songs like the others,' Ringo said in 1965. 'I've tried, but I just can't. I can get the words all right, but whenever I think of a tune and sing it to the others they always say, "Yeah, it sounds like such-a-thing."' However, in December 1973, when Ringo's eponymous third album – *Ringo* – crashed into the top ten on both sides of the Atlantic, charting higher than his own album, *Mind Games*, John Lennon sent Ringo a telegram: 'CONGRATULATIONS. HOW DARE YOU? AND PLEASE WRITE ME A HIT SONG.'

It Don't Come Easy

Announced with a shimmering cymbal and a descending guitar riff – played by George Harrison – 'It Don't Come Easy' revolved around a three-chord riff accented by staccato drum rolls and a chorus of voices singing the song title. Coming after the outmoded *Sentimental Journey*, Ringo Starr's debut solo single was an unexpected cheer of upbeat pop. Both urgent and uplifting, the record celebrated love: 'Peace, remember peace is how we make it / Here within your reach / If you're big enough to take it.'

Then known as 'You Gotta Pay Your Dues', the song was written before The Beatles' demise. George offered it to Badfinger, who at the time were riding high in the hit parade with a version of Paul's 'Come and Get It'. Wary of recording another Beatles-related tune, Badfinger passed up the opportunity. George then proposed the song to Ringo. A session was booked at Abbey Road, and over two days – 18–19 February 1970 – they recorded the song, now retitled 'It Don't Come Easy'. 'That was a gas,' Stephen Stills told Richard Williams of *Melody Maker*.[3]

---

3   Stephen Stills was a member of the folk rock supergroup Crosby, Stills, Nash & Young.

There was Ringo, me, George Harrison, and Klaus [Voormann], plus George Martin. George said the session was for Ringo's 'surprise single,' and I guess that could be right. Ringo came in with this little tune – that is, he sat down and played eight bars and said, 'That's it.' So we all made suggestions, like how about adding a bridge here, and playing this little intro, and this little tag, and it came along very nicely. I could see why George Martin has been so important to The Beatles particularly in the form of the songs, in the more sophisticated elements. I thought he was tremendous. I suggested this thing where we should use a major seventh chord, and it sounded strange at first and the other guys couldn't hear it but Martin could, and he made another suggestion which made it work perfectly.

On the second day of recording, with George unable to attend the session, Eric Clapton added electric guitar to the track. Dissatisfied with the finished mix, George booked Trident Studios and on 8 March began to rework the track. 'George put down a vocal to give Ringo an idea of the phrasing of the song so he could sing it better,' studio engineer Ken Scott explained to *Daytrippin'* in 2012:

With Ringo, his whole thing was that he was a great drummer, anything beyond that he needed help with. 'It Don't Come Easy' was the perfect example. Same way we had to put down a guide vocal for Ringo to learn how to sing 'Good Night' the way it was written [on the 'White Album']. George knew exactly what he wanted and we just got down to it. It was great seeing him as both the writer and working with other artists.

The demo recording of 'It Don't Come Easy', circulated online, makes for fascinating listening. Where Ringo's delivery is atonal and deadpan, George injects depth and wisdom. It brings to mind how Ringo's songs were enhanced on Beatle recordings: how, in 1963, Ringo's plucky vocal on 'I Wanna Be Your Man' was elevated in the chorus by John and Paul's screaming ad-libs; how, in 1967, the forlorn tone of Ringo's narration on 'With a Little Help from My Friends' was energized by John and Paul's memorable backing vocals; asking questions in the verses and harmonizing with Ringo over the chorus; and how, in 1969, the guitar riff establishing the rhythm track on 'Octopus's Garden' was complemented by animated piano chords and a bed of 'oohs' and 'ahs' all performed by Paul and George.

On 11 March 1970 – and then latterly in October – George added further overdubs on 'It Don't Come Easy', recording a blistering eight-bar guitar solo, a horn section and a chorus chant of *Hare Krishna*, courtesy of Tom Evans and Pete Ham of Badfinger and of Natalie Workman.[4] 'George Harrison really was quite a talented producer. He knew what he wanted, and he was a very different person when he wasn't on Beatles sessions,' Geoff Emerick wrote in *Here, There and Everywhere*, before adding with a touch of malice, 'Perhaps that was because he didn't have to

---

4   In 1971, Workman added backing vocals to John Lennon's 'Power to the People'.

contend with being second guessed by Paul, or John...or Yoko.'

Released in April 1971, 'It Don't Come Easy' somewhat unexpectedly became the most popular solo Beatles record of the year – outselling John's 'Power to the People', Paul's 'Another Day' and George's 'Bangla Desh' and going on to peak at number four on both the UK and Billboard charts. 'Undoubtedly one of the best, thumpin'est things the Starr man has ever done,' Alan Smith raved in the *New Musical Express*, 'That's a very strong hook he's got there, and George Harrison has given the record a fat, pumping backing full of guts and stuff.' Ending on an optimistic note, Smith predicted, 'One day he may even write a masterpiece.'

I'm the Greatest

In August 1963, Cassius Clay – rapping on his debut spoken-word album for Columbia Records – predicted the 'dismemberment' of Sonny Liston in the 1964 World Heavyweight Championship title fight, signing off with the swaggering declaration, 'I am the greatest!'[5] On 18 February 1964, on a day off during their first visit to America, The Beatles were invited to meet Clay at his training camp at the Fifth Street Gym, in Miami, Florida. Posed in the ring by photographer Harry Benson, John, Paul, George and Ringo were shot receiving a knock-out punch from their host. 'When Liston reads about The Beatles visiting me. He'll get so mad, I'll knock him out in three!' Clay enthused to a rabid press.

---

5   On 6 March 1964, Clay changed his name to Muhammad Ali.

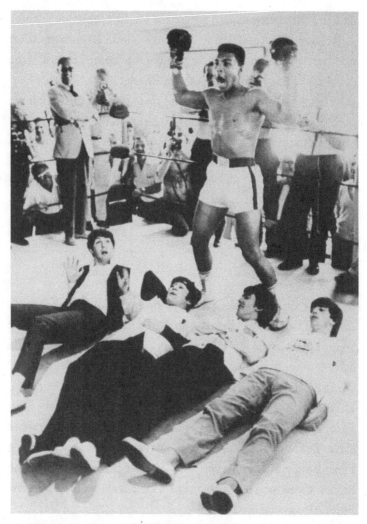

Cassius Clay in the ring with The Beatles two days after their second appearance on the *Ed Sullivan Show,* 18 February 1964.

Reflecting on the encounter in 1995, Ringo told *Anthology*, 'I sparred with Cassius Clay. I taught him everything he knew. That was a thrill, of course, and I was putting my money on Liston, so I *really* knew what was happening!' A week later, on 25 February 1964, Clay won his first world title, knocking Liston out in the seventh round[6] while The Beatles returned to England to act in their first feature film, *A Hard Day's Night*. Six years later, these two seemingly unrelated events prompted John Lennon to write a song that would become the opening track for Ringo Starr's third album, *Ringo*.

On 28 December 1970, *A Hard Day's Night* premiered on British television at 4.05pm on BBC One. Watching the film at home in Ascot, John reflected on his youth and nostalgically conjured up images of the past 'Way back home in Liverpool'. Accompanying himself on piano, John laid down a rudimentary recording, ending each of the three short verses – about boyhood, being a teenager, and manhood – with the pronouncement 'My mama told me, I was great.' 'It's the Muhammad Ali line,' John explained to *Playboy* in 1980. 'I couldn't sing it, but it was perfect for Ringo. He could say "I'm the greatest" and people wouldn't get upset. Whereas if I said "I'm the greatest," they'd all take it so seriously.'

Before giving the song to Ringo, John in fact attempted to record 'I Am the Greatest' in February 1971 during a session to record his fourth solo single, 'Power to the People'. While retaining its original simplicity, the expanded version included the telling line 'Yoko told

6 Having hedged their bets before the fight in 1964, three years later The Beatles included a wax model of Liston on the front cover of *Sgt. Pepper*. Ali did not feature.

me, I was great' and the outline of an as yet un-worded middle-eight section. However, despite recording two further self-penned albums – *Imagine* (1971) and *Some Time in New York City* (1972) – John did not commercially record the song.

In 1973, in need of material for a third solo album, Ringo turned to his former bandmates. Although they hadn't worked together since The Beatles split, Paul responded to Ringo's request and offered 'Six O'Clock' – co-written with Linda – with the illuminating chorus line 'I don't treat you like I should'. George contributed three songs – 'Sunshine Life (Sail Away Raymond), 'You and Me (Babe)' (co-written with Mal Evans) and 'Photograph' (co-written with Ringo) – and, dropping by the studio[7] on 10 March to hear the initial recordings, announced, 'I'm knocked out by what you've done.' Two days later, John arrived at the session with an updated version of 'I'm the Greatest'. Keen to record the song, John – playing piano – led Ringo and Klaus Voormann through numerous takes in an attempt to record a guide vocal and backing track.

Counting in the band, John begins to sing 'When I was a little boy' but during the chorus abruptly stops. 'That's corny,' he says. 'A bit slow isn't it?' Counting the band in for a second time, John again stops at the same point. 'No, no, no,' he says. 'It seems a different speed to me, does it to you?' Ignoring the disruption, Ringo and Voormann play on, but again John is not satisfied. 'Okay,' he says, halting the rhythm section. 'Let's go,' he directs but, with the tempo still at odds, soon snaps, 'It's changing speed.' '1, 2, 3, 4,' he pronounces assertively.

---

7   Sunset Sound Recorders Studios, Los Angeles, California.

Two bars in, John loses his patience. 'No,' he shouts, determined to get the groove right. Adopting a slower pace, the band successfully reaches the middle passage of the song, and John, now relaxing into his performance, sings with a gruff timbre, 'Yes, I'm Billy Shears have been for all those years.' 'Shit hot!' he laughs. 'Let's do another one! Okay boys, this is it!'

Explaining what happened next, producer, Richard Perry – in 1982 – told the authors of *The Record Producer*: 'The song wasn't quite complete...Then the phone rang. It was George [Harrison], who said, "I hear there's a track going down. Is it okay if I come down?"' Turning to John, the response was unequivocal. 'Hell, yes!' John beamed. 'Tell him to get down here and help me finish this bridge.' Soon after, George arrived and 'without saying a word joined in', much to Perry's delight: 'There was The Beatles' magic unfolding right before my eyes!'

'We were like big girls again,' Ringo told Bill Minkin. 'We were all looking at each other smiling. We were just smiling while we were playing. It was nice.'

In fact, the session marked the first occasion John, George and Ringo had been in a recording studio together since Wednesday, 20 August 1969, when all four Beatles oversaw the editing of 'I Want You (She's So Heavy)' for their last album, *Abbey Road*. Although The Beatles it was not, the release of *Ringo* – on 2 November 1973 – saw a reunited John, Paul, George and Ringo on a single disc. The album opened with 'I Am the Greatest', and Ringo singing the poignant lyric 'I was in the greatest show on earth'.

Early 1970

Across four verses in 'Early 1970', Ringo surmises the domestic lifestyle of The Beatles at the start of the new decade: John 'laying in bed, watching TV' with his Japanese 'mama'; Paul on his farm among the sheep and his 'brand new wife and a family'; the 'long-haired' George in his 'forty acre house...in the garden picking daisies for his soup'; 'And when I go to town', Ringo concludes, 'I wanna see all three.' 'I keep looking around and thinking where are they?' Ringo told *Look* magazine in February 1970. 'What are they doing? When will they come back and talk to me?' Two months later, Ringo had his answer when Paul quit The Beatles.

On 3 October 1970, during a Plastic Ono Band session at Abbey Road, John, Ringo and Klaus Voormann improvised a backing track, with the working title 'When I Come to Town'.[8] Eager to develop the idea, Ringo booked a recording studio in New York and enlisted the help of George. By coincidence, John and Paul were both in town, and with the future of The Beatles still uncertain, John invited Paul to the session. 'The meet was bait,' John revealed to authors Peter McCabe and Robert Schonfeld in September 1971. 'Paul would have forfeited his right to split by joining us again. We tried to con him into recording with us. Allen [Klein] came up with this plan. He said, "Just ring Paul, and say, "We're recording next Friday, are you coming?"'"

On 12 December, responding to an overactive rumour mill, the *New Musical Express* announced that 'The Beatles are said

---

8   Sometimes identified as 'When Four Knights Come to Town'.

to be closer [to re-forming] than at any time for the last eighteen months.' 'It got round that we were recording together again because EMI heard that The Beatles had booked recording time,' John commented. 'But Paul would never, never do it, for anything, and now I would never do it.' Optimistically, George remarked, 'Stranger things have happened!'

In John and Paul's absence, Ringo recorded 'Early 1970' with George on board playing a distinctive fuzz-tone, bottleneck lead guitar line. Charming and unassuming, 'Early 1970' was carried by subtle key changes, tempo shifts, a bluesy bar-room piano and Ringo's infectious deadpan delivery. But by the fourth verse, Ringo concedes his musical shortcomings – 'I play guitar, A, D, E,' he sings. 'I don't play bass 'cause that's too hard for me. / I play the piano if it's in C.' Correspondingly, each line ends with a four-bar solo played by the associated instrument. It was a device that Roxy Music would similarly employ in 1972 on 'Re-make/Re-model', the opening track of their eponymously titled debut album. In turn, each member of the band punctuates a four-bar silence with a musical homage: Phil Manzanera, the guitar figure from Eddie Cochran's 'C'mon Everybody'; Graham Simpson, the bass riff from The Beatles' 'Day Tripper'; and Andy Mackay, a screeching saxophone motif from 'Ride of the Valkyries'.

It is difficult to resist the temptation and speculate how each Beatle would have filled the space on 'Early 1970'. Would John have played a snatch of Buddy Holly's 'That'll Be the Day' as a tribute to his mother, Julia, who taught him the song on the banjo?[9] Perhaps Paul would have

9   Recorded by The Quarry Men on 12 July 1958 by John (guitar/vocals), Paul (guitar/vocals), George (guitar), John Lowe (piano) and Colin Hanton (drums).

opted for the riff from his favourite Eddie Cochran song, 'Twenty Flight Rock', which he played to John when they first met at the Woolton garden fete on 6 July 1957. And, in keeping with the thematic link, would George have played the lead line of 'Raunchy', the song with which he ingratiated himself to John on the upper deck of the school bus on 6 February 1958, assuring his place in The Beatles.[10]

In the event, when 'Early 1970' was released on 9 April 1971 – as the B-side of 'It Don't Come Easy' – it inauspiciously marked the first anniversary of Paul quitting The Beatles.

Coochy-Coochy

'It all came together because I sent my car to pick up Pete Drake at the airport when he came in to record with George,' Ringo told the *Nashville Scene* in 2008. 'He noticed I had a lot of country music in my car. Everyone always knew I liked country music.'

Drake was a highly respected Nashville steel-guitar player who had played on Bob Dylan's albums *Nashville Skyline* and *John Wesley Harding*. However, his knowledge of pop music was non-existent, as he told *Guitar Player* in 1973. 'One day my secretary buzzed me and said, "George Harrison wants you on the phone." I said, "Well, where's he from?" She said, "London." And I said, "Well, what company's he with?" She said, "The Beatles." The name just didn't ring any bells – well, I'm just a hillbilly. Anyway, I ended up going to London for a week where we did the album *All Things Must Pass*.'

---

10 Recorded by Bill Justis in 1957.

Striking up a friendship over a shared passion for country music, Ringo asked Drake if he would produce an album for him. 'I was trying to get it together over here, in Britain, and fly in twelve guys from Nashville,' Ringo explained. 'I was talking to Pete and he said, "Look here, son, why don't you come to Nashville? I'll get it together in a week." I said, "Come on, you can't get an album together in a week, it's impossible!" He said, "But Dylan's only took two days!" I said, "Okay, you go back and fix it up and I'll fly out a few days later."'

Arriving in Nashville in late June 1970, Ringo recorded a selection of newly written country and western songs over three days, backed by an array of session musicians. D J Fontana recalled a degree of scepticism, as he told Tim Ghianni of the *Nashville Scene* in 2008.[11] 'We were thinking he was going to be a jerk. I mean, The Beatles, the No. 1 act in the world. This guy's got all these big monster records. But he came here and it was, "Whatever you guys want to do, let's do it. You guys play the way you've been playing and I'll try to catch up.'

'We did the album in two nights,' Ringo marvelled. 'I was only there three days recording. I'd learn five songs in the morning and I'd go and record five songs that night. It was really good.' Described as a 'pretty typical' Nashville recording, much admired studio guitar player Charlie Daniels added, 'It was not a Beatles-type leisurely session. It was work.'[12] At eight o'clock on the final evening, and revelling in the productive atmosphere, Ringo introduced a new

11 As a drummer, Fontana cut over 400 records with Elvis Presley between 1954 and 1968.

12 On 11 February 1962, The Beatles recorded ten new songs for their debut album, *Please Please Me*, in little more than 12 hours.

composition, 'Coochy-Coochy'. 'I wanted to play guitar because Pete had bought George and me guitars as gifts,' Ringo said. 'So I was playing this incredible Harmony guitar and I went to this band of Nashville professionals and said, "I've written this song and it's in E." Only E – it didn't go anywhere.' The song was conceived as a simple ditty: Ringo sings of having 'everything that I ever wanted' and yet, despite both 'waiting' and travelling 'all over', in the chorus he asks, in an exasperated tone, 'Where are you, / my coochy coochy coochy coochy, coo?'

In the *Oxford English Dictionary* 'coochy' is a term used to elicit a smile or laughter from a baby, especially in combination with tickling. However, in American street slang, 'coochy' is a vagina, possibly derived from 'hoochie coochie', a term used in the nineteenth century to describe a sexually provocative belly dance. Perhaps ignorant of this cruder definition, the musicians recorded a 28-minute version of 'Coochy-Coochy'.[13] But Ringo was not satisfied, and a week later oversaw a new edit of the song combining two previous takes – an act reminiscent of John Lennon's request to George Martin in December 1966 to splice together two versions of 'Strawberry Fields Forever' recorded in different keys and different tempos.

Discussing the backing track, D J Fontana said of the skipping country rhythm:

> You couldn't pry Ringo off the beat if you tried. People say
> "He don't do a lot." Well, he don't have to do a lot. What

---

13 Some accounts suggest, somewhat contradictorily, that the song took over 100 takes to complete.

amazed me, he never varied from that tempo. He had the greatest conception of tempo I've ever heard in my life. I have never heard anybody play that steady. He was the glue for The Beatles. He put it together for them. That's what they needed. That's the whole secret of drumming. If you wanna do something fancy, go ahead and do it. If not, just play the beat.

'It was really fantastic,' Pete Drake raved in *Guitar Player*. 'It was good for Nashville and I really wanted Nashville to get credit for it. Those guys, Ringo and George Harrison, really dig country music. And they're fine people too, just out of sight.'

Country music had always been a key element of The Beatles' sound and can be traced back to a teenage John Lennon seeing merchant seamen – commonly known as 'Cunard Yanks' – trading cowboy clothing at the Liverpool docks in the 1950s. Indeed, as Pete Shotton noted in *John Lennon: In My Life*, the manager of The Quarry Men, Nigel Whaley, had 50 business cards printed bearing the inscription 'Country. Western. Rock 'n' Roll. Skiffle'. Inspired to buy his first guitar after seeing a photograph of the country and western singer Slim Whitman, George often quoted the formative musical influence in his playing, heard in songs such as 'I Don't Want to Spoil the Party' and, as John revealed in 1964, 'I Feel Fine': 'George and I play the same bit on guitar together,' John said. 'That's the bit that'll set your feet a-tapping, as the reviews say. I suppose it has a bit of a country and western feel about it, but then so have a lot of our songs.' Referencing 'I'm a Loser' and 'Nowhere Man', Paul told Barry Miles in 1995, 'We used to listen to quite a lot of country and western songs and they are all about sadness and *I lost my truck*.' Evolving from the home-grown Merseybeat style, Ringo would also sing lead vocals on two country and western-influenced Beatles songs: a cover of Buck Owen's 'Act Naturally' (*Help!*) and 'What Goes On' (*Rubber Soul*), both released in 1965. Asked, in the same year, at a press conference at the Atlanta Stadium, Georgia, if The Beatles had any plans to record in the home of country and western, Ringo replied, 'I do like country and western, but we have no plans of recording in Nashville.'

Released in the US in October 1970 – as the B-side of Ringo's debut solo single, 'Beaucoups of Blues' – 'Coochy-Coochy' bombed, making no notable impact on either the charts or the buying public. Nevertheless, it was not to be Ringo's last involvement with the record, as singer-songwriter Ray Wylie Hubbard explained to the *Riverfront Times* in 2012:

> I ended up going to Ringo's house in Beverly Hills and I told him I really liked his songwriting. He said, 'What do you mean? Nobody thinks of me as a songwriter.' I told him one of my favourites was 'Coochy-Coochy' and that I was thinking about cutting it. He said, 'I'd like to hear that!' So we cut it and sent a copy to him. He called and said he 'loved it' and 'wanted to play on it but the drums are so good, maybe I'll just sing and play shaker.' And that's what he did. He even double tracked his vocals like The Beatles used to do. So what you hear is what he heard when I sent it to him, but with a fucking Beatle on it! It was a real thrill.

When Every Song Is Sung

The story of 'When Every Song Is Sung' – written by George Harrison and recorded by Ringo Starr in 1976 – is a fascinating tale of frustration, disappointment and eventual threats of legal action. The story begins in 1970 with the writing of the song. 'I got the chord sequence,' George wrote in *I Me Mine*, 'and *when every song is sung* were the first words to come out of my mouth and it developed from there. I tried several times to record it: Ronnie Spector had a go at it, Cilla Black, Leon Russell and his wife Mary, and in the end Ringo.'

The song was recorded during sessions for *All Things Must Pass*, and a six-minute outtake reveals George exploring a possible arrangement of the song – then titled 'Whenever' – tentatively backed by a rhythm section and a mournful trumpet accompaniment. But, despite its haunting quality, the song was not included on the subsequent triple-album release. Then, in December 1970, rejuvenated from a summer top-ten hit with a cover version of The Beatles' 'Something' and making a welcome return to the UK charts after a seven-year absence, Shirley Bassey told Phil Symes of *Disc and Music Echo*, 'It would be lovely if [George] wrote a song for me; I think we're a great combination. Like Burt Bacharach and Dionne Warwick it could be Shirley and George.'[14]

Responding to the article, George noted, 'I thought ['Whenever'] would be a good one for her.' United Artists, Bassey's record label, disagreed and, overlooking George's suggestion, opted for another

---

14 Bassey simultaneously celebrated success with a solo album, *Something*, titled in honour of George's song.

Beatles song, 'Fool on the Hill', instead.[15] Undeterred, George included 'Whenever' among a batch of six songs – alongside 'Try Some, Buy Some', 'Love Me La-Di-Day', 'Tandoori Chicken' and 'You' – intended for Ronnie Spector's proposed comeback album in 1971. When neither the song nor the album materialized, George offered 'Whenever' to Cilla Black.

Recorded in August 1972, Black's version of the song now retitled 'I'll Still Love You (When Every Song Is Sung)' featured an all-star line-up of Ringo on drums, Klaus Voormann on bass, Eric Clapton on guitar and George producing. 'George phoned me up and said I've written this song for you,' Black recounted on her website in 2003. 'I was doing a summer season at the time in Blackpool. I came down on the Sunday and we all went into Apple studios and it was really nice. Then we went our separate ways and I never heard anything more about it.' Two years later, Black re-recorded the track with producer David Mackay, but 'even then', Black said, 'it didn't have the magic it deserved. It should have had a "Yesterday" type arrangement.'

By 1976, Ringo was enjoying great artistic success, having secured seven straight top-ten singles on the Billboard chart, including the number-one smash 'Photograph'. Choosing songs for a fifth studio album – *Ringo's Rotogravure* – Ringo turned to George. 'I asked him to write a song,' Ringo told the *New Musical Express*. 'But there was an old one of his – "When Every Song Is Sung" – that was never released by anybody that I always loved. I was on the session when it was recorded so in the end I asked him if, instead of writing one,

---

15 The song was written by Paul McCartney and included on the *Magical Mystery Tour* EP. Bassey's version reached number 48 and stayed in the chart for one week.

could I have that old one? He said fine; it saved him a job.'

Recorded in Los Angeles, Ringo's version of 'I'll Still Love You' retained all its earlier majestic fineness and was supplemented by a soaring guitar solo played by Lon Van Eaton, one of the first acts to sign to Apple Records. Further enhanced by a dramatic orchestral arrangement and an ARP String Ensemble, overdubbed by producer Arif Mardin, the track rested on Ringo's ability to carry a grandiose backing. 'Singing with the boys used to be easy because John used to take me through the lyric,' Ringo told Philip Norman of the *Sunday Times* in 1976. 'I'd stand there, thinking I was Stevie Wonder: then I'd go in the control box and find out I was Bing Crosby. I've got a lot more confident, but I can still feel it shaking in here [pulling on his Adam's apple]. I've got the range of the common housewife.'

Unimpressed with the finished recording, George sensationally threatened to sue Ringo if the track was ever released. They agreed on an out of court settlement, but the incident was nevertheless not forgotten. A decade later, when both George and Ringo appeared as guests on *Aspel & Company* in 1988, the issue was unexpectedly raised in front of a live television audience. After reminiscing about their days in The Beatles, Michael Aspel asked his guests, 'What makes you cross with each other now?' Seizing the initiative, Ringo answered, 'The last time we were cross was when George was suing me.' Then, miming holding a receiver in his left hand, Ringo re-enacted a telephone call between them: "'I'm going to sue you." "Now, come on George." "No, I'm going to sue you because I don't like what you've done."' Dressed in a grey suit, black shirt and matching tie, George sat with his head in his hand and attempted to laugh off the anecdote. Unperturbed, Ringo, wearing a pair of dark sunglasses, finished his story, 'because [George] wrote this song and I had it mixed by somebody else. He didn't like the mix so he was going to sue me. In the end I said, "Sue me if you want but I'll always love you."'

Suicide

'Stand up, Daisy!' John shouts as Paul finishes playing 'Don't Let the Sun Catch You Crying' – a hit for Gerry and the Pacemakers in 1964. It is Sunday, 26 January 1969 and The Beatles are at Apple for a sixth consecutive day of recording, sitting around drinking coffee and eating a round of morning toast. Reading the weekly music papers, John reacts to an eye-catching feature. 'Has anybody heard the Motherfuckers? This American group?' 'Oh, really!' George asks. 'Yeah, the Motherfuckers,' John repeats. 'What a thing to give yourself; you know you're never gonna get in *Billboard*. If they get a number one, imagine it: "Number One this week is the Motherfuckers followed by Engelbert Humperdinck."' As the banter subsides, Paul launches into a burlesque-flavoured melody, singing 'if when she tries to run away'. Familiar with the song, John injects a harmony and quips, 'Stand up, baby.' Playing a simple 4/4 rhythm, Ringo joins in as Paul picks out a flourish of jazzy notes on the top end of the piano. Fifty seconds later the improvisation peters out and the only known Beatles version of 'Suicide' comes to an unceremonious end.

Written in 1956, when Paul was living at home at 20 Forthlin Road, 'Suicide' was an unusual song for a 13-year-old boy to write. 'Rock and roll was about to happen,' Paul explained to Mike Read on BBC

Radio 1. 'So I was still a little bit cabaret minded.' Lying in bed, half asleep, Paul hastily located a piece of paper and pencil – handily kept by his bedside for such moments – and scribbled out a stream of ad-hoc phrases running through his head: 'ruin I'd…doin' I'd…suicide.' 'The rhymes are painful,' Paul elaborated in conversation with Paul Du Noyer. 'I used to do it as a joke: [adopts cabaret crooner voice] *when she tries to* …"Good evening ladies 'n' gentlemen! Bop-bee-bop yeah! Welcome to Las Vegas!" That kind of thing. Like I'd do "Michelle": "Ello [adopts comic French accent] welcome to mah French clurb…" You had a few party pieces and "Suicide" was the Rat Pack one.'

Unmistakably owing a debt of gratitude to the show style of Frank Sinatra with its bouncing rhythm and slurred vowels, 'Suicide' told the tale of a girl 'under the thumb' always 'giving into her man'. An icon of the pre- and post-war age, Sinatra was a music and screen star who attracted an audience hysteria John and Paul could only dream of in the late 1950s. 'I had my Dad's old piano at home that I used to tinker about on when there was no-one in the house,' Paul told Paul Du Noyer. 'And my feelings were, then, that if you were ever going to be a songwriter, the height of it all was Sinatra. That would be the greatest stuff that you could do. So around that time I wrote "When I'm 64" and this other thing ["Suicide"], which I thought would be a bit Rat Pack, smoochy, with words like *when she tries to, uh-huh…* Boom! And stabs from the band.'

The Beatles' fondness for old-fashioned standards made 'Suicide' a compelling candidate for Ringo to record as the final track on the imagined *Four Sides of The Beatles*. In 1968, his lilting execution of 'Good Night', with its antiquated sonorous melody written by John and cinematic orchestration by George Martin, oozed sentimentality. Similarly, Ringo delivered Hoagy Carmichael and Mitchell Parish's standard 'Stardust', recorded a year later, with an assured timbre, accompanied by Paul's lavish arrangement, played by the George Martin Orchestra. Both 'Good Night' and 'Stardust' offer an enticing blueprint for 'Suicide' had The Beatles recorded it after the release of *Abbey Road*. Added to which, Ringo's side of the record would further be balanced by song contributions from each of The Beatles: 'I'm the Greatest' by John, 'Suicide' by Paul, and 'It Don't Come Easy' and 'When Every Song Is Sung', both by George. It is also worth noting that the four-sided disc would close with Ringo singing 'They call it suicide', its dark humour somewhat in contrast to the elegiac finale of *Abbey Road*: 'And in the end / The love you take / Is equal to the love you make.'

At this point in 1969, having now achieved worldwide recognition and unparalleled commercial success, The Beatles' writing catalogue came to the attention of Frank Sinatra. During an acclaimed Las Vegas residency, Sinatra described 'Something' – written by George Harrison – as 'one of the greatest love songs of the past fifty years'. 'He used to introduce it as his favourite Lennon/McCartney song,' Paul chafed in *Anthology*. 'Thanks Frank!' 'I'm more thrilled now than I was then,' George added, unimpressed. 'I wasn't really into Frank – he was the generation before me.' Nonetheless, when George recorded 'Far East Man', co-written with Ronnie Wood, in 1974, he dedicated it to the self-styled 'King of the Swingers'. 'This is for Frank Sinatra,' George said. 'We love you Frank and we hope you play this one at Caesars Palace on your next live album.'

Not to miss out on the group veneration, John made his own appeal to his childhood hero in 1980. 'I always imagined Sinatra singing ["Nobody Loves You When You're Down and Out"],' John told David Sheff. 'He could do a perfect job with it. Ya listenin', Frank? You need a song that isn't a piece of nothing. Here's one for you. The horn arrangement – everything's made for you. But don't ask me to produce it!' Such was his revered status among all four Beatles, a recording of 'Suicide' was an opportunity to pay a musical homage to Sinatra, much in the way as 'I'm Down' or 'Norwegian Wood (This Bird Has Flown)' had to Little Richard and Bob Dylan, respectively, in 1965.

In 1970, Paul included a nine-second snippet of 'Suicide' on *McCartney*, where it was heard crossfading out of the preceding instrumental track, 'Hot As Sun/Glasses'. Although the song was greatly truncated, its inclusion was sufficient for it to be mentioned in the album's accompanying press release, with appropriate succinctness: '...the end is a section of a song called SUICIDE – not yet completed'. But perhaps the best version of the song, suggesting how The Beatles might have recorded it, came four years later, when Paul revived 'Suicide' for the Wings documentary *One Hand Clapping*.

Filmed at Abbey Road in 1974, Paul performed 'Suicide' on the piano to its full length, complete with an exaggerated forties-style vocal delivery, playfully conjuring the spirit of Frank Sinatra. Shortly after, whether by design or accident, Paul received a request from Sinatra for a song. 'I spoke to him on the phone and told him about it. "Great, Paul, send it along." "Thank you, Frank." I sent it him and apparently he thought it was an almighty piss take. "No way!" he's supposed to have said to one of his people. "Is this guy having me on?"'

The Beatles at the Liverpool Docks, 20 February 1963.

10. **Extended Play**

'The items lined up on this EP have been designed to pass the audio spotlight very fairly from Beatle to Beatle, exposing four contrasting facets of the quartet's vocal and instrumental ingenuity.' In July 1963, these words, written by press officer Tony Barrow, introduced the first Beatles four-song extended play. 'At one end of the scale,' Barrow wrote, 'we have the all-action, all-raving rocker, "Twist and Shout"; at the other we have the more subdued mood of "A Taste of Honey".

Writing on the reverse of the record sleeve – which portrayed John, Paul, George and Ringo silhouetted against a grey sky, jumping jubilantly above the ruins of a London bombsite[1] – Barrow introduced the record-buying public to each of the performers' unique styles: John's 'wild' and 'compelling' interpretation' of the 'violently exciting' 'Twist and Shout'; easing the tension, Paul's 'clear, sturdy voice' turning 'A Taste of Honey' into a 'haunting piece of *atmosphere* balladeering'; on the flipside, George tempering his vocal delivery on 'Do You Want to Know a Secret' with an 'intriguing blend of warmth and wistfulness'; and for the finale, John and Paul's self-penned composition 'There's a Place' boosted 'with a fair amount of Ringo's percussive pressure'.

Between 1963 and 1967, The Beatles issued 12 further EPs, variously collating tracks from their studio albums, film soundtracks,

---

1   Photographed by Fiona Adams.

and, in the case of *Long Tall Sally* and *Magical Mystery Tour*, a set of previously unavailable recordings.[2] To give fans value for money, The Beatles' inviolable rule was not to issue singles already available on an album. 'You can't after the LP's been out,' John told *Top Gear* presenter Brian Matthew in 1964. 'A lot of people do,' Matthew replied. 'Well, in America they do…' Paul chipped in. 'Well, they're different over there, aren't they?' John jibed. 'In America they do that,' Paul qualified, 'but it's a bit of a drag. Yes, a drag, that!'[3]

A four-track EP, featuring one song from each Beatle, would act as a perfect introduction to this new imagined album, *Four Sides of The Beatles*. It is, of course, an irresistible opportunity to keep the dream of The Beatles alive just that little bit longer. All the same, I hope, as the reader, you find the inclusion of a bonus disc both credible and a natural home for four wonderful and original songs

With an abundance of material to select from, the choice of songs on the EP reflects four very different faces of The Beatles at the turn of the new decade. Exploring an overt form of songwriting self-

---

2   Released in June 1964, the *Long Tall Sally* EP featured: 'Long Tall Sally', 'I Call Your Name', 'Slow Down' and 'Matchbox'. *The Magical Mystery Tour* EP (December 1967) introduced five songs: 'Magical Mystery Tour', 'Your Mother Should Know', 'I Am the Walrus' (previously issued in November 1967 as the B-side of 'Hello Goodbye'), 'The Fool on the Hill', 'Flying' and 'Blue Jay Way'.

3   The Beatles issued 12 singles as standalone releases: 'From Me to You', 'She Loves You', 'I Want to Hold Your Hand', 'I Feel Fine', 'Paperback Writer', 'All You Need Is Love', 'Hello Goodbye', 'Lady Madonna', 'Hey Jude' and 'The Ballad of John and Yoko'. Additionally, 'Day Tripper' / 'We Can Work It Out', 'Yellow Submarine' / 'Eleanor Rigby', 'Penny Lane' / 'Strawberry Fields Forever' and 'Something' / 'Come Together' pioneered the concept of the double A-side single.

analysis, John's visceral description of withdrawal from heroin, 'Cold Turkey', is a brutal window into 'thirty-six hours' of a man 'rolling in pain'. Softening the edges, the Oedipally influenced tale of 'Teddy Boy', jealous of his mother 'finding herself a man', is draped with an innocent sweet melody by Paul. Perhaps foreseeing the fading days of The Beatles' existence, George delivers a seductive meditation on regret and breaking 'each other's hearts' in the epic 'Isn't It a Pity'. And Ringo brings the EP to a close by 'Taking a Trip to Carolina', keeping his journey strictly in the key of C.

Cold Turkey

In what is known as the 'Two Junkies' interview, recorded for Canadian television on 14 January 1969 at Twickenham Studios, John and Yoko are sitting on matching wooden chairs. Dressed in a brown mink jacket with a cigarette in hand, drinking tea from a cup and saucer, John looks visibly pale. 'I've forgotten what I was saying,' he slurs mid-answer. Laughing off the comment, Yoko defends John's absent-mindedness. 'We've just got up,' she says. Then, politely excusing himself from the interview, John promptly throws up off camera. 'The two of them were on heroin,' Paul acknowledged to Barry Miles in 1998. 'This was a fairly big shocker for us because we all thought we were far-out boys but we kind of understood that we'd never get quite that far out.'

The Beatles' taste for drugs had begun with Benzedrine and Preludin, back in the late 1950s. 'The only way to survive in Hamburg, to play eight hours a night, was to take pills,' John told *Rolling Stone* in

1970. 'I've always needed a drug to survive. The others, too, but I always had more, more pills, more of everything because I'm more crazy probably.' They occasionally experimented with other stimulants, but it wasn't until an infamous encounter with Bob Dylan on 28 August 1964 at the Delmonico Hotel, New York, that marijuana became a drug of choice within the group. Peter Brown recounted in *The Love You Make*:

> When Dylan offered a joint to the band, Brian [Epstein] and The Beatles looked at each other apprehensively. 'We've never smoked marijuana before,' Brian finally admitted. Dylan looked disbelievingly from face to face. 'But what about your song?' he asked. 'The one about getting high?' The Beatles were stupefied. 'Which song?' John managed to ask. Dylan said, 'You know...' and then he sang 'I get high, I get high.' John flushed with embarrassment. 'Those aren't the words,' he admitted. 'The words [to "I Want to Hold Your Hand"] are *I can't hide, I can't hide, I can't hide*.'[4]

A year later, in April 1965, John and George were both introduced to lysergic acid diethylamide (LSD), which, as George explained in *Anthology*, was soon sampled by the rest of the band. 'John and I had decided that Paul and Ringo had to have acid, because we couldn't relate to them anymore because acid had changed us so much.' Naturally, with an increased use of mind-altering chemicals the

---

4   In 1965, John would write 'It's Only Love' for *Help!* with the opening line, 'I get high when I see you go by'.

music also radically changed – from the marijuana-influenced 'Got to Get You into My Life' to the LSD references of 'Day Tripper' and 'Tomorrow Never Knows'. Then, in 1968, and perhaps predictably as John searched for greater highs, heroin entered the picture. Although his drug use was kept from public knowledge for many years, the morphine derivative was subtly alluded to in many of his songs, from 'I need a fix 'cause I'm going down' to 'The deeper you go the higher you fly'. Significantly, both these songs, 'Happiness Is a Warm Gun' and 'Everybody's Got Something to Hide Except Me and My Monkey', were written a year after Brian Epstein's death from an accidental overdose of sleeping pills. The 'clean-cut' presentation of The Beatles, which Epstein had assiduously promoted to the outside world, was now increasingly challenged by John in an attempt to free himself from the straitjacket of the group's public image.

On 9 September 1969, at a board meeting at Apple, John raised the subject of a new single. 'I went to the other Beatles and said, "Hey lads, I think I've just written a new single," 'But they all said, "Umm… arrr…well."' This had 'happened once before', John told *Melody Maker*, 'when I wanted to put "Revolution" out as a single, but "Hey Jude" went out instead…so I thought, "Bugger you I'll put it out myself."' Stark to the point of distressing, the new song bristled with unbridled honesty – 'Cold turkey has got me on the run.' 'I was just writing the experience I'd had of withdrawing from heroin,' John explained, 'and saying this is what I thought when I was withdrawing.'

John's and Yoko's battles with addiction were chronic and prolonged. Reflecting on The Plastic Ono Band performance in Toronto on 13 September 1969, John confessed to *Rolling Stone*, 'We were full of junk. I just threw up for hours till I went on. I nearly threw up in "Cold Turkey". I could hardly sing any of [the songs] I was so full of shit.' Performing in front of a paid audience for the first time in three years, John apprehensively announced, 'We've never done this number before...best of luck...it's called "Cold Turkey".' Reading the lyrics from a piece of paper held up by Yoko, John rattled through the song, elongating vowels 'Cold turk-eee has got meeee on the run', accompanied by the ad-hoc wailing of Yoko. 'Yeah, that,' John said, as the song petered out over an uninspired instrumental passage. Then, gesticulating to the audience, he added, 'Come on! Wake up.'

On 15 December, The Plastic Ono Band performed 'Cold Turkey' again at the Lyceum Ballroom, London, for a UNICEF benefit concert, this time in front of a huge backdrop boldly declaring 'War Is Over'. Standing stage left, dressed in a familiar all-white suit and shoulder-length hair, John's introduction was simple and to the point. 'We'd like to do a number. This song's about pain.' Extended over eight minutes, 'Cold Turkey' ebbed and flowed with John's teasing, gritty delivery backed by an ensemble including Eric Clapton – doubling the guitar riff reminiscent of the MC5's 'Kick Out the Jams' – and The Who's Keith Moon banging out a heavy tom-tom rhythm. Post-performance, John was jubilant. 'I thought it was fantastic. We were doing the show and George [Harrison] and Bonnie and Delaney, Billy Preston and all that crowd turned up.' Performing with him for the first since the Apple rooftop gig in January, George stood in the shadow of John playing a Gibson hard-top, dressed in a long overcoat, his face partly shaded beneath a checked cloth cap.

Live, 'Cold Turkey' was a far cry from the plainer demo version, recorded three months earlier when, if circumstances had been different, we might have witnessed Bob Dylan contributing to a Beatles record. On Monday, 1 September 1969, the day after an appearance at the Isle of Wight Festival,[5] Dylan returned with John and Yoko to Tittenhurst Park. 'He came over to our house with George when I had written "Cold Turkey",' John told Jann Wenner. 'I was trying to get him to record. We had just put him on piano for "Cold Turkey" to make a rough tape but his wife was pregnant or something and they left.'

Subsequently recording the song over three days – 25 and 28 September and 5 October – at Abbey Road and Trident Studios, with Ringo on drums, Klaus Voormann on bass and Eric Clapton on lead guitar, John presented a double-tracked vocal with quivering vibrato, clearly indebted to Yoko's unique quavering influence. Quickly packaged and released, 'Cold Turkey' entered the UK top 20 on 2 November, three places below 'Come Together' and in effect putting John in competition with The Beatles.[6] John told the *New Musical Express* on 13 December:

5   Bob Dylan played the Isle of Wight Festival on 31 August. Promoter Rikki Farr told *Q* magazine: 'We had been trying to convince The Beatles to get back together and play, but it never quite happened. We did have a kind of spontaneous superstar jam session in the afternoon at a mock Tudor house where Bob Dylan was staying. The Beatles came down to watch the show, but in the afternoon they all got together in the house and I saw on stage the most incredible super group: Dylan, The Beatles, Eric Clapton, Jackie Lomax all just jamming. Ginger Baker would get off the drum stool and Ringo would step in. Eric Clapton would take a solo, and then George Harrison would take the next one. It was amazing.'

6   'Cold Turkey' – credited to 'Lennon' – would peak at number 14 while 'Come Together' – credited to 'Lennon/McCartney' – would climb to number four.

You have to realize that there's a peculiar situation, in that if 'Cold Turkey' had the name Beatles on it, probably it would have been a No. 1. 'Cold Turkey' has got Ringo and me on it, and yet on half The Beatles' tracks off *Abbey Road* I'm not on, or half the tracks on [the 'White Album'] – and even way back. Sometimes there might be only two Beatles on a track. It's got to the situation where if we have the name 'Beatle' on it, it sells. So you get to think: What are we selling? Do they buy it because it's worth it or just because it says 'Beatles'? That's the drag.

After three weeks climbing the chart, 'Cold Turkey' dropped a place, prompting John to make an audacious political statement. On her first day at Apple, Diane Robertson, a 20-year-old secretary, was asked to type a letter to Her Majesty the Queen on Lennon's behalf. It read: 'Your majesty, I am returning this MBE in protest against Britain's involvement in this Nigeria-Biafra thing, against our support of America in Vietnam and against "Cold Turkey" slipping down the charts. With Love John Lennon of Bag.'[7]

---

7   Copies of the letter – written on Bag Productions notepaper – were sent to the Prime Minister and the Secretary of the Central Chancery. On 26 October 1965, The Beatles were honoured by the Queen for their unprecedented achievement in the history of world show business, In an interview for BBC Radio 4, on 25 November 1969, John told David Bellan that Brian Epstein had persuaded him to accept the award but that he had been considering returning it since learning about the My Lai massacre in Vietnam by American soldiers on 16 March 1968. Upon receipt of John's letter and MBE, a spokesman for Buckingham Palace responded, '[It's ironic] that he should return the medal, as the first M.B.E.s that were returned were from people protesting that Mr. Lennon and the other Beatles were given the award in the first place.'

Teddy Boy

Partly written in 1968 while on retreat in India, 'Teddy Boy' was a deceptively simple song that behind its overt acoustic ease demonstrated Paul McCartney's wily understanding of music. Principally set around four chords – D, A, A minor and E minor – the song seamlessly embraced a subtle shift from major to minor chords before modulating and repeating the cyclical trick in a second unrelated key. The practice of slipping between unexpected chords was a distinct feature of many of Paul's songs and played a key part in The Beatles' sound. Take, for example, the dramatic shift in 'Things We Said Today', from the album *A Hard Day's Night*, which abruptly lifts at the end of the second chorus, in A minor, to the wonderfully liberating middle section – 'Me, I'm just a lucky kind' – played in A major. Similarly, in 'Penny Lane' as the banker sits 'waiting for a trim' in B major, 'the fireman rushes in' over a mood-changing B minor drop.

Like 'Penny Lane', 'Teddy Boy' was a fictional story drawing on Paul's skill to write characters, like Desmond and Molly in 'Ob-La-Di-Ob-La-Da' or the lonely spinster Eleanor Rigby who was buried 'along with her name'. Wishing to please his mother by being 'good', 'Teddy Boy' is saddened by the loss of his 'soldier dad' and runs 'far away' when his mother finds herself 'another man'. Told over two verses, the tale is short and seemingly undeveloped. By contrast 'Rocky Racoon', written in the same year as 'Teddy Boy' and also formulated around four repeating chords, recounts the story of a young boy who lived 'somewhere in the black mountain hills of Dakota'. Over eight verses, Rocky hunts down his rival and, after a comic verse about 'his woman', variously called Magill, Lil or Nancy, loses out in a 'showdown' to the fast-shooting Daniel.

On 24 January 1969, Paul introduced 'Teddy Boy' to The Beatles as a work-in-progress, accompanying himself on acoustic guitar. 'Keep going,' engineer Glyn Johns encourages, 'it sounds great.' 'Okay,' Paul says, repeating the song until he reaches an impasse. Then searching for direction at the end of the second verse, Paul observes, 'It's nice, that key change.' 'What is it?' John asks. 'I forget what it is now,' Paul says. 'I had something going on there.' After a brief discussion to establish the next chord, Paul repeats the song with John tentatively picking out the melody: first on guitar, then whistling, and finally mimicking in a mock country tone 'take your partners do-si-doh hold them tight and don't let go and when you've got it – jump up.' 'That's one for consideration,' Paul says, unfazed. 'Do you remember that at one of Maharishi's lectures?' he adds. 'What?' John says. Paul sings, 'This is the story of a boy named Ted.' 'What did Maharishi say?' John asks, confused. 'No, I said it to you.' Paul clarifies. Still unsure, John asks, 'Writing it, then?' 'Yeah,' Paul says. 'Writing and telling you, "What do you think about that bit?"'

In 1996, a combination of two performances of 'Teddy Boy' were edited together and presented on *Anthology 3*. 'You can hear on it that the band wasn't very interested in it,' Paul commented. 'I don't know why. Maybe I hadn't finished it enough or something. Maybe it was just tension coming in. The bit I'd like to keep actually was John sort of making fun of it. He starts towards the end of it, going, "Grab your partners, do-si-doh," so we've kept that in. And while it was, in some way, indicative of friction, it was good-humoured friction.'

As the *Get Back* sessions drew to a close, The Beatles discussed outstanding songs for the upcoming show. '"Teddy"'s nice,' George says, 'but we haven't learnt it. It's just busking.' On 29 January – the day before the rooftop gig – The Beatles spent 20 minutes developing 'Teddy Boy'. With Ringo keeping a straight 'four-on-the-floor' beat and George picking out a guitar melody, Paul gave instructions for the necessary chord changes. 'It's like a full cycle,' he says to John, adding, 'You should do a bit more, like George is doing.' 'I just wanna know it,' John says. 'Yeah, okay,' Paul acknowledges. As the song begins to take shape, an intriguing backing vocal emerges, with John slurring a two-note 'da-da' over the verse prompting George to double its effect on guitar. 'That's as far as it's going to get unless I finish writing it,' Paul says, bringing the rehearsal to an end. Two days later, Michael Lindsay-Hogg included 'Teddy Boy' in a list of songs still to be recorded. 'I thought maybe we can come back after a week or something,' Paul says hopefully.

Passed over in 1969, and again in 1970 when Phil Spector made two stereo mixes of 'Teddy Boy' for *Let It Be*, Paul re-recorded the track for his solo album *McCartney*, by which point many of the ideas developed at Apple had been either forgotten or overlooked. Asked whether any of the tracks on the album had been originally written with The Beatles in mind, Paul answered, '"Teddy Boy" was for *Get Back* but something happened.'

Isn't It a Pity

'I've been thinking about all the tunes I've got and they're all slow-ish,' George says during a conversation with Paul on 3 January 1969. 'Yeah,' Paul sympathizes. 'Most of mine are too.' 'I've got that "Taxman Part Two: Taxman Revisited",' George continues. 'It should be very sad, with maybe a string or two.' Finding the chords on the guitar, George illustrates the song with a three-second burst: 'when you're smiling'. The exciting prospect of a sequel to 'Taxman', the stunning opening track on The Beatles' 1966 album, *Revolver*, is frustratingly not reviewed further. But three weeks later, on 25 January 1969, an ambiguous connection is made during a conversation at Apple between John and George. 'What's that?' John asks at the end of the day. 'It's one I wrote about three years ago,' George replies, picking out the melody of 'Isn't It a Pity' on an electric guitar. 'I think I sang it to you at the time.' 'It didn't impress me much,' John responds with laconic disinterest.

The following morning, chatting to Beatles roadie Mal Evans, George says, 'There's a nice song that I wrote…way back in the Fifties… about three years ago and I sung it to John and he said, "It's too much like fucking…" I don't know, but I thought it was good.' Lighting a cigarette and asking for a coffee, George then explains how, at the time, Reprieve Records were seeking out songs for Frank Sinatra to record. 'I was thinking, "That'd be nice, Sinatra singing one of my songs" so I went to see him. Sinatra doesn't sing anyway. He sings them all shit! He's great and everybody digs him but he just comes in after the band have learnt it, walks in, and does it in maybe two takes. So I thought,

"Fuck that! I'm not letting him sing it. I'm going to do it myself.'"
Picking up an acoustic guitar, George plays a beguiling version of
'Isn't It a Pity', wrapping his soft delivery around the cascading melody.
Talking over himself, George says, 'It can be any speed you want.' After
two verses, he stops and briefly plays a clipped, up-tempo rhythm to
demonstrate the song's versatility, but thinking better of it returns to
the smoother approach before ending the rendition with a mouthed
trumpet solo.

Asked in 2000, by *Billboard* editor-in-chief Timothy White
whether 'Isn't It a Pity' was intended as a song 'just for you', George
replied:

> No, I mean, this is the funny thing: imagine if The Beatles
> had gone on and on...well, maybe some of the songs I would
> probably only just got round to do now, you know with my
> quota that I was allowed! 'Isn't It a Pity' would just have been a
> Beatles song, wouldn't it? That could be said for each one of us:
> 'Imagine' would have been a Beatles song, but it was with John's
> songs. It just happened that The Beatles finished.

Probing for inspiration behind 'Isn't It a Pity', George explained
that it was 'just an observation of how society and myself were or are'.
Quoting the song's lyrics, he said:

> We take each other for granted, *forgetting to give back*. That was
> really all it was about. It's like love lost and love gained between
> fourteen-to-twenty year-olds. But I must explain: At the time

I was at Warner Bros and I wrote 'Blood from a Clone' [1981], they were having all these surveys out on the street to find out what was a hit record. And apparently, as I was told, a hit record is something that is about 'love gained or lost between fourteen-to-twenty year-olds,' or something really dumb like that. So that's why I wrote 'Isn't It a Pity': I thought, 'Oh, I'll get in on that!'

Despite the tongue-in-cheek timeline contradiction – writing a song in 1981 that had already been released in 1970 – George clarified his thinking in his memoir, *I Me Mine*: '"Isn't It a Pity" is about whenever a relationship hits a down point – instead of whatever other people do (like breaking each other's jaws) I wrote a song. It was a chance to realise that if I felt somebody had let *me* down, then there's a good chance *I* was letting someone else down. We all tend to *break each other's hearts*, taking and not giving back – *isn't it a pity*.'

Like many songs showcased during January 1969, The Beatles never recorded 'Isn't It a Pity'. But when George cut the track in June 1970 for his solo album *All Things Must Pass*, accompanied by Ringo on drums, he incorporated a knowing nod to his erstwhile bandmates. The song clocks in at over seven minutes, with the final three minutes building seductively, matched by a choral chant of 'Isn't it a pity?' until, nearing the finale, the distinctive vocal coda of 'Hey Jude' – 'na na na' – is prominently heard. Whether it was incorporated as a pointed comment implying 'Isn't It a Pity' belonged among the venerated ranks of Beatles classics or simply an improvised moment, George never stated. But, like the burst of 'She loves you, yeah, yeah, yeah' sung over the fading backing track of 'All You Need Is Love', the cross-pollination of past and present united The Beatles, whether they were together or alone.

In 1972, touched by the compassionate heart of the song, Nina Simone recorded an electrifying 11-minute version of 'Isn't It a Pity'. Breathing an emotional profundity into George's composition, Simone's reading invoked the desperation of the ongoing Vietnam War and the horrifying Civil Rights race struggles dominating the streets of America. Later, describing his own song 'The Answer's at the End', George would write that 'Simone's version of "Isn't It a Pity" influenced the mood.'

On 6 April 1992, at the Royal Albert Hall – his debut UK solo performance and a benefit for the Natural Law Party to promote Transcendental Meditation ahead of the 1992 General Election – George revisited many Beatle tracks, including 'Taxman', 'I Want to Tell You' and 'Old Brown Shoe' before encoring with 'Isn't It a Pity'. Responding to the explosive applause, George thanked the audience. 'It's really overwhelming,' he said, adding with touching candour, 'I'm always paranoid about whether people like me. I don't know.'

Taking a Trip to Carolina

What to do for Ringo? It was a question to challenge John, Paul and George at the beginning of each new Beatles record.

By 1969, Ringo had featured as a lead vocalist on only one single, 'Yellow Submarine' – two if you included 'Matchbox' from the 1964 EP *Long Tall Sally*. With the exception of three further songs – 'What Goes On', 'Don't Pass Me By' and 'Octopus's Garden' – Ringo's songwriting contribution to Beatle albums rested upon John and Paul, who tended to use Ringo as a buffer for their less commercial or novelty compositions. In 1968, a year before its inclusion on *Abbey Road*, Paul suggested that the dark tale of 'Maxwell's Silver Hammer' should be sung by Ringo. And the following year there was 'Carry That Weight', which Paul introduced to Ringo at Twickenham as a song that 'might interest you, like a story, a bit like "Act Naturally" where the tag line keeps coming up'.

Ever the optimist, Ringo arrived at Twickenham Studios on 3 January 1969 with two new ideas. Sitting down at the piano – left vacant after Paul's morning warm-up, practising 'Let It Be' – Ringo began to play a simple 12-bar blues in C major about taking a trip, rhyming 'ocean liner' with meeting a 'girl in Carolina', which was met with mild amusement. Paul's and George's attention is then lost to the morning papers. 'The True Story of The Beatles!' George reads. 'Accompanied by his current steady, American photographer Linda Eastman, Paul spent the December week in Portugal visiting The Beatles biographer, Hunter Davies.'

Conversation drifts to the music of The Band, and George tells

Ringo that their favourite track on the 'White Album' is 'Don't Pass Me By'. 'Are you going to write another?' Paul asks. 'Yes, I am,' Ringo says. 'He's a got a great one,' George chips in. 'Picasso?' Paul asks 'Yeah,' Ringo says, 'but I can't fit it in when I play it. That's the only drag with that.' 'Because it's a fast one?' 'Too fast for me,' Ringo quips, pounding the rhythm. 'Just sing it down the octave,' Paul suggests, as Ringo struggles to pitch the first line. 'Oh Picasso, I wanna Picasso,' Ringo improvises over a structure identical to his last song. Playing G major to resolve the blues pattern, Ringo falters. 'See,' he says, 'I need to do something there.' Paul sings, *'Oh baby.'* George: *'It looked like it wouldn't show.'* 'Make it twice as long,' he says, 'and then do *oh baby.*' Spurred on by their suggestions, Ringo switches back to 'Taking a Trip to Carolina' but, partly forgetting the words, substitutes 'oh baby' (suggested for 'Picasso') at the end of the chorus – to the delight of Paul and George. 'The words aren't very good,' Ringo apologizes, 'Carolina. Oh baby!'

Three days later, on 6 January, the subject of a song for Ringo is once again raised. Strumming an acoustic guitar in the style of George Formby, John bursts out with *'Just take a look at Annie, oh my oh my'*. 'It's one I wrote for Ringo,' he says, prompting Paul to join in over a repeated rendition of the chorus. 'There's one Dylan wrote for Ringo!' George adds to the party, singing the repeated line 'Maureen'. Then, firing out a successive stream of rhymes, *'finger-pickin', being sick, and lookin''*, Paul duplicates George's rapid delivery, rounding off with an improvised round of 'Maureen... Maureen'. Soon after, as Ringo's marriage began to falter, George and Maureen had a brief affair. According to Apple employee Chris

O'Dell, writing in *My Hard Days and Long Nights*, 'George said, "You know, Ringo, I'm in love with your wife," to which Ringo replied with a shrug…"better you than someone we don't know".' Talking to *Starts at 60* in 2018, Pattie Boyd added, 'I became aware [of the affair] when she would turn up at midnight and she'd still be there the next day. I'd have to be pretty stupid not to notice! It was towards the end of our marriage.'

Despite the sexual trysts, 'Maureen' – alongside 'Taking a Trip to Carolina', 'Picasso' and 'Annie' – never materialized beyond a brief introduction at Twickenham and Apple. As Ringo remarked in an interview in 1967, much depended on the willingness of John, Paul and George to push his ideas over the finish line. 'I try,' Ringo said, alluding to a tape of demo recordings he kept at his home. 'I have a guitar and a piano and play a few chords, but they're all just chinga-lingas. No great tune comes out as far as I'm concerned.'

11. And in the End...

On 29 August 1970, Paul acknowledged that the dream was over. 'Dear Mailbag,' he wrote in a handwritten letter to *Melody Maker*. 'In order to put out of its misery the limping dog of a news story which has been dragging itself across your pages for the past year, my answer to the question, "Will The Beatles get together again"...is no.' Signed off with a sketch of a set of grinning teeth, Paul's admission was a devastating blow to any hope of reconciliation.

'The only way The Beatles can get together again is if Allen [Klein] wasn't there,' George responded in a conversation with Allan Steckler, head of Apple US. 'I'm ready to do it, so is Ringo and I think we can persuade John to go along with it. But if we're going to work with Paul, we need to get rid of Klein.' It was the first of many 'what ifs' proposed by the individual Beatles, but in reality the future of the band had been determined a year earlier when on 9 September 1969 John suggested that The Beatles record a new album and then 11 days later, on 20 September, declared that he wanted 'a divorce'.

The premise of *The Lost Album of The Beatles* rests on Paul, George and Ringo acquiescing to John's first suggestion. Had the four Beatles agreed to record a new album, it would have unleashed an incredible alternative series of events and a dramatic rewriting of popular culture. We know that, in late 1969, Paul charged the managing director of Apple Corps, Neil Aspinall, with obtaining as much television and film footage as could be located on the rise and fall of

The Beatles. Subsequently labelled *The Long and Winding Road*, the collected material was edited into a 105-minute documentary. After the split, Aspinall sent each Beatle a copy of the film, which, as he told *Mojo* in October 1996, 'they all quite liked. Then I put it on the shelf.' The project lay dormant for almost a quarter of a century until Aspinall resurrected the idea in the early 1990s. The result was an eight-part television series, *Anthology*, first aired on British television on 23 November 1995. Nostalgia is a powerful medium, and had the film been acted upon by The Beatles in 1970, its catalytic effect could have played an influential role in the group's future. Whether it would have been sufficient to placate the fraught unease between them is debatable, but it may have acted as a powerful reminder of what they had achieved in the past, and arguably created a balm between them for the future.

But, ahead of such surrogate speculation – and accepting that *Four Sides of The Beatles* was released in 1970 – one outstanding question was in need of an answer: what was to become of *Let It Be*? The question presents a variety of possible outcomes. First, that the album remained in the EMI vaults or at least until such a time that all four Beatles sanctioned its official release.[1] Or perhaps, depending upon

---

1   The 'lost' album holds a special place in the hearts of music fans. In 1975, Columbia issued *The Basement Tapes,* a double album's worth of unreleased songs recorded by Bob Dylan and The Band in 1967–8. In the intervening years, many of the songs had made their way into the public domain either through Dylan's publishers or illegal pressings. In an attempt to shut down the bootleggers, CBS issued an official release of the tapes. In 1985, a long-rumoured Velvet Underground album, recorded between the band's third and fourth records, was released as *V.U.*, collating a set of songs recorded in the late 1960s.

how far its manufacturing had advanced, copies of the album would surreptitiously circulate on the black market. In either scenario, at least three of the eleven tracks marked for *Let It Be* would have reached the buying public: 'Get Back' and 'Don't Let Me Down', from the April 1969 single release, and 'Across the Universe', which first appeared on the charity record *No One's Gonna Change Our World* in aid of the World Wildlife Fund on 12 December 1969.[2] Furthermore, it is reasonable to suppose that the song 'Let It Be' – backed by 'You Know My Name (Look Up the Number)' – would still have been issued as a single in March 1970.[3]

A second scenario envisions the release of *Let It Be* after *Four Sides of The Beatles*, perhaps as late as 1971, although the notion of promoting a record two years after its original recording would come with understandable problems and maybe even inter-band reluctance. This would leave a final option of a simultaneous issue of both *Four Sides of The Beatles* and *Let It Be*, with the latter being strictly promoted as a soundtrack album to the accompanying film documentary. It is this option that seems most plausible and indeed more appealing. Yet, as we know from the ancient philosopher Heraclitus of Ephesus (*c.*535–*c.*475 BCE), 'We both step and do not step in the same rivers. We are and are not.' Thus, as we change the

---

2   Recorded in February 1968, the track was re-edited in 1970 by Phil Spector, who slowed down John's vocal and embellished the arrangement with orchestration and a choir.

3   'Let It Be' reached number two in the UK chart, denied the number one position by Lee Marvin's 'Wand'rin' Star'. A week later, The Beatles record slipped down to number three and was leapfrogged by Simon & Garfunkel's tour de force, 'Bridge Over Troubled Water'.

course of history with one step, the river changes for the second. Consequently, with the release of a new Beatles album in 1970, there would be no *Plastic Ono Band*, *McCartney* or *All Things Must Pass*. With many of the songs from those records shaping *Four Sides of The Beatles*, each subsequent solo record would be different from how we know them today. John Lennon's debut would conceivably be a mixture of both *Plastic Ono Band* and *Imagine*, bringing together on one record the attractive prospect of 'Mother' and 'Crippled Inside', 'Working Class Hero' and 'How Do You Sleep?' Similarly, Paul's outstanding recordings from *McCartney* would serve as wonderful demos to bring forward on *RAM*, delivering 'That Would Be Something' with 'Too Many People' and 'Man We Was Lonely' with 'Monkberry Moon Delight'.

And what of the effect on popular culture? Would The Beatles have returned to the live arena and performed at the 1970 Isle of Wight Festival alongside Jimi Hendrix and The Who? And with Led Zeppelin and The Rolling Stones enjoying incredible ascendency on both sides of the Atlantic, would The Beatles' influence on fashion and musical innovation still have the potency of the previous decade? Or perhaps an unbowed Beatles would inspire Simon & Garfunkel to continue after the gargantuan success of *Bridge over Troubled Water* or conversely inhibit the rise of acts such as David Bowie or Elton John or even hinder the oncoming onslaught of glam rock. Would it be churlish to suggest that one more Beatles record would have enough impact to offset the explosion of punk half a decade later? It seems unlikely. But, as author Craig Brown fancied in *One, Two, Three, Four: The Beatles in Time*, but for differing circumstances he could have been writing about the world phenomenon Gerry and The Pacemakers. In Brown's preposterous alternative world, The Beatles become 'mainstays in sixties revival tours throughout the 1980s and 1990s', with George 'following a successful career as a session musician', John and Paul 'touring Britain' with their 'Tribute to Gerry and The Pacemakers' and Ringo pursuing an 'earlier ambition, managing a successful chain of hairdressing salons through the North-East'.

Ultimately debating the great 'lost' Beatles album and the infinite 'what ifs' is a daring game, played and replayed with ever increasing vagaries and manipulations. Just as in 1994 when Paul, George and Ringo played their own version of *The Lost Album of The Beatles* by recording first 'Free as a Bird' and then 'Real Love', pretending John had not been callously murdered 14 years earlier but had simply popped out of the studio. Inventing a scenario where John was away on holiday, Paul imagined his writing partner phoning up and saying 'Just finish this track for us, will you? I'm sending the cassette – I trust you.' 'That was the key thing,' Paul told *Anthology*. '"I trust you, just do your stuff on it."' In Ringo's imagination, John had just 'popped out' for a cup of tea. 'That's the only way I could get through it.' Taking a more philosophical view, George saw it as an opportunity for John to be with them again and 'to let all the past turbulent times go down the river and under the bridge.'

Appendix 1: Single Album

In September 1969, John Lennon proposed that the next Beatles album should be comprised of four of his songs, four of Paul's, four of George's and two of Ringo's.[1] If the idea had been adopted, this is the selection and running order I would choose.

Side One

1.	What Is Life?	George
2.	Gimme Some Truth	John
3.	Another Day	Paul
4.	It Don't Come Easy	Ringo
5.	Instant Karma!	John
6.	Not Guilty	George
7.	The Back Seat of My Car	Paul

Side Two

1.	Maybe I'm Amazed	Paul
2.	My Sweet Lord	George
3.	I'm the Greatest	Ringo
4.	Come and Get It	Paul
5.	Jealous Guy	John
6.	God	John
7.	All Things Must Pass	George

---

1 Five Beatle albums had previously featured 14 songs: *Please Please Me* (1963), *With The Beatles* (1963), *Beatles for Sale* (1964), *Help!* (1965) and *Revolver* (1966).

Appendix 2: Timeline

The outlined events adhere to the authentic history of The Beatles. They draw upon key events detailed in the text leading to the dissolution of the group and offer a guide to the solo output sourced for the compiling of *Four Sides of The Beatles*. All release dates are for the UK.

1966

August 29: Candlestick Park, San Francisco. The Beatles last date of their North American tour

1967

June 1: *Sgt. Pepper's Lonely Hearts Club Band*
August 27: Brian Epstein dies

1968

August 30: 'Hey Jude' / 'Revolution'
November 22: *The Beatles* ('White Album')

1969

January 2: Rehearsals begin at Twickenham Studios
January 10: George walks out of rehearsals
January 21: Rehearsals continue at Apple, 3 Savile Row
January 30: Rooftop concert
April 11: 'Get Back' / 'Don't Let Me Down'
May 30: 'The Ballad of John and Yoko'
July 4: 'Give Peace a Chance' by The Plastic Ono Band
August 20: 'I Want You (She's So Heavy)'. The last recording session with all four Beatles together

September 9: Meeting at Apple; John proposes a new record

September 13: John performs at the Toronto Rock and Roll Revival Festival

September 20: Meeting at Apple; John: 'I want a divorce'

September 26: *Abbey Road* released

October 6: 'Something' / 'Come Together'

October 29: 'Cold Turkey' by The Plastic Ono Band

December 5: 'Come and Get It' by Badfinger

December 15: Plastic Ono Band perform at the Lyceum, London

1970

January 3: Paul, George and Ringo record 'I Me Mine'

February 6: 'Instant Karma!' by Lennon/Ono with The Plastic Ono Band

March 6: 'Let It Be' released

March 27: *Sentimental Journey* by Ringo Starr

April 10: Beatles split

April 17: *McCartney* by Paul McCartney

May 8: *Let It Be* release

May 13: *Let It Be* film world premiere New York

September 25: *Beaucoups of Blues* by Ringo Starr

November 6: *Let It Be* standard release

November 27: *All Things Must Pass* by George Harrison

December 9: *John Lennon / Plastic Ono Band* by John Lennon

December 31: Paul McCartney files a lawsuit against John, George and Ringo at the High Court, London

1971

January 15: 'My Sweet Lord' / 'What Is Life?' by George Harrison

February 19: 'Another Day' by Paul McCartney

April 9: 'It Don't Come Easy' / 'Early 1970' by Ringo Starr

May 21: *RAM* by Paul and Linda McCartney

August 13: 'The Back Seat of My Car' by Paul and Linda McCartney

September 9: *Imagine* by John Lennon

1973

November 2: *I'm the Greatest* by Ringo Starr

November 16: *Mind Games* by John Lennon

References

I have drawn on a wide variety of sources and in the main have referenced these throughout the book. On occasion, I have opted to keep the text clean and free-flowing for the benefit of the reader. As a result, may I take this opportunity to thank all the authors, writers, journalists and broadcasters I have sourced information from and hope the list below is sufficient to honour your fine work. In a few instances, I have not been able to discover original quotes. For these, the publisher and I will happily update the necessary credit, if notified, for any future editions of the book.

Epigraphs

'There was the possibility we could have carried on...': *The Beatles Anthology*, Episode 8, UK 1995 (1 hr 09 mins), dir. Kevin Godley, Bob Smeaton and Geoff Wonfor

'If people need The Beatles so much...': *The Beatles Tapes from the David Wigg Interviews*, Polydor, 1976

'When the spinning stops...': Apple press release, 10 April 1970

Part 1: Don't Upset the Apple Cart
1 Transition
End of Touring

'I think the troubles really began...': 'The Ex-Beatle Tells His Story', *Life*, 16 April 1971

'We'd like to carry on, now...and all for one...'; 'We'd like to carry on... carry on, certainly'; 'Definitely... definitely': 'The Long Goodbye', *Mojo*, October 2000, p73

'That's it...Beatle any longer': 'George: The Friendliest Beatle', *The Beatles Book Monthly*, August 1988

'An excuse to go mad...blamed it on us': *The Beatles Anthology* (Cassell/ Weidenfeld & Nicolson, 2001) [henceforth *Anthology*]

'It was great at first...there was no satisfaction at all': Hunter Davies, *The Beatles: The Only Authorized Biography* (Jonathan Cape 1985), p291

'It was wrecking our playing...we didn't give anything': Davies, *The Beatles*, p292

'One big sameness…what would it be?': Davies, *The Beatles*, p292

'One of your countrymen was here yesterday…two queers': Los Angeles Press Conference 1966; www.youtube.com/watch?v=O8MgItRRaTo

Death of Brian Epstein

'After we stopped touring…': *Anthology*, p267

'Even before we got into our own company…become a bit redundant': *Anthology*, p265

'There was a huge void…chaos after that': *Anthology*, p268

'We collapsed…fuckin' had it': Jan S. Wenner, *Lennon Remembers*, new edn (Verso, 2000), p24

'I know now that the original concept…': 'Beatles Are on the Brink of Splitting', *New Musical Express*, 13 December 1969

'Suddenly, the lunatics had got hold of the asylum': *Anthology*, p268

Yoko Ono

'If there was one simple reason… arrival into John's life of Yoko Ono': Davies, *The Beatles*, p436

'It was midnight when we finished… it was very beautiful': 'Lennon Remembers', *Rolling Stone*,

21 January 1971

'We were in…and she went to see him': SIRIUS XM Radio, 18 October 2001

'[Paul] sent them a hate letter once… you could see the pain in John': Francie Schwartz, *Body Count* (Straight Arrow, 1972), p86

'There was a definite vibe…talking in corners': *Anthology*, p308

'We didn't get it…and it put a strain on it': Barry Miles, *Paul McCartney: Many Years from Now* (Vintage, 1998), p552

'There's only two answers…silly neither of us compromising': *Something about The Beatles* podcast, Episode 158: 'January 1969 part one', 12 February 2019

'There were negative vibes at that time…hanging out with us': *Anthology*, p316

'Yoko freed me completely…Don't put me down': Wenner, *Lennon Remembers*, p54

'Yoko only wants to be accepted'; 'Well, she's not a Beatle, John': 'Why The Beatles Broke Up', *Rolling Stone*, 3 September 2009

'It's going to be such an incredible… bringing this girl along': *Something about The Beatles* podcast, Episode 40: 'Winter of our discontent; part one: Twickenham', 4 February 2016

'I understand it all now...but I understood how they felt': BBC Radio, 1 December 1980; Andy Peebles, *The Lennon Tapes* (BBC Publications, 1981), p16

'I haven't broken it off...married when we're about seventy': *Dee Time*, BBC One, 20 July 1968

'Another reason for people taking a dislike of you...the media': BBC One, *Parkinson*, 17 July 1971

'Yoko didn't split The Beatles... simple as that': Wenner, *Lennon Remembers*, p44

'Sycophant slaves...what it was to be Elvis Beatle': 'The Real John Lennon', *Newsweek*, 29 September 1980

'At the time we split up...and The Beatles wives': *The Last Resort with Jonathan Ross*, Channel 4, 16 October 1987

The 'White Album'

'The tensions arising in the world... The Beatles was created': 'We, The Beatles', introduction by Paul McCartney to The Beatles / The 'White Album' 50th Anniversary Super Deluxe Edition, Universal Music, 2018

'We wrote about thirty new songs between us...he wrote his first song':

Anthology, p305

'Paul was always upset about the "White Album"...which really meant more Paul': Peter McCabe and Robert D Schonfeld, *John Lennon: For the Record* (Bantam Books, 1984), p366

'I left because I felt two things... around knocking to bring it to a head': *Anthology*, p311

'I think it was one of the only...I think George played bass': Miles, *Paul McCartney*, p288

'The only regret I have about past numbers...like on "She Said She Said"': Robert Rodriguez, *Revolver: How The Beatles Reimagined Rock 'n' Roll* (Backbeat Books, 2012)

2 *Get Back* Sessions
Twickenham

'George Martin no longer had an equal...lost the classroom': *The Beatles White Album Anniversary Edition*

'There's some really great songs...and we go, "Urghhhh"': Jonathan Cott and David Dalton, *The Beatles Get Back* (Garrod & Lofthouse, 1969)

'To come back into the winter of discontent...a lot of trivia and games being played': *Anthology*, p316

'Start off with a corny one...I give up':

Cott and Dalton, *The Beatles Get Back*

'That period was the low of all time... getting at me about the way I was playing': *NME*, March 1971

'We can find the bit...'; 'Or we can stop and say it's not together'; 'it's complicated...if we can get it simpler'; 'It's not complicated'; 'I'll play just the chords, you always get like that'; '...that's all I'm trying to do'; 'You always get annoyed...'; 'You don't annoy me, Paul'; 'Well': *Something about The Beatles* podcast, Episode 158: 'January 1969 part one', 12 February 2019

'I've learnt that bit... no pretending about that', *Something about The Beatles* podcast, Episode 40

'I just can't think of any solution out of here...please you, I'll do it': *Let It Be*, UK 1970, dir. Michael Lindsay-Hogg

'It doesn't matter what's gone wrong... that's what I'm onto': *Something about The Beatles* podcast, Episode 158

'It's passé...put an ad in the *New Musical Express*': Peter Doggett, *You Never Give Me Your Money* (Vintage, 2010), p60

'Got up went to Twickenham...chips later at Klaus': Olivia Harrison,

George Harrison: Living in the Material World (Abrams, 2011)

'I decided I'd had enough...there's where I had left'; 'It's Open Warfare': Alan Smith, *New Musical Express*, 6 March 1971

'At the morning rehearsal...as good and not such a headache': Michael Lindsay-Hogg, *Luck and Circumstance* (Alfred A Knopf, 2011)

'Okay, George...every day I think what fun we had when we was The Beatles playing and rocking around the world': *Something about The Beatles* podcast, Episode 40

'If George doesn't come back by Monday or Tuesday we ask Eric Clapton to play', *Daily Express*, 30 August 2020

'The day George Harrison Quit': Stefan Kyriazis, *Daily Express*, 30 August 2020

'The point is if George leaves do we want to carry on The Beatles? I do': 'Why The Beatles Broke Up', *Rolling Stone*, 3 September 2009

'Maybe for the show you can say George was sick'; 'No...he leaves'; 'What is the consensus...show and the work?'; 'Yes...get Clapton'; 'JOHN...WHAT!'; 'anything you say...stop that!...just go on as if nothing's happened'; *The*

Beatles Naked podcast, Episode 17: 'Twickenham Mind Games – George Walks, Yoko Wants a Mic'

'Yeah, rock it to me baby...sock it to me!': *Something about The Beatles* podcast, Episode 40

'The meeting was fine..., apart in the end'; 'For what?'; 'It doesn't matter...see you in a year's time'; '...I don't believe you'; 'That was a key moment'; 'That's why George said it twice...'; 'The thing is...just been the four of us'; 'Yoko was doing all...'; 'In the middle...I'll see you'; 'He was waiting...meeting without Yoko'; 'That's a big crunch': *Something about The Beatles* podcast, Episode 190B: 'Memo To Peter Jackson Part Two', 8 March 2020

'I don't think The Beatles revolves... too hard'; 'It's really hard working...'; 'I know...there's far more inside us': *Something about The Beatles* podcast, Episode 190B

'The point that we both...'; Within ourselves,' Paul surmises, 'we reach something that's nearly perfect': *Something about The Beatles* podcast, Episode 190B

'Let's go now, shall we...he's gone to Liverpool': *Something about The Beatles* podcast, Episode 158

Apple. The Rooftop Performance

'The others asked me to return...so that we all benefited': *NME*, 6 March 1971 (Ultimate Uncut); Keith Badman, *The Beatles Diary Volume 2: After the Break-up, 1970–2001* (Omnibus, 2001), p26

'There's that famous old saying...into something bigger than it was': *Scene and Heard*, BBC Radio 1, 21 January 1969

'The idea of us just doing it and there's no overdubs or you can't get out of it is much better really. Because you know that all the time recording, you're thinking, "Ah, it's all right, we can do that later," so you never get even the most out of that moment, really': *Let It Be... Naked, Fly on the Wall*, Bonus Disc, Track 28, *Fly on the Wall*, Apple, 2003

'We stopped touring...that's what we all missed': *Anthology*, p322

'"I Dig a Pygmy" by Charles Hawtrey and the deaf-aids,' he randomly shouts out before a rehearsal of 'Dig a Pony'; 'Phase one, in which Doris gets her oats!' Cott and Dalton, *The Beatles Get Back*

'What's your practical answer to...and see how it went'; 'Is it a

documentary...to get in my head';
'All that footage and film...make
about half a dozen films': *Something
about The Beatles* podcast, Episode
46: 'Winter of our discontent; part
two: Savile Row'

'Timing it...sun came up on the
middle eight'; 'We'd be stuck with a
bloody big boat of people...insane!';
'It's too far...it puts us in...Not
another fucking album': *Let It Be...
Naked, Fly on the Wall*, Bonus Disc,
Fly on the Wall, Apple, 2003

'Say it's his number...quiet number or
something like that...': *Let It Be...
Naked, Fly on the Wall*, Bonus Disc,
Fly on the Wall, Apple, 2003

'I would dig to play on stage...';
'I don't want to go on the road
again'; 'I just feel as though we...
we're in the studio'; 'I don't want
to do any of my...I just wanna
play'; 'It's such a high when you get
home': *Something about The Beatles*
podcast, Episode 46

3 The End Game

'We're always waiting for the big
man with a cigar': Press conference,
August 1965

'The Fifth Man: Brian Epstein and
The Beatles': *New York Times*, 2015

Arrival of Allen Klein

'Ever since Mr. Epstein passed away...
make it positive or should we fuck
it?': Cott and Dalton, *The Beatles
Get Back*

'Your daddy goes away at a certain
point of your life...need a bit more if
we are going to get on with it': Cott
and Dalton, *The Beatles Get Back*

'After Brian died...we went round
in circles?': Wenner, *Lennon
Remembers*, p46

'I can find you money you never even
knew you had': *Mojo*, October
2000, p75

'We've haven't got half the money
people...broke in six months': *Disc
& Music Echo*, January 1969

'One of the things that impressed
me about Allen...all the defences
and see what I'm like': McCabe and
Schonfeld, *John Lennon*

'I wanted to tell you all at once...we
were both stunned'; 'Allen Klein's
here – look out!': *Something about
The Beatles* podcast, Episode 40

'In the very early days of The
Beatles...very strong individuals
in our own right': 'Q&A: Paul
McCartney', *Rolling Stone*, 30 April
1970

'Of necessity, we developed a
pattern...it worked quite well';

'Apple was full of "hustlers" and "spongers"'; 'He dismissed incompetent...appeared in the Apple offices'; 'close as we had ever been'; 'After Mr. Epstein's death...'; 'Mr. McCartney and me...here checking the accountants': Badman, *The Beatles Diaries*, vol.2, p23

'That was just the irreconcilable difference...I'll buy it for you': *Life*, 16 April 1971

'We were all from Liverpool...much easier if we went with him too': *The Beatles Anthology*, Episode 8, 1995

'You imagine that situation...Paul's living with the Eastmans': WABC-FM radio, New York City, 1 May 1970

'Eastman's a WASP Jew...can you imagine it!': Wenner, *Lennon Remembers*, p125

'Allen had a very good way of persuading people...and she wasn't even in the group': *Anthology*, p326

'Mr. Lennon had challenged my statement...John would have said if he heard the remark': L Badman, *The Beatles Diaries*, vol. 2, p30

'They all accused me of stalling...the dark horse, the problem': 'A Rose by Any Other Name', *Club Sandwich*, No. 63, Autumn 1992

'That was actually the night we broke

The Beatles...it never came back together after that one': ibid.

'I was having dreams that Klein...they held me to that contract': Miles, *Paul McCartney*, p570

'The outcome of this whole financial business...and that'll be that': Alan Smith, 'Beatles music straightforward on next album: an interview with John Lennon', *NME*, 3 May 1969

'I don't like doing the business bit...it's just force of circumstance': BBC Radio 1, *The Beatles Tapes*, 1976

'Great bond of friendship...they're good lads, I tell you': *Light and Local*, BBC Radio Merseyside, 15 May 1969

'Klein is certainly forceful to an extreme...to which he was not entitled': Badman, *The Beatles Diaries*, vol. 2, p27

'I wasn't gonna tell you till after we'd signed...I'm leaving the group': Miles, *Paul McCartney*, p561

Abbey Road

'It's his own fault...a lousy district'; 'Well, we'll try it...chance to be loud': *Abbey Road Anniversary Edition* deluxe box set, 2019

'Why did we spring "Get Back" on the public...Get it out tomorrow':

Alan Smith, 'Beatles music straightforward on next album: an interview with John Lennon', *NME*, 3 May 1969

'John and Yoko came round to see me...you could play drums': *Abbey Road Anniversary Edition*, p66

'like an old-time ballad...Johnny B. Paperback Writer': Alan Smith, 'Beatles music straightforward on next album: an interview with John Lennon', *NME*, 3 May 1969

'The story came out that only Paul...'; 'and he couldn't come that night': ibid.

'I didn't mind not being on the record...then I would have been on it': *Anthology*, p333

'Suddenly, when we were working... we were doing really well': *Anthology*, p355

'By the time we made *Abbey Road*... anything he hadn't written himself': *Life*, 16 April 1971

'We made the album from a large number...'; 'I'd just put fourteen rock songs on': Barry Miles, John Lennon/Yoko Ono interview, September 1969; available at www.rocksbackpages.com

'Paul came racing out of the front door...even though the studio was booked'; 'We're waiting for The Beatles': *Mojo*, October 1996

'John was really angry...know he couldn't make the session'; 'We're a damn good little band': ibid.

'If George Martin hadn't been there... we'd be back doing another album': Geoff Emerick, *Here, There and Everywhere: My Life Recording the Music of The Beatles* (Gotham Books, 2006), p304

'The nastiness...the horror show that was *Let It Be*': ibid.

'I didn't know at the time...so much going on all the time': *Anthology*, p343

'Show me any other group packing so much originality of composition and honest pop music on to one album. Show me!': *NME*, September 1969

**4 *Get Back*. Phil Spector.
*Let It Be***

'Remember that idea you had... Nobody could face looking at it': Wenner, *Lennon Remembers*, pp101–2

'The idea...what the public expected': *Something about The Beatles* podcast, Episode 51

'It's a strange album...you when you try and make a record': WABC-FM New York City, December 1969

'He'd done a very straightforward mix...it had a lot of character': BBC Radio 1, 12 October 1987

'It's very rough in a way...this is really not like that': 'The Beatles Today', *Scene and Heard*, a one-off special, BBC Radio 1, 30 March 1970

'*Get Back* is The Beatles with their socks off...them out with their music': 'August LP surprises', *Beatles Book Monthly*, No.72, July 1969

'It was a very, very difficult...I got my guitar and went home': *Anthology*, p316

'He had this idea that we would rehearse...eight in the morning or ten or whatever it was': Wenner, *Lennon Remembers*, p100

'It's very quick...any idea what we'll play?': *Something about The Beatles* podcast, Episode 158: 'January 1969 part one', 12 February 2019

'Sounds like it'll be a good...the idea of the waltz': ibid.

'[It's] a very strange song...in the studio and re-record it': 'The Beatles Today', *Scene and Heard*, BBC Radio 1, 30 March 1970

'You all will have read that Dave Dee...always gone down in number two': Mark Lewisohn, *The Complete Beatles Recording Sessions* (Hamlyn, 1988), p195

We got an acetate each...cause he's got no idea': Wenner, *Lennon Remembers*, pp101–2

'When Spector came around...would break the myth': ibid.

'If there is anything you'd like... about anything regarding the album tonight': Peter Doggett, *You Never Give Me Your Money: The Battle for the Soul of The Beatles* (Vintage 2010), p123

'There's really good songs on it...than the average studio recording.' 'The Beatles Today', *Scene And Heard*, BBC Radio 1, 30 March 1970

'You can't blame Spector...too happy about the whole thing.' *McCartney on McCartney*, BBC Radio 1 (41 mins), 21 December 1989

'We all said yes...he didn't put it down.' *Melody Maker*, 7 August 1971

I don't like *Get Back* being held back...I don't even remember making it.' *Rolling Stone*, 30 April 1970

'It's been held up because...we think it's this and we think it's that': 'The Beatles Today', BBC Radio 1, *Scene and Heard*, 30 March 1970

'There was a bit of hype on the back... it didn't sound commercial enough':

Melody Maker, November 1971

'A betrayal...Over-produced by Phil Spector': 'Produced by George Martin', *Arena*, 25 April 2011

'If anybody listens to the bootleg version...Spector did a terrific job': Philip Norman, *John Lennon: The Biography* (Harper, 2009), p645

'If the new Beatles' soundtrack album...again the face of pop music': 'New LP Shows They Couldn't Care Less', *NME*, 9 May 1970

'It was set-up by Paul...I felt sick': Wenner, *Lennon Remembers*, p23

'There are scenes in it like the rooftop concert...': *The Beatles Diary*, vol 2, p8

'...I don't like it': *The Beatles Diary* vol 2, p8

'The *Get Back* film is a good film... moments': 'Q&A: Paul McCartney', *Rolling Stone*, 30 April 1970

4 The Love We Make
Divorce

'By the time we got to *Let It Be*... longer creating magic': *Imagine: John Lennon*, directed by Andrew Solt, 1988; *Anthology*, p317

'Taking roughly a 9–4 gamble on getting away with it': *Record Mirror*, 18 May 1970

'I never intended it to mean I'd quit... the one to say the party's over': *Evening Standard*, 21 April 1970

'I absolutely did believe...life was worth living': *Anthology*, p352

'The world reaction was like...we'd known it for months': ibid.

'A lot of people knew I'd left...I was just – "shit"': 'Lennon remembers', *Rolling Stone*, 21 January 1971

'I was speechless...don't tell anybody yet'': 'My part in The Beatles' break-up', *Daily Mail*, 26 August 2016

'We got this phone call...we went the next morning': *Anthology*, p347

'I dug performing at Toronto...I'm bound to now I've had a taste of it': *OZ*, 23 September 1969

'We should get back to our roots... like my divorce from Cynthia': *Anthology*, episode 8; Miles, *Paul McCartney*, p561

'That just hit everyone...not going to say anything': *Life*, 16 April 1971

'I blab off...God knows what I'm saying': Wenner, *Lennon Remembers*, p28

'When we've done a month of this... and then we split': *Something about The Beatles* podcast, Episode 158: 'January 1969 part one', 12 February 2019

'We should have a divorce...Dick James': ibid.

'I was talking to Neil... "The Beatles have broken up"': ibid.

'If Brian was around today...Allen Klein to be on our own men': *Anthology*, p265

'With the introduction of Allen Klein...that they would split up': Miles, *Paul McCartney*, p542

'Nobody could break The Beatles up...they were a bit stifled with The Beatles': *John Lennon,* Ray Coleman (Futura, 1984), p331

'By the time The Beatles were at their peak...that my whole life is a misery': interview with David Wigg in 1971, later used on *The Beatles Tapes*, 1976; *Anthology*, p316

'It was like a wind down to a divorce... Oh, let's end it': *Anthology*, p329

'It was like an army song...would come true': Chris Salewicz, 'Paul McCartney: An Innocent Man?', interview with Paul McCartney, *Q* magazine, October 1986

'You know the song...the moment I met Yoko': *Playboy* interview, 12 September 1980, later published in David Sheff, *The Playboy Interviews* (New English Library, 1982)

'John asked me...and "What's The New Mary Jane"', Emerick, *Here, There and Everywhere*, p312

'You Know My Name (Look Up the Number)' is probably my favourite...And I want to do it like a mantra!': Lewisohn, *The Complete Beatles Recording Sessions*, p15

'It's my escape valve...I'll have to wait and see': 'Beatles are on the brink of splitting', *NME*, 13 December 1969

The Beatle thing is over...and partly by other people': *Life*, 7 November 1969

'I told him I was leaving...have accepted it mentally': *Life*, 16 April 1971

Indecision

'Everybody had tried to leave...leaving for years': *Anthology*, p348

'After a confrontation...it's all over!': Anthony Fawcett, *John Lennon: One Day at a Time: A Personal Biography of the Seventies* (New English Library, 1976), p101

'It just depends how much we all want to record together,' he said, 'I go off and on it': *NME*, 13 December 1969

'It'll all be okay...we all do': WABC-FM, 1 May 1970

'I don't know what all this business …
just a phase they're passing through':
Alanna Nash, 'A visit with Aunt
Mimi', www.meetthebeatlesforreal.
com/2016/07/a-visit-with-aunt-
mimi.html

'Just being bitchy to each other…
round the cycle again': WABC-FM,
1 May 1970

'When John and I used to meet…
Well, serve him right, ha, ha, ha':
Miles, *Paul McCartney*, p567

'It's like when people decide to get
a divorce…you get frustrated': *The
Beatle Tapes*; *Anthology*, p349

'I don't want to spend six months…
maybe it'll sort itself out': *NME*,
December 1969

'We always carved the singles up
between us…I've pushed it a bit
more': Fawcett, *John Lennon: One
Day at a Time*, p96

'I know what he's saying…Well,
you had Eric or somebody like
that': ibid.

'When we get in a studio…That's
always been': ibid., p97

'What I do is bring out the numbers…
to make an impact': *NME*,
1 November 1969

'Even on *Abbey Road*…and away
you go': WABC-FM,
1 May 1970

'The trouble is that we've got too much
material…can't get more albums out
faster': *Melody Maker*, September
1969

'Even before they began…all of Paul's
on the other': Lewisohn,
*The Complete Beatles Recording
Sessions*, p193

'It seemed mad for us to put…People
who like music like that,' he said,
'like Mary [Hopkin]': Fawcett, *John
Lennon: One Day at a Time*, p95

'Paul preferred "pop-type"…
contributed to our success': *The
Beatles Diaries*, vol. 2, p27

'All right, let's move on. We'll do
another album. We'll all do four
songs. How's that? That's fair': Mark
Lewisohn, 'Hornsey Road Lecture',
Bloomsbury Theatre,
28 September 2019

'All right…How about a Christmas
single? Y'know, we finish it with a
Christmas single. I think it's a great
idea. I'm in': ibid.

'In the future…we all have as much on
the album': *NME*,
1 November 1969

'It was just over the last year…but I'd
rather be Harrison': WABC-FM
radio, 1 May 1970

'It's the end of The Beatles…free to be
individuals at the same time':

BBC Radio 1, 30 March 1970

'All we have to do is accept...then I'm not going to be with him': WABC-FM radio, 1 May 1970

'Everything's fine...can't do everything at once': *NME*, 14 March 1970

'Ringo's just completed...ready to do a new Beatle album': *Scene and Heard*, 30 March 1970

'I've no idea if The Beatles will work... probably be rebirth': *Scene and Heard*, 6 February 1970

'We've got to a point where...the natural course of events': *Disc*, 5 April 1970

'Ringo came around to see me...me to work in as an artist': *Evening Standard*, 21 April 1970

'Paul went completely out of control..., put my coat on and get out. I did so': *The Beatles Diaries*, vol. 2, p28

'He said, "Well, on behalf of the board...but it was near enough"': *Anthology*, p351

'There was nothing *against* Paul...Let *Let It Be* breathe!': Wenner, *Lennon Remembers*, pp131–2

'I had to do something in order... pummelled about the head, in my mind anyway': Miles, *Paul McCartney*, p572

'All I want for The Beatles is their individual happiness...remains to be seen': *Scene and Heard*, 6 February 1970

'I never thought we'd be so stupid... people come between us and that's what happened': *Anthology*, p349

'We all have to sacrifice...if The Beatles don't record together': WABC-FM, 1 May 1970

Resolution

'I quite fancy giving some live shows... We've got to come to an agreement': *NME*, 3 May 1969

'one colour television show...best parts of the three': *Beatles Monthly*, December 1969

'I wanted to get in a van...there'd be no press and we'd tell nobody about it. John thought it was a daft idea': *Melody Maker*, November 1971

'My best playing days ...but it's what I want to do with this new group': ibid.

'You'd come up with a *Magical Mystery Tour*...the energy to turn 'em out and get 'em on as well': Fawcett, *John Lennon: One Day at a Time,* p92

'When we get into the studio...if he wants them': Fawcett, *John Lennon: One Day at a Time*, p93

Part 2: *Four Sides of The Beatles*

'I do what I like, Paul does...we've all turned into pure Beatle': *OZ*, 23 September 1969

'We always regarded ourselves... threes': James Paul McCartney v John Ono Lennon, George Harrison, Richard Starkey and Apple Corps Limited, High Court, witness box, 1971

'If The Beatles had continued...': *Undercover*, 1994

'If we weren't all...': Paul Du Noyer, *Mojo*, June 1998

5 The Concept

'We don't really write together any more...': *OZ*, 23 September 1969

'I think this is a good way if we do our own albums...do my songs their way': WABC-FM radio, 1 May 1970

'John screamed with laughter... that line, aren't you?': Miles, *Paul McCartney*

'In the Beatle days...bit embarrassed by it, we'd say it': Badman, *Beatles Diary*, vol.2, p5

'It's a stupid expression...it sounds like a parrot' and offering to 'fix-it'; 'You won't!' John responded, aghast; 'That's the best line in the song': *Anthology*, p297

'I was lucky enough to work with John...be said to lack something': McCartney interview with Derek Taylor, *Mojo*, October 2000

'No it hasn't got the right number of syllables...It's meaningless. It's a fill-in-word': Hunter Davies, *The Beatles*, p345

'I was at John's...that record is a different song': *Acoustic Guitar*

'It's hard to describe...we were writing, I don't know': *Playboy* interview, 12 September 1980, later published in *The Playboy Interviews* by David Sheff (New English Library, 1982)

'In short...were in a room together': Emerick, *Here, There and Everywhere*, p304

6 Side One: Lennon

'It's another slow one...tired when I got in': *Something about The Beatles* podcast, Episode 40

'Haven't you written anything... When I'm up against the wall... just wish you'd come up with the goods...across the conversation'; 'I was hoping for the same thing myself.' *Something about The Beatles*, Episode 40

'I got a message on acid...And I just was nothing. I was shit': Wenner,

Lennon Remembers, p54

'When I was a Beatle...but it wasn't made right', *Playboy* interview, 12 September 1980, later published in David Sheff, *The Playboy Interviews* (New English Library, 1982)

'We start from scratch...doing it the hard way': Davies, *The Beatles*, p345

'John got disenchanted...'He wanted authenticity': *Anthology*, p340

'Even "Strawberry Fields?"'Especially "Strawberry Fields": 'Produced by George Martin', *Arena*, dir. Francis Hanly, BBC One, 25 April 2011

'[George] is more Paul's style of music than mine': 'Lennon Remembers', *Rolling Stone*, 21 January 1971

"I always keep saying I prefer the double album...like productions so much.' Wenner, *Lennon Remembers*, p116

'I'm fond of Phil's work a lot...': Peebles, *The Lennon Tapes*, p36.

'The fact is The Beatles have left school...or *Abbey Road*': *NME*, August 1971; last line in Tim Riley, *Lennon: The Man, the Myth, the Music* (Andersen Press, 2012), p526

Instant Karma!

'Ecstatic, bubbling with excitement... He'll get the sound I want'; 'Well, we'll just pick one up on the way': Fawcett, *John Lennon: One Day at a Time*, p153

'John phoned me up...that's the whole point: Instant Karma!': *Anthology*, p350

'Can you be at the airport...thing to have happened?': *Music Radar*, 11 September 2009

'[Spector] said, "How do you want it"...it in just about three goes': Wenner, *Lennon Remembers*, p91

'It was like the idea of *instant* coffee... something in a new form': Sheff, *All We Are Saying: The Last Major Interview with John Lennon and Yoko Ono*, 1980; *John Lennon*, Coleman, p358

'I want records to be like news-papers...care what name goes on it': *The Beatle Tapes*, February 1970

'This is an American record...intro is slightly like "Instant Karma!"': WNEW-FM New York, 28 September 1974

'To hell with it...Who will know?': Emerick, *Here, There and Everywhere*, p318

Jealous Guy

'"Mother Nature's Son" was...the same lecture by Maharishi': *Playboy*, 12 September 1980

'We'll probably write some fast ones here, together, all of us': *The Beatles Abbey Road Anniversary Edition*, 'The Route to Abbey Road', Apple 2019, p15

'Do you have anything more you're writing...'; 'You're writing all the time, aren't you John?'; 'Yes...I've got the energy': Cott and Dalton, *The Beatles Get Back*

'If we get a repertoire that's...into the ballads'; 'It'd be nice if you could play Hawaiian guitar ... proper lead to go with it'; 'Just try and gig it...'; 'fruity at the beginning'; 'If you can play Hawaiian...fruity old band, for that part'; 'That's it, really': *Let It Be... Naked, Fly on the Wall* Bonus Disc, *Fly on the Wall*, Apple, 2003

'The words were silly...I sang it to Yoko...Yoko's help, I did'; 'I don't believe these tight-skinned people...possess them to death': *Woman's Hour*, BBC Radio 4, 28 May 1971

'I was just hysterical...taking out all my frustrations on her': Davies, *The Beatles*, p56

'John was true to his word...he was never again physically violent to me': Cynthia Lennon, *John* (Hodder & Stoughton, 2002)

'I told John I was uneasy...and my head, around my neck': Mark Lewisohn, *The Beatles Tune In* (Little Brown, 2013), p210

'Not only did we dress like James Dean...that's how you do it': *Hattford Courant*, 26 November 1972

'I was a very jealous, possessive guy... he feels like playing with her': *Playboy*, 12 September 1980

Love

'It's like a child's song...I'm not even known for writing melody': Wenner, *Lennon Remembers*, p94

'We'll probably get a feel for it...and do it slower': John Lennon/Plastic Ono Band, *The Ultimate Collection* deluxe box set, Universal, 2021

'"Imagine", "Love"...fucking stuff that was ever done': *Playboy*, 12 September 1980

Make Love Not War

'The last bunch of pickets...like they were capable of doing either': *What about Ronald Reagan?*, CBS News, 12 December 1967

'I wanted to write...what my job and our job is'; 'It was one of the biggest moments of my life': Wenner, *Lennon Remembers*, p93

'Okay..."What was the French one...
Not Love New War," you know!'":
*Gimme Some Truth: The Making of
John Lennon's Imagine Album*, dir.
Andrew Solt, 2000
'"Make Love Not War" was such
a cliché...peaceniks were idiots':
Playboy, 12 September 1980
'We all have to face the reality...just
keep doin' it': *Playboy*, 1980
'That was a fun track because...they
didn't know what reggae was then':
Peebles, *The Lennon Tapes*, p54
'I sat down at the piano and worked
something out...George Martin,
who produced it with us': Keith
Badman, *The Beatles: Off the
Record Vol.2 – The Dream is Over*
(Omnibus, 2009)

Gimme Some Truth

'I've got one. "Gimme Some Truth"...
remember your hangman bit?';
'Yeah!'; 'It started in D, didn't it...
Maybe we had Capos then?'; 'Oh
yeah'; 'The only trouble about the
slow ones...that hypocrite's one';
'Do you know the other bits...We
should change it there...that's just as
exciting as the other one': *Something
about The Beatles* podcast,
Episode 190
'For the first time, because the

people...' https://avalon.law.yale.
edu/default.asp
'The Beatles have been a real force for
anti-American spirit': https://www.
archives.gov/exhibits/nixon-met-
elvis/assets/doc_3.1_transcript.
html
'I've seen those famous Nixon
transcripts...the toilet full of them!';
'Presley tried to have us banished
from America, because he was very
big with the FBI': *Anthology*, p192
'Sharp solo with his steel finger...';
'half the money anyway and vice
versa': 'Sometime in L.A. Lennon
plays it as it lays', *Crawdaddy*,
March 1974
'The only reason Ringo wasn't on it...
but then it was more diplomatic':
NME, February 1972
'Side Two opens with a "2001...
neurotic...psychotic"': *NME*,
11 September 1971
'I like the overall sound...go out and
buy it': Hunter Davies, *The John
Lennon Letters* (Weidenfeld &
Nicolson, 2012), p220

God

'Where Paul's press release...':
*Composing outside The Beatles:
Lennon & McCartney 1973–1980*,
dir. Rob Johnstone, 2009

'It's excruciating: you are forced to realise…': *Red Mole*, 21 January 1971

'Incredible…he was sixteen': *Classic Albums: John Lennon: Plastic Ono Band*, dir. Matthew Longfellow, TV programme, first broadcast in the UK 24 June 2008

'Like a lot of the words…don't believe in the dream anymore': Wenner, *Lennon Remembers*, p134

'Most people channel their pain… kind of Heaven': *Red Mole*, 21 January 1971

7 Side Two: McCartney

'I tried to avoid any Beatle cliché…': Tom Doyle, *Man on the Run: Paul McCartney in the 1970s* (Polygon, 2013), p45

'And that was it…*lock me away…* "Yes, okay!"': Press conference, Milwaukee, Wisconsin, 4 September 1964

'We missed the collaborative thing… conscious of it': Paul Du Noyer, *Conversations with McCartney* (Hodder & Stoughton, 2015)

'George's real expertise was in vocal harmony…but very effective': Lewisohn, *The Complete Beatles Recording Sessions*, p83

'If Paul has written a song, he comes into…': Davies, *The Beatles*, p345

'After *Let It Be*, I never thought… Why should I when I have you?': *RAM* (Deluxe), Universal, 2012

'Dear Sir, In future no one…Don't ever do it again': www.theguardian.com/uk/2002/jan/12/thebeatles.immigration

'I felt, "What am I going to do."': *Melody Maker*, 1 December 1973

'It was a barrelling…': *Playboy*, April 1984

I was going through a bad time…': Miles, *Paul McCartney*, p570

'I felt I'd outlived my usefulness… became really very difficult': ibid.

'"That Would Be Something" and "Maybe…they could've sounded better"': Howard Smith NY Radio, May 1970, in Keith Badman, *The Beatles: Off the Record Vol. 2* (Omnibus, 2009), p5

'I thought Paul's was rubbish… frightened into it': Werner, *Lennon Remembers*, p18

'I expected [Paul's] solo albums to be better…': *Melody Maker*, 22 May 1971

Come and Get It

'Demo, take one…headphones and I'll track it': Lewisohn, *The Complete Beatles Recording Sessions*, p182

'I would have liked to sing harmony...': *Evening Standard*, October 1970

'I was lying in bed trying to get...I knew it was a very catchy song': *The Word*, October 2005

'I said to Badfinger...and they were good': *Anthology*, p289

Another Day

'I better go and put in some piano practice...'; 'We can film it'; 'Don't tell me!'; 'Candidly, so you're not noticing': *Something about The Beatles* podcast, Episode 40

'I liked the idea of writing songs...was especially pleasing': Paul McCartney and Mark Lewisohn (ed.), *Wingspan: Paul McCartney's Band on the Run* (Little Brown, 2002)

'We were sitting in Studio A2... Paul never said anything about it': Gary Eskow, 'Classic Tracks: Paul McCartney's "Uncle Albert/ Admiral Halsey"', *Mix*, 1 August 2004, https://www.mixonline. com/recording/classic-tracks-paul-mccartneys-uncle-albertadmiral-halsey-375127

Maybe I'm Amazed

'Nowhere near as good as Paul played it...that can happen in a relationship':

The Ronnie Wood Show, Sky Arts, 25 June 2012

'Might have been personal...*Mother Mary*, which was her name': Miles, *Paul McCartney*, p538

'At the time...but we never did': Paul Gambaccini, *Paul McCartney: In His Own Words* (Putnam, 1983)

'Maybe I'm Amazed...included on say *Abbey Road*': *Melody Maker*, 18 April 1970

Every Night

'The Apple wagon again hits the road': Cott and Dalton, *The Beatles Get Back*

'If he does not appear in court... No comment': *The Beatles: Get Back*, trailer, dir. Peter Jackson, 2021

'I remember one tune [Paul] played for me...I've always kept quiet': Davies, *The Beatles*, p434

'It's a song about a dog!'; 'What key you in?'; 'E'; 'It should just go on straight'; 'How I Inspired a Beatles Song': Hunter Davies, *The Times*, 31 December 2020

'When we started off as Beatles... They're good lads!': *Light and Local*, BBC Radio Merseyside, 15 May 1969

'We are a good combination...': *Light and Local*, BBC Radio Merseyside, 15 May 1969

Junk

'Heroin...we were in real pain':
'Lennon Remembers', *Rolling Stone*,
21 January 1970

'He paused in the middle of singing a
line...': Davies, *The Beatles*, p398

'When we came to sing it...but
we forgot all about it': Radio
Luxembourg, 27 September 1969

The Back Seat of My Car

'They flew to Sardinia...in his Aston
Martin with Maggie': Philip
Norman, *Paul McCartney: The
Biography*, p340

'Too many people going what...can't
all be hearing things': Davies, *The
John Lennon Letters*, p220

'There was one tiny little reference...
your lucky break and broke it in two':
Playboy, December 1984

'I felt John and Yoko were telling...got
to be a thing about them': Paul Du
Noyer, *Conversations with McCartney*
(Overlook Press, 2016), p96

'I thought *RAM* was awful...had a
lucky break to be with him': *Hit
Parader* magazine, February 1972

'There was a line that...he loved it':
Playboy, 11 November 1971.

'It's what you might call an "angry
letter"...': *Gimme Some Truth*, dir.
Solt

'I think the truth...were missing each
other': Du Noyer, *Conversations with
McCartney*

'"Back Seat of My Car" is the
ultimate teenage song...is s
nogging, making love': *Billboard*,
16 March 2001

'Another instantly...song for others to
cover': *Melody Maker*, 22 May 1971

8 Side Three: Harrison

'We're the grooves and you two
just watch it': BBC Radio 1,
December 1974

'They'd written all or most of their...':
Anthology, p194

'He came to me because Paul
wouldn't have...': *Playboy*,
September 1980

Shall we do other people's tunes
as well...never mind strangers':
Badman, p410

'I've got so many songs...'; 'On your
own?'; 'If we put out an LP...I
don't think they need much':
Something about The Beatles
podcast, Episode 46

'Out of the new records from Apple...
to do something for myself': *NME*,
14 March 1970

'His talents have developed over the
years...but I consider George's less':
Wenner, *Lennon Remembers*, p135

'Like the *McCartney* album...
overshadowed by its average':
'George Harrison: All Things Must
Pass', *New Musical Express*,
5 December 1970, p2

'He took me over to Eric Clapton's
house...And I did too': Graeme
Thomson, *George Harrison: Behind
the Locked Door* (Omnibus, 2013),
p220

What Is Life?

'I wrote it very quickly...while Billy
was playing his funky stuff': George
Harrison, *I Me Mine: The Extended
Edition* (Genesis, 2017), p156

'Sort of disappeared': Dave
Thompson, *Phil Spector: Wall of
Pain* (Sanctuary, 2005)

'Band track was fine...further tracks
are necessary': Allen Goldstein
collection, 19 August 1970

'I tried having this piccolo trumpet
player...it very staccato like
a classical player': *Billboard*,
December 2000

My Sweet Lord

'George came up to me one night after
a show...that was the end of it': Marc
Shapiro, *All Things Must Pass: The
Life of George Harrison* (Virgin UK,
2000), p101

'We had a piano in the dressing
room...': *George Harrison: Living
in the Material World*, dir. Martin
Scorsese, 2011

'I immediately called George up...';
'It's not exactly the same.' Shapiro,
All Things Must Pass, p101

'I remember Eric [Clapton] and
Delaney & Bonnie..."Oh Happy
Day" which became "My Sweet
Lord"': Badman, *The Beatles: Off the
Record Vol.2* (Omnibus, 2009)

'The plaintiff had huge charts made
up...': Harrison, *I Me Mine*, p174

'I received a call from George...hearsay
and wouldn't allow it': Shapiro, *All
Things Must Pass*, p101

'I wasn't consciously aware...because
of the sound and its simplicity':
Harrison, *I Me Mine*, p174

'George was very unlucky...I'd have
sued if I'd wanted some money':
Melody Maker, October 1976

'[George] walked right into it...':
Playboy, September 1980

'I was just thinking of a way to
combine...strong enough then
you should say it': BBC Radio 1,
1 February 1977

Not Guilty

'The lyrics are a bit passé...': *Rolling
Stone*, 19 April 1979

'...Paul-John-Apple Rishikesh-Indian friends, etc.': Harrison, *I Me Mine*, p136

'Me getting pissed off at Lennon and McCartney...I was sticking up for myself': *Billboard*, 30 December 2000

'I don't mind if we keep on doing it but I don't think it's going anywhere'; 'Not Guilty': *The Beatles Anniversary Edition*, Apple 2018

'I think that's the best so far...'; 'George asked us to put his guitar amplifier...through to the chamber': Lewisohn, *The Complete Beatles Recording Sessions*, p149

George had this idea that he wanted to do it...'; 'Bloody hell, the way you lot are carrying on you'll be wanting...': ibid.

'I forgot all about...for Peggy Lee or someone': *Rolling Stone*, 19 April 1979

Wah-Wah

'It had given me a wah-wah...I had such a headache with that whole argument': *Crawdaddy*, February 1977

'George drives home after "tiff"" with John...I don't know what started it': 'Two Beatles row in TV studio', *Daily Sketch*, 16 January 1969

'It says swung "a few vicious phrases at each other...and that's Housego': *Something about The Beatles* podcast, Episode 46

'It may have been the first time reports...they traded a few punches': Michael Housego, 'The end of a beautiful friendship?', *Daily Sketch*, 16 January 1969

'Drugs, divorce, and a slipping image...left most people agog'; 'fed up'; 'their own private way'; 'less reliant on each other for guidance and comradeship'; 'I can say definitely': ibid.

'There was no punch-up...': Riley, *Lennon*, p431

'There's no truth in it...It's quite untrue': ibid.

'I got tired of being with The Beatles... able to be happy in this situation': WABC-FM radio, 1 May 1970

'Paul is the greatest bass player...': Badman, *The Beatles: Off the Record Vol.2* (Omnibus, 2009), p28

'If you've known a guy when... he's still nine months older!': *Anthology*, p27

'It was sounding really nice...thought, "I hate it. It's horrible"': *George Harrison*, dir. Scorsese

'The sound in your headphones... What are you doing to my song?':

Mojo, November 2014

'Coated in a wash of reverb...'; 'a grand cacophony of sound!' *Rolling Stone*, 21 January 1971

'A phone call came and John picked it up...': *John Lennon Anthology*, box set sleeve notes, EMI, 1998

'I was asked to play...might have had second thoughts about it': *Melody Maker*, 20 November 1971

Try Some Buy Some

'I stopped singing when I married Phil...': *Disc and Music Echo*, May 1971

'"Try Some Buy Some" was written on the organ...I had a friend write it down for me': Harrison, *I Me Mine*, p232

'The first verse didn't exactly grab me...a different approach with that one!': Ronnie Spector, *Be My Baby: The Autobiography of Ronnie Spector* (Harmony, 1990)

'It's Sixties...but it's a good record': *Disc and Music Echo*, 8 May 1971

'If you want to do some comparison shopping...which is what we did': Peebles, *The Lennon Tapes*, p51

'Even though the words are mundane...spiritual for me and has more meaning': Harrison, *I Me Mine*, p232

All Things Must Pass

'Because there's no solo or anything...'; 'Just play it through'; 'What key's it in?'; 'Maybe you should just play...'; 'What does it do all the time?'; 'I know what it is until I do a chord...it's really A flat minor'; Cott and Dalton, *The Beatles Get Back*

'Really I should play this on acoustic guitar...so how am I going to do that on the famous TV show?'; 'Do you fancy doing it just on your own with an acoustic?': ibid.

'Fuckin' hell...Electric shocks...'; 'You're gonna cop it!': *Let It Be*; Cott and Dalton, *The Beatles Get Back*

'When I wrote "All Things Must Pass"...Robbie Robertson-Band sort of tune': Harrison, *I Me Mine*, p180

'There's some players who can play... his own personnel prowess': *Classic Albums: The Band: The Band*, dir. Bob Smeaton, 1997

'I got [the title] from Richard Alpert/ Baba Ram Dass...': *Billboard*, December 2000

'We're pretending to be The Band... I'd like the backing group, The Raelettes': 'Okay, do that bit then'; 'If John sings what...that will be The Raelettes!': Cott and Dalton, *The Beatles Get Back*

'This guy, who Paul is looking...really fantastic': Cott and Dalton, *The Beatles Get Back*

'It sounds a bit like a synthesiser... notes bend'; 'It's one of those, it's easy...'; 'It's just getting to know it'; 'There's so much you can do in it because it's so easy'; 'In the beginning was the word. The word was scribble. And they scribbled': *Something about The Beatles* podcast, Episode 46

'Go through it from the beginning again...It's sounding alright'; 'Or if you can think of...anything wrong it's fine'; 'It's just a matter... feel how to do it'; 'Just to get it...do everything really mechanical...all good after that'; 'Okay. Now there's where...I expected you to go...'; 'It's getting like...The Chambers' Sisters'; 'That idea would be good...get a quick breath': *Something about The Beatles* podcast, Episode 47

9 Side Four: Starr

'About five words...and I haven't done a thing since': Capitol Records Tower press conference, Los Angeles, 24 August 1966, www.youtube.com/watch?v=O8MgItRRaTo

'I wrote "Don't Pass Me By" when I was...'I only play three chords... everyone was really helpful': *Anthology*, p306

'It was written as a country and western...knocked me out', Interview with Bob Rogers, 26 June 1964, New City Hotel, Dunedin, New Zealand, https://amoralto.tumblr.com/post/160814860637/june-26th-1964-new-city-hotel-dunedin-new/amp

'Was coming along...he's the Dylan Thomas of Liverpool!': *Top Gear*, BBC Light Programme, 14 July 1964

'It was for John that I did an off-the-wall introduction...score was scrapped': George Martin, via www.beatlesbible.com/songs/dont-pass-me-by/

'I think it's the most wonderful thing...': Radio Luxembourg, Abbey Road Studios, 6 May 1968, www.beatlesinterviews.org/db1968.0605.beatles.html

'It's lovely...but the lyrics are great'; 'For me, I find very deep meaning... cosmic songs without noticing': *Let it Be*; Peter Doggett, *Abbey Road* (Schirmer Books, 1998), p106

'I got an idea to record an album of songs...so for want of a better idea I thought I'd do that': *Anthology*, p349

'Just go in a studio with whatever…':
  Anthology, p349

'Ringo can't sing…tiredest junk ever
  written'; 'The Beatles *Let It Be*; Paul
  McCartney *McCartney*; Ringo
  Starr *Sentimental Journey*': John
  Gabree, *High Fidelity* magazine,
  August 1970, p. 110

'*Sentimental Journey* may be
  horrendous…at least it's classy':
  'Sentimental Journey', *Rolling Stone*,
  14 May 1970

'A couple of years back…I hear no
  important points of connection':
  'Ringo Stars', *The Guardian*,
  19 December 1970

'I used to wish that I could write…
  Yeah, it sounds like such-a-thing':
  Ray Connolly, *The Beatles: Complete*
  (Wise, 1983), p14

'Congratulations…how dare you…':
  Nicholas Schaffner, *The Boys from
  Liverpool: John, Paul, George, Ringo*
  (Methuen, 1980), p165

It Don't Come Easy

'That was a gas…which made it work
  perfectly'; 'Genius, Hard Work and
  Steve Stills': *Melody Maker*,
  28 February 1970

'George put down a vocal…writer
  and working with other artists':
  Daytrippin', 25 July 2012, https://
  daytrippin.com/2012/07/25/
  beatles-recording-engineer-ken-
  scott-reveals-behind-the-scenes-
  details-on-working-with-the-fab-
  four/

'George Harrison really was
  quite a talented producer…second
  guessed by Paul, or John…or
  Yoko', Emerick, *Here, There and
  Everywhere*, p319

'Undoubtedly one of the best…
  one day he may even write a
  masterpiece': *NME*, 24 April 1971

I'm the Greatest

'When Liston reads about The
  Beatles visiting me…': 18 February
  1964, press conference, 5th Street
  Gym, Miami Beach, Florida

'I sparred with Cassius Clay. I taught
  him…': *Anthology*, p123

'It's the Muhammad Ali line…they'd
  all take it so seriously': *Playboy*,
  September 1980

'I'm knocked out by what you've
  done': Badman, *The Beatles: Off the
  Record Vol.2* (Omnibus, 2009), p92

'That's corny'; 'A bit slow isn't it?';
  'It seems a different speed'; 'It's
  changing speed'; 'Let's do another
  one! Okay boys, this is it!': *The
  Lost Lennon Tapes*, radio series,
  Westwood One Radio Network

'The song wasn't quite complete...
magic unfolding right before my
eyes!': John Tobler and Stuart
Grundy, *The Record Producers* (BBC,
1982), p70

'We were like big girls again...It was
nice': Bill Minkin interview, 1977,
Something about The Beatles podcast,
Episode 96

Early 1970

'The meet was bait...Friday, are you
coming?': McCabe and Schonfeld,
John Lennon, p46

'The Beatles are said to be closer...last
eighteen months': *NME*,
12 December 1971

'It got round that we were recording
together...would never do it':
McCabe and Schonfeld, *John
Lennon*, p46

'Stranger things have happened!':
NME, 12 December 1970

Coochy-Coochy

'It all came together because...
always knew I liked country music':
Nashville Scene, 3 July 2008,
www.nashvillescene.com/news/
article/13016270/nashville-starr

'One day my secretary buzzed me...':
Guitar Player, September 1973

'I was trying to get it together..."I'll

fly out a few days later"': Bill Harry,
The Ringo Starr Encyclopaedia
(Virgin Books, 2004)

'We were thinking he was going...':
Nashville Scene, 3 July 2008

'We did the album in two nights...
It was really good': Bill Harry, *The
Ringo Starr Encyclopedia* (Virgin
Books, 2004), p83

'pretty typical Nashville...It was
work': *Nashville Scene*, 3 July 2008

'I wanted to play guitar because Pete...
it didn't go anywhere': Michael Seth
Starr, *Ringo: With a Little Help*
(Backbeat, 2016)

'You couldn't pry Ringo off the
beat...play the beat': *Nashville Scene*,
3 July 2008

'It was really fantastic...just out of
sight': *Guitar Player*, September
1973

'George and I play the same bit on
guitar together...so have a lot of our
songs': *Anthology*, p160

'We used to listen to quite a lot...
and *I lost my truck*': Miles, *Paul
McCartney*, p176

'I do like country and western...'
press conference Atlanta Stadium,
Georgia, 18 August 1965

'I ended up going to Ringo's
house in Beverly Hills...':
Riverfront Times, 27 April 2012,

www.riverfronttimes.com/
musicblog/2012/04/27/ray-wylie-
hubbard-on-the-grifter-blues-
songwriting-and-ringo-starr

When Every Song Is Sung

'I got the chord sequence...and in the
end Ringo': Harrison, *I Me Mine*,
p246

'It would be lovely if [George]
wrote a...'; 'Shirley's beef about
a Beatle', *Disc and Music Echo*,
12 December 1970

'I thought ["Whenever"] would be a
good one for her': ibid.

'and said I've written this song...have
had a "Yesterday" type arrangement':
Alan Clayson, *George Harrison*
(Sanctuary, 2003), p32

'I asked him to write a song...'; 'saved
him a job': Badman, *The Beatles
Diary*, Vol. 2, p191

'Singing with the boys...range of the
common housewife': 'Ringo: A
Starr Is Bored', *Sunday Times*, 1976;
Philip Norman, *The Road Goes on
Forever* (Corgi Books, 1982), p80

'What makes you cross with each
other now...but I'll always love you':
Aspel & Company, ITV,
5 March 1988

Suicide

'Stand up, Daisy!'; 'Has anybody
heard the Motherfuckers...
followed by Engelbert
Humperdinck'; 'Stand up, baby':
Something about The Beatles,
podcast, Episode 40

'Rock and roll was about to happen...
little bit cabaret minded': BBC
Radio 1, 12 October 1987

'The rhymes are painful..."Suicide"
was the Rat Pack one': Du Noyer,
Conversations with McCartney

'I had my Dad's old piano...Boom!
And stabs from the band': ibid.

'He used to introduce it as...Thanks,
Frank': *Anthology*, Episode 8

'I'm more thrilled now than...
generation before me': ibid.

'I always imagined Sinatra singing...
But don't ask me to produce it!':
Playboy, September 1980

'I spoke to him on the phone...is this
guy having me on?': Miles, *Paul
McCartney*, p183

10 Extended Play

'The items lined up on this EP...
subdued mood of : A Taste of
Honey"': Tony Barrow, *Twist and
Shout* EP sleeve notes, 1963

'wild' and 'compelling'; 'with a fair
amount of Ringo's percussive

'pressure': ibid.

'You can't after the LP's been out…a drag, that!': *Top Gear*, BBC Light Programme, 14 July 1964

Cold Turkey

'I've forgotten what I was saying… we've just got up': Canada's CBC-TV, 14 January 1969

'The two of them were on heroin… we'd never get quite that far out': Miles, *Paul McCartney*, p567

'The only way to survive in Hamburg…I'm more crazy probably': *Rolling Stone*, January 1971

'"We've never smoked marijuana before"…*I can't hide*': Peter Brown and Steven Gaines, *The Love You Make: An Insider's Story of The Beatles* (Pan, 1983), p135

'John and I had decided that Paul and Ringo…': *Anthology*, p190

'I went to the other Beatles and said, "Hey lads…I'll put it out myself"': 'John and Yoko', *Melody Maker*, 6 December 1979

'I was just writing the experience…I was withdrawing': Peebles, *The Lennon Tapes*, p28

'We were full of junk…was so full of shit': Wenner, *Lennon Remembers*, p19

'I thought it was fantastic…': Peebles, *The Lennon Tapes*, p32

'He came over to our house with George…pregnant or something and they left': Wenner, *Lennon Remembers*, p148

'You have to realize that there's a peculiar…That's the drag': *NME*, 13 December 1969

'Your majesty, I am returning this MBE…': Fawcett, *John Lennon: One Day at a Time*, p57

'We had been trying to convince…': 'The road to Abbey Road', *Q* magazine special edition, *The Beatles: Band of the Century*, January 1999, p133

Teddy Boy

'Keep going…sounds great'; 'It's nice that key change'; 'I had something going on there'; 'That's one for consideration…one of Maharishi's lectures?'; 'What do you think about that bit?': *Something about The Beatles* podcast, Episode 40

'You can hear on it that the band… good-humoured friction': *The Beatles Anthology 3*, liner notes, Apple, 1996

'"Teddy"'s nice…'; 'It's like a full cycle…like George is doing'; 'I just wanna know it'; 'That's as far as it's going to get...'; 'I thought maybe we can...': *Something about The Beatles* podcast, Episode 40

Isn't It a Pity

'I've been thinking about all the tunes..."Taxman Part Two"...a string or two'; 'What's that?... It didn't impress me much': *Something about The Beatles* podcast, Episode 158

'There's a nice song that I wrote...I thought it was good'; 'I was thinking...I'm going to do it myself'; 'It can be any speed you want': ibid.

'just for you...'; 'I thought, "Oh, I'll get in on that!"': *Billboard*, 30 December 2000; www.billboard.com/articles/news/80788/george-harrison-all-things-in-good-time

'"Isn't It a Pity" is about whenever a relationship...': Harrison, *I Me Mine*, p166

'Simone's version of "Isn't It a Pity" influenced the mood': ibid., p320

Taking a Trip to Carolina

'Accompanied by his current steady, American photographer...Hunter Davies': *Something about The Beatles* podcast, Episode 158

'Are you going to write another?';

'Too fast for me'; 'I need to do something there'; 'Make it twice as long'; 'Carolina. Oh baby!': *Something about The Beatles* podcast, Episode 40

'It's one I wrote for Ringo'; 'There's one Dylan wrote for Ringo!': *Something about The Beatles* podcast, Episode 158

"You know Ringo, I'm in love ...': Chris O'Dell, *My Hard Days and Long Nights with The Beatles, The Stones, Bob Dylan, Eric Clapton, and the Women They Loved* (Atria, 2009)

'I became aware [of the affair]...': *Starts at 60*, 19 April 2018, https://startsat60.com/media/lifestyle/entertainment/pattie-boyd-george-harrison-affair-ringo-starrs-wife-maureen

'I try...as far as I'm concerned': *Something about The Beatles* podcast, Episode 158

11 And in the End...

'Dear Mailbag...is no': *Melody Maker*, 29 August 1970

'The only way The Beatles can get together...we need to get rid of Klein': Peter Doggett, *You Never Give Me Your Money: The Battle for the Soul of The* Beatles (Vintage, 2010), p202

'mainstays in sixties revival tours…
salons through the North-East':
Craig Brown, *One, Two, Three, Four:
The Beatles in Time* (Fourth Estate,
2021), p602

'I invented a little scenario…just do
your stuff on it': 'God in heaven,
what was I on', *Mojo*, November
1995, p54

'We had to imagine he'd just gone for
a cup-of-tea…could get through it':
John F Kelly, 'All he's got to do is act
naturally', *Washington Post*, 14 July
1995

'We had the opportunity…to be with
us again': Elliot J Huntley, *Mystical
One: George Harrison: After the
Break-up of The Beatles* (Guernica
Editions, 2004), p256

Index

Page numbers in *italics* refer to illustration captions.

Picture Acknowledgements

The publishers would like to acknowledge and thank the following for permission to include images in this book.

Alamy Stock Photo Trinity Mirror/Mirrorpix 196, 264

Getty Images Bettmann 236; C. Maher/Daily Express 85; Clive Limpkin/Daily Express 30; Evening Standard/Hulton Archive 81; George Stroud/Daily Express 154; John Downing 14; Keystone-France/Gamma-Rapho 276; Koh Hasebe/Shinko Music 26, 35; Michael Ochs Archives 190; Photoshot 268; Steel/Mirrorpix 99; Watford/Mirrorpix 113

Iconic Images Baron Wolman 231; Michael Brennan 181, 212; Michael Ward 41, 150, 294; Terry O'Neill 89, 127, 228

Author's Acknowledgements

An idea for a book always begins with a conversation with my literary agent, Carrie Kania. Her generosity, encouragement and conviction transform what is in my imagination into reality, for which I am truly grateful (Baby's in Black).

While not predating my infatuation with The Beatles, Susie McDonald's presence in my life is now more than four times greater than the Fab's existence. Such tolerance, of them and me, is a mindblower. Thank you: for your love and your keen editing skills (And I Love Her). While maybe struggling with the daily bombardment of Beatles records and films: Lottie, Eleanor and Lily your love...that means a lot (All Together Now).

At Octopus (Garden), Joe Cottington has offered unstinting backing, belief and support in the idea (Sun King). Helping to execute his faith have been Robert Anderson (copy editor), Alex Stetter (project editor), Jonathan Christie (creative director), Karen Baker and Matthew Grindon (publicity). (Dig It).

To Laurence Cairns-Smith for your computer wizardry and expertise (Fixing a Hole).

And of course, to John, Paul, George and Ringo whose unparalleled creativity has been the soundtrack of my life (All You Need Is Love).

I thank you all.

And finally...to Simon Fowler: this was your idea as much as mine – all those years ago – perhaps I should have known better! (I Am the Walrus – 'No, You're Not!' said Little Nicola.)

Daniel Rachel, summer 2021 (Paperback Writer)